8007 T

THATCHED VILLAGE

To the memory of
my mother and father
Helen and James Buchan

THATCHED VILLAGE

James Buchan

HODDER AND STOUGHTON
LONDON SYDNEY AUCKLAND TORONTO

Also by James Buchan

The Expendable Mary Slessor

British Library Cataloguing in Publication Data
Buchan, James
Thatched village.
I. Title
Copy to follow

ISBN 0 340 32666 2

Printed in Great Britain for Hodder and Stoughton Limited,
Mill Road, Dunton Green, Sevenoaks, Kent by
St Edmundsbury Press, Bury St Edmunds, Suffolk.
Typeset by Hewer Text Composition Services, Edinburgh.

Hodder and Stoughton Editorial Office:
47 Bedford Square, London WC1B 3DP.

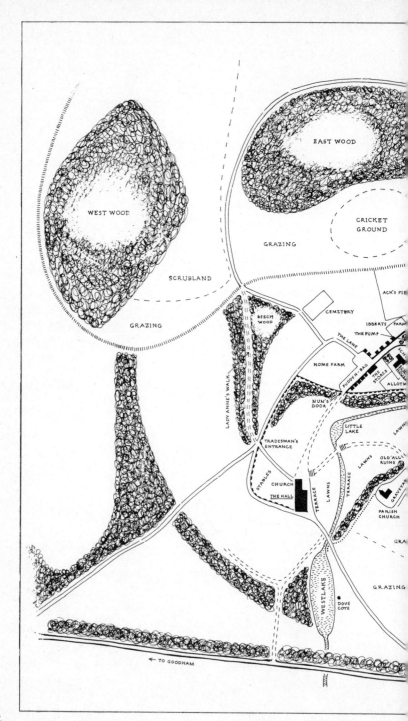

PROLOGUE

COTTAGES WITH honey-coloured thatch over grey stone walls ringed the Green which was canopied by giant sycamore trees. Dogs lay sleeping in the sun in the rutted streets where sparrows fluffed deeper into their dust-baths, scooped powder over themselves with their wings, and chirped in ecstasy. Tethered to the white railings outside the Fox and Geese Inn, a saddled horse lazily flicked its tail. On the other side of the Green, Amos the blacksmith, hammering at a horse-shoe, beat out music on his anvil: 'Ting—ting—tang . . . Tang—ting—ting . . . Tang—ting—ting.' A bucket clattered. A door slammed. A horse clopped slowly along Top Street towards Pudden Bag. It was summertime in Overton and the village dozed in the heat like a cat on its hearth-rug. In a wood above the village the towering pillars of the beech trees divided into arches which supported a shimmering roof of leaves. Birds sang. The sun lanced down on a patterned pavement of green.

At the window of my mother's room in Aberdeen I remembered Overton. I saw again the village, which once was all my world, as I had seen it so often in the places to which six years of soldiering and thirty years of television had taken me: in Brazil, in South Africa, in Egypt, in France, in Italy, in Germany, and the rest.

But had it really been idyllic? No, of course it hadn't. How about the poverty, the hunger, the patched threadbare clothes, the damp, chill, homes, the primitive sanitation, and the bullying of the gamekeepers? Behind me on my mother's desk was the file of notes which she had written when she planned to write a book about Overton. She had been teacher, nurse, and social-worker there, all rolled into one, for thirty-four years. Now that I was sixty-two and retired I was thinking of writing the book for her.

It would not be a 'Fairies-At-The-Bottom-of-My-Garden' book. It would be about what it was really like to live in the 1920s in a Leicestershire village without piped water, electricity, radio, or even, for a few years, buses or motors; what it was like to live in the little cut-off worlds which villages used to be. And that kind of living would soon be forgotten.

It was the summer of 1978 and my mother had died in January. Before she retired in 1953 and came to live with us in Scotland, my wife and I had spent part of our holidays each year with her in Overton. But in the last twenty-five years—my travelling years—I had only made a few brief visits to our village. And even then, because the Fox and Geese offered no accommodation, I had stayed in a hotel in Plantham or Ashborough, the nearby towns. But if I wanted to write the book that would not be enough. I would have to find a way to live in Overton again. Why not do that and see what happened? Would the old life come alive again for me? Or had it all been swept away?

Was the Fox and Geese on the telephone these days? I rang enquiries and asked for the number. To my surprise I got it.

A voice said, 'Mr. Findon here'. I recognised the name. He and his wife had taken over the management of the inn a few years before my mother retired. Unfortunately I had never met them.

I explained who I was and what I wanted. 'I'm sorry,' he said, 'we never put people up.'

'No. I know you don't usually. But I don't want anything posh. I was brought up in the village.'

'Hang on,' he said, 'I'll get the wife.'

I told Mrs. Findon my tale but she too said 'I'm sorry, we never . . .' then she paused. '*Who* did you say you are . . . Mrs. Bookin's son? Oh, that's different, I'll put *you* up.'

I got a lump in the throat at the knowledge that the name of the woman who for the last two years of her life had been a cripple in a wheel-chair, was still an Open Sesame in Overton.

In August I drove down from Aberdeen along the A1. Remembering the trials and tribulations of travel in my boyhood, I still looked on Plantham as being a long, long, way from our village. Although I knew it was stupid of me, I was surprised to find that, using the new wide road which runs across to the south of our village between Plantham and Ashborough, the eight miles took only ten minutes. Yet Plantham had once seemed to me to be on the rim of the world.

I turned off the new road at Springwell village and drove along past Glebe Farm and Cuckoo Spinney. I didn't go down Brooks Hill and up through Plantham End but carried on to the parallel road into Overton up Oss Pond Hill because that is the way I know best.

As I topped the hill I saw the cottages, the Green with its sycamores, and the old inn on the far side of it. They looked just as they had always looked.

I was late. So I only had time for a quick drive round the centre of the village. The Earl who owns it came into money after the war. I was pleased to see that he had spent a good deal of it on restoring cottages which had been shabby when I was a boy. The work had obviously been done by a master craftsman. The new thatch and the front gardens full of flowers fairly glowed in the evening sunshine.

I got out at the school where my mother had been Headmistress. It had been closed down after she retired. The building was now used as a community centre. The beautiful tar-macadam surface which replaced the mud in the playground, and for which we had worked so hard to raise the money, was cracked, and pitted with puddles, and dotted with weeds. The door in our front garden wall was split and hanging by one hinge. But the garden inside was well kept and the old schoolhouse looked in good order too, although nobody answered my knock at the front door.

I walked round to the vegetable garden. A fluffy black cat was sunning itself on the wall. It was so right for my pet, Smuttie, to be there that, for a moment, fifty years flicked away, then, when the cat didn't get up and run to me, flicked back again. What a strange thing is time.

Back in the playground I stood where my mother used to stand when she bowled for us at rounders. I could see her again, jumping high to catch the ball. I used to field beyond the porch, Mike across the street in front of the left hand cottage, Agnes in front of the centre one, and Leftie the right hand one. Mike, I knew, was dead, shot down in his Spitfire. I wondered where the others were.

Blanche, who had been my mother's assistant teacher, had written news of the village to me every year at Christmas time. I knew from her that many of my old friends were dead. But others were alive and still living in the village. Some had written to say how sad they were to hear from Blanche of my mother's death. Dan had written that they had found my mother's old high-backed headmistress's chair in a shed, and had cleaned and varnished it, and put it in the centre of her old classroom and held a little service there in her memory. She would have been pleased about that.

I had written to Blanche to tell her about the book and that I was looking forward to seeing her again. But I had received no reply. Instead Dan had written again to say that she too had died. I had missed her by only three weeks.

After supper in the Fox and Geese, which I had in the big kitchen with the family, I went into the bar. The old smoke-stained panelling and battered oak bar which had known so many 'characters' had been ripped out and replaced by anonymous chipboard and plastic veneer edged with chromium.

It was Monday and a quiet night. Mrs. Findon, who was serving behind the bar, gave me news of the village. But she kept using proper Christian names instead of the nicknames which even to this day Overton men get in boyhood and by which they are known for the rest of their lives. There are so many families with the same name in the village that nicknames are the quickest way of identifying them. For example John George Taylor is Bummie and John William Taylor is Scrabby. And that's easy to remember. My own nickname is 'Son'—short for 'teacher's son'.

A grey-haired stoutish man came in. 'You'll know Leslie Dalby, Mr. Bookin,' said Mrs. Findon.

I knew I ought to know him and his face was familiar. So I put on my best 'Great-to-see-you-again' BBC manner, to hide the fact that I hadn't the faintest notion who 'Leslie Dalby' was. I was quite sure that I had been successful. But when Mrs. Findon moved off up the bar I asked him, 'Where did you use to live?'

'On Top Street next door to Mary's mam.'

'Tabbie!' I said and without thinking slapped him on the shoulder.

He grinned. 'That's right, Son. Wondered why you didn't know me.'

Later Crum and Speedie came in, grey-haired too, but still looking as leathery as they always did. They looked suprised and pleased to see me. But in our village you don't go falling on people's necks.

''Allo, Son,' Crum said as we shook hands. 'Weer the 'ell 'ave you bin this last five years?'

After we had sunk a couple of pints Speedie said, 'Now you've retired, Son, you could come back and live in Overton.'

'Takes a long time to get accepted by the village,' said Mrs. Findon. 'Took us fifteen years.'

'Ah, yes, it would,' said Speedie. 'But you don't belong Overton—'e does.'

That, I discovered, was one of the nicest things anybody has ever said to me.

During the next few days several old friends put their memories together with mine and my mother's notes to turn the clock back sixty years. We had all known each other since school-days. Their background was my background and they loved what I loved. Soon it all began to come alive again.

CHAPTER ONE

IT WAS dawn on 9th October 1918. The big black cat was slowly strangling my mother. Its body curled more tightly round her neck and its green eyes glared into hers. Just as her lungs seemed about to burst she wakened screaming and set me off screaming too in my cot. Gran came rushing in from her own bedroom and comforted us both. My mother, sobbing, told her about the nightmare.

Afterwards Gran went to the window and peeped round the curtains. 'It's dawn, Neldie,' she said. 'It will soon be daylight. You'll be fine now. I'll go down to the kitchen and make us a cup of tea.'

Gran's mother was of Irish descent and had the sight. Gran too was a bit fey. Down in the kitchen, while she waited for the kettle to boil, she decided that there would be a meaning in the nightmare. So she found a pencil and was just going to ring the number eight on the calendar which hung on the wall, when she remembered that it was dawn. So she ringed the nine instead. The ninth day of the last full month of the First World War.

A few days later my mother received one of the War Office telegrams which the wives and families of all servicemen dreaded. It told her that her husband, James Buchan, had been killed in action on that day. A fortnight later she received a letter from one of his friends. He told her that a shell had hit my father's dug-out at dawn and buried him and three other men. It had not been my mother who was choking to death but my father.

It was customary for the forward batteries on the Western Front in France to leave some of their guns loaded overnight and to fire them at dawn to clear the dew out of the barrels and to make sure that it had not seeped into the charges. If the range of one particular German gun had been just a touch different the thatched village would never have been all my world, nor would it have lived in my memory ever since. For, six months after my father's death, my distraught mother ran away from everything and everyone she knew—except from Gran and me—and went to hide her hurt in what she had been led to believe was the suburb of the county town of an English shire, where she was to be a headmistress. It turned out to be a poverty-stricken, primitive village called Overton.

At first she was furious at the trick played on her and made up her mind to resign immediately and return to Scotland. But when she saw how ragged and ill-fed some of the school children were, and found that they had been so badly taught that they were almost illiterate, she changed her mind. Besides I was a delicate child, the country air would do me good and, when I was old enough to begin school, it would be in her own Infant Department. I was all that she had left of James Buchan and she was very much afraid that I would vanish too.

She decided that she would stay for a few years in Overton and then go back to Scotland and take up her career again. Before her marriage she had been a lecturer at Notre Dame Training College for Teachers in Glasgow. But she never really recovered from the shock of my father's death. She remained a widow and stayed all those years in the village, which she grew to love, and where she became an institution.

She coaxed, led, bullied, or thumped generations of children along the path of learning and of citizenship. She even helped some of the boys to pass Senior Scholarship examinations for entry into the famous public school at Ashborough and that involved teaching them Latin, French, and Higher Mathematics. After the Second World War she stayed on at the school because she knew that if she left it would be closed.

We arrived at Ashborough's tiny railway station on 20th April 1919. My mother, Gran, and I had been travelling from Aberdeen all the previous night and half that day so we were not at our best.

When she had seen our trunks safely unloaded from the luggage van my mother asked the elderly porter to get us a taxi.

Porters wore a shiny black hat flat on top and with a peak at both ends, rather like a small, sawn-off witch's hat. He took his off and scratched his head. 'Taxi? We ain't got no taxi.'

'Then how are we to get to Overton?'

'*Overton*? And you wants a *taxi*?'

He sounded as indignant as if she had asked for a golden coach to go to a slum.

'Mrs. Bewcannon?' a voice asked behind her.

She turned. 'Buchan,' she snapped. (We *hate* being called 'Bewcannon'!)

The small, bronzed man backed away a bit and raised his cap. She noticed that he had three fingers missing on his left hand. 'My name's Stanwell. I have been sent to meet you.'

'Thank goodness for that!' said my mother and shook hands with him. 'This is my mother, Mrs. Duncan, and this,' pointing to the bundle in Gran's arms, 'is my son.'

Gran was small, in her fifties, with green eyes and auburn hair sprinkled with grey. She was tough as whipcord, quick-tempered, quick with her tongue, and quick on her feet. She would explode with temper and then, usually, her strong sense of humour would take over and she would start wisecracking. She had been convinced that her daughter had gone mad ever since she heard of the plan to rush off to the back of beyond. By now she was past caring. As shock followed shock that day, all she could do was laugh in a kind of horrified disbelief that such things could be happening to her.

My mother was of medium height, good at cricket and tennis, and like her mother she had a quick temper and a rapier tongue. She was twenty-seven, with dark, waving, chestnut hair which the sun bleached to auburn in summer. She had big, striking blue-grey eyes which could gleam with fun and laughter or glint like steel when she glared. Their glare got to be famous. Strong men would back off, hands out in front of them. 'Now! . . . Ey-up Teacher! . . . Don't lose your temper!'

I was a sweet child not yet three years old, with blue eyes and beautiful golden, curly, hair. Ah well! Nothing lasts for ever!

With Mr. Stanwell leading and the porter following with our luggage on a barrow, we went into the station-yard. My mother looked round. All she could see was a brown pony between the shafts of an open trap: a high vehicle with two large wheels and kept up at the front by the pony.

'Are we to go in *that*?' she asked.

'Er . . . yes!' said Mr. Stanwell.

'Mechty!' said Gran. 'Where's the Red Indians?'

'We don't have motors in the village, you see,' explained Mr. Stanwell.

'What village?'

'Overton.'

'Wi' wigwams?' asked Gran.

'No. Thatched cottages mostly.'

'Oh! Luxury!' sighed Gran. She was so horrified she forgot to laugh.

Mr. Stanwell helped my mother up on to the vehicle's only bench seat. Then he handed me up to her before helping Gran up too. He then loaded one trunk into the back, but decided that the other two would be too much weight for Kitty, the pony. He promised to come back later and fetch them. He covered our knees with a black leather rug lined with wool and off we went, with Kitty clopping along the muddy five-mile road to Overton.

It was then that he explained, what was to them, the awful truth about Overton.

When we came to Barnswell Hill, three miles out of Ashborough, he got down to lighten the load on Kitty, and led her up the steep, winding hill.

'I hope the poor beastie can manage,' said Gran. 'I'm nae for pushin' this thing.'

Once up the hill Kitty trotted into a mile long avenue where the trees almost met overhead.

Mr. Stanwell told my mother that he had come from Australia to fight in the War, had married an Overton girl, and after a year running the Stores was enjoying life in the village. He said though, that since it was run on feudal lines, it was very different from life 'down under'. And that was not welcome news to my mother either.

'There's the main entrance to the Hall Grounds,' he said, and pointed ahead to high wrought-iron gates painted black with the Family crest on each picked out in gold. They were hung between wide stone pillars and on either side of the pillars was the house of the lodge-keeper, split in two by the gates.

'We call that the Double Lodge,' Mr. Stanwell said, 'there's another side-entrance to the Grounds further on which we call the Single Lodge.'

'Do we go through this one?' asked my mother.

'Oh no,' he said hastily. 'Village folk aren't allowed in there.'

He turned Kitty to the right into a road which has a spinney running along the left-hand side of it. Round about Overton you never get far away from trees. A mile further on the road turns left past the Single Lodge, then down Ashborough hill with the high wall enclosing the Grounds on the left and Green's farm on the right, then past the Oss Pond and up another hill into the village where we saw for the first time the cottages, the Green, and the inn.

Kitty had been a circus pony before Mr. Stanwell had bought her at Melton market. When first she came to Overton the Green had held a strong fascination for her. She would fight the reins and canter anti-clockwise round it until he had to get down and lead her away from it. However on this day she ignored it. She trotted straight on up the street between the cottages on the right and allotment vegetable gardens on the left until we saw ahead of us, where the road slopes upwards, a triangle of rough ground with a huge horse-chestnut tree at each corner and between them, supported on six circular brick pillars, a red-tiled roof shaped like a

Chinese hat. This is the Pump, so-called because once there used to be one under the hat.

Here the street forks. One section goes straight on to the right of the triangle and joins Top Street, the other curves away to the left along a high stone wall.

Mr. Stanwell pointed his whip at the wall and the tall stone building with a slate roof showing above it. 'That's your play-ground wall, Mrs. Buchan,' he said 'And that's your school.'

The building is T-shaped. The school is the top, with the playground above it, and the schoolhouse is the upright with the front garden to the right of it, the vegetable garden running across the gable below the upright, and the kitchen, pantry, wash-house, lavatory and outbuildings, on the left of it. The gardens are each about the size of a tennis court with a fence dividing them from the allotments on the right hand – the south side – and a stone wall surrounding the rest of the premises.

My mother and Gran were surprised to hear Mr. Stanwell call the school 'the Convent'. He explained that from 1906 until 1916 it had been run by nuns, and after calling it 'the Convent' for ten years, the village hadn't yet got out of the habit. It was another five years before it did. So you could say that I was reared in a convent. That, however, would be misleading. Overton life was rugged rather than refined.

There are steps leading up through the playground wall opposite the Pump. But Mr. Stanwell passed these and pulled Kitty up at the gate which leads to the door in the wall round the north side of the schoolhouse. He explained that to get to the front door you had to go up the steps and across the muddy playground to the door in the wall on the south side. Because of the mud the front door was seldom used.

After he had let us into it and brought in the trunk, my mother and Gran inspected the musty, damp, neglected house. It had obviously not been lived in for some months. They found that it had two rooms about twenty foot square downstairs and two of the same size upstairs. Each had a sash window of twelve panes overlooking the front garden. Between the rooms was a hall from which a wide staircase with a mahogany banister on wrought-iron supports led up to a landing off which was a boxroom. The staircase was elegant and the best feature of the house but a waste of space in such a small building. The room on the right of the hall was the sitting-room with a door leading off it into the school. The other room on the ground level had a floor of black and red tiles laid in a diamond pattern with a door into a walk-in cupboard under the staircase and another into the kitchen. Built into the back wall of the kitchen was a rusty 'range' with an oven on one side of the grate and a small boiler for heating water on the other. On the left of the range under a window in the side wall which overlooked the vegetable garden was a stoneware sink with a cold water tap but no hot. In the wall opposite the window was a door leading into a passage. A short section of this turned left to the back door and a longer one led past the pantry on the left into the wash-house. Beyond the wash-house was a lavatory which consisted of a zinc tub under a wide wooden seat with a hole in it and a wooden lid to cover the hole. There was no bathroom.

The Chairman of the Management Committee had written 'there is furniture in the house'. This turned out to be two old iron bedsteads with damp mattresses, a scrubbed wooden kitchen table, a few kitchen chairs, some pots, pans, and cutlery, and an old piano.

When they had finished their inspection, my mother and Gran, tired and depressed, sat on two of the kitchen chairs in the dining-room.

'Ah weel,' said Gran, 'you would come. You would come. Nae electricity or gas. Nae bathroom. Nae hot water. Nae trams, buses, nor taxis. Nae proper streets, just mud and manure. Nae real shops. Nae theatres nor picture-houses. Nae restaurants. I think I'll awa oot to Australia and bide wi' my sister Isie. I'm ower auld to put up wi' the Wild West.'

'We'll just have to make the best of it for a few weeks,' said my mother, 'until I can get a job in Scotland again. Now we better light a fire, boil a kettle, and finish off the sandwiches.'

At that point, as if in answer to a prayer, the old bell on the kitchen wall tinkled. It was attached to a wire which ran along through a hole in the frame of the backdoor to a brass mounting with a hinged T-shaped handle. This, my mother discovered, had been pulled by a tall, bony woman with sandy brown hair sticking out from under a man's cap. 'I'm Mrs. Walton,' she said in a deep, hoarse voice. She was wearing a sacking apron over a long blue skirt and a grey blouse and she had little gimlet eyes set close to a long nose above a jutting chin. Even with a parrot on her shoulder she couldn't have looked more of a pirate. 'Mr. Stanwell reckons yer might need a bit o' 'elp seein' as 'ow nobody 'as seen fit to get this place ready fer yer. Which I must say is a dang disgrace and no mistake. Would yer like me to come in and set abaht it?'

'I would indeed,' said my mother, 'we've been travelling since yesterday evening.'

'Clean the ole 'ouse for three shillin'.' She looked anxious and her big red hands clutched into the sacking apron. 'That all roight?' Clearly she would be glad of any work that was going.

'Done!' said my mother.

'Right, Teacher.' The grim face twitched into a grin, then she turned, went to the door in the wall and trumpeted 'Lizzie! . . . 'Enry! . . . Come 'ere!'

As if by magic her two eldest children appeared in the doorway. They were bony and pale-faced like their mother. Lizzie was thirteen and 'Enry twelve. Each wore a darned jersey with a patched skirt for the girl and patched shorts for the boy, over scuffed boots.

'Come on! 'Enry get some coal and sticks outta the shed and start loightin' fires. Lizzie yer'll take a note round to the Stores soon as we find out wot's wanted. I reckon there won't be owt in the pantry 'cept mice dirt.'

So Emma Walton came into our lives. She was tough, poor, honest, and heavy-handed. When Emma was around everything went with a bang, clatter or thump. Doors, buckets, pans, cups, plates. They were all one to Emma. She made sure they went where she wanted them to go and stayed there. She handled her five children in much the same way, so that, perforce, they grew up to be as tough as she was. Her war-cry was, 'I'll soon sort that out,' and in she went 'Muck or nettles', as we say in Overton. One way or another she did sort it out; though if anything of a delicate constitution was involved, it might never be the same again.

Without Emma to help her and to teach her how to deal with primitive cooking facilities, paraffin lamps, cockroaches, beetles, and other pests, I think my mother would have gone straight back to Scotland.

That evening she and Gran had a scratch meal beside the fire in the dining-room. The chimneys were damp and needed sweeping, so the fires belched a cloud of smoke every time a door was opened, and the house stank now of coal-gas. They had just finished eating and were having a cup of tea when tinkling music began somewhere in the house. 'Mechty! Ghosts!' said Gran and spilt hers. 'It must be the last of the Mohicans.'

They listened. Someone had begun playing the old piano in the sitting-room. But that was impossible. The door into the School and the front door were locked. My mother picked up a candle and the two of them tiptoed into the hall and across to the sitting-room door. Surrounded by pitch blackness they stared at each other in the circle of light from the flickering flame which sent long shadows up the staircase and over the walls. Someone was gently striking notes at random. 'Mebbe the ghosts of the old nuns dinna like us,' said Gran, who was beginning to think it was no laughing matter.

My mother opened the sitting-room door. The fire glowed on a room empty except for the piano. And the lid of that was shut. But 'Ting . . . ting . . . ting' went the notes.

My mother was just stretching out her hand to open the lid when a squeaking inside the instrument blended with the music. Quickly she pulled her hand back. Was the thing alive? Then, 'It must be mice!' she said.

Sure enough they found that the wee beasties had built nests made of chewed paper and cloth among the hammers.

'Ah weel,' said Gran, 'It's nae everybody that has musical mice.'

When she heard about the music Emma was not amused. 'My guy!' she said, 'the 'ouse must be overrun with the little darvels. Wot yer needs is traps.' She went to the back door and trumpeted again, 'Lizzie!' and when her daughter shot round the corner, 'Go you round to the Stores and get six mice traps and arf a pound o' cheese on Teacher's bill. I'll show yer 'ow to bait 'em, Teacher.'

Next evening the ghostly music gave way to the snapping of the traps. My mother got sick of cremating the bodies in the sitting-room fire.

CHAPTER TWO

IT WAS two days before our furniture arrived from Aberdeen.
During them we camped in the house. Mr. Stanwell kindly
bought us some new lamps in Ashborough to back up the one
ancient lamp left in the house and the few enamel candlesticks.

Mr. Stanwell was particularly proud of two of the lamps which
he had bought. They were made of brass, except for the glass
bowl into which you poured the paraffin. 'These two have a new
kind of burner,' he said, 'and they are two-hundred candle-power!'

At night, unless there was a moon, the village was in almost
total darkness. There were no street lamps and the lamps behind
the curtains of the cottages did no more than glow. Some folk
went about with 'bulls-eye' paraffin lanterns, so-called because
they had a big magnifying lens on the front, or with candle
lanterns. But the paraffin ones were a pest to keep filled and the
candle ones smoked their glasses so most folk went about in the
dark and struck a match if they dropped anything. In later years

they carried electric torches for emergencies. But just after the war batteries for them were hard to get.

Inside your house it was like living in a perpetual power failure. You either had to carry a box of matches with you when you went out or else be careful to leave a box along with a candle where you could be sure of finding it when you got home. But even in the best-run homes misunderstandings occurred, toes were stubbed, things were knocked over, and a good deal of cussing and bad-temper went into 'finding them bloody matches'.

For my mother and Gran living without electricity took a bit of getting used to. Lamps had to be filled and the wicks in the burners kept level by trimming: a messy, smelly, business.

Emma was most alarmed when she heard that they had been carrying lighted lamps about the house. 'No, no, Teacher. Yer mustn't never do that. If yer goes and drops one, the paraffin spills out and catches alight and up goes yer 'ouse.'

In Overton and the villages round about folk were even more afraid than usual of setting fire to their houses. The only fire-brigade was at Ashborough and by the time it arrived buildings had usually burned to the ground. Besides, few families could afford to insure their possessions so that a fire could mean losing everything.

So my mother and Gran carried candles. But the draughts, particularly from opening or closing a door, often blew the flame out unless you had a hand free to curl round it to shield it. One night, after two unsuccessful attempts to get upstairs with a candlestick in one hand, a hot water bottle in the other and books under her arm, Gran came down in a temper. 'Here tak the useless thing. I'll gang up in the dark.'

This, they found, was the way to do it. You left lamps or candles with a box of matches in bedroom, pantry and lavatory, and moved between them in the dark, just as you moved about in the dark outside, and memorised the position of any gates you had to go through and the number of any steps you had to go up.

Emma arranged for Mr. Harport to come and sweep the chimneys so that, after the first day, the fires burned well. But the 'range' contraption in the kitchen was not so easily tamed. Mr.

Harport, liberally sprinkled with soot, like the kitchen, was saying, 'I dunno. It ought to be 'eatin' up the oven but it ain't', when there was a pull at the backdoor bell. Gran went to investigate. She came back and reported, 'There's a mannie wi' the artus gripes. I think it's a disease.'

'Tell him we don't want it,' said my mother, who was beginning to get a trifle out of temper with the soot, the oven, and Mr. Harport.

'Tell him yourself. I canna understand these redskins.'

To my mother's surprise it turned out that what was involved was hot-house grapes from Ashborough. So she bought some.

Emma's view of the range was, 'Yer don't want to mess about trying to roast in that there oven, Teacher. They ain't no good no 'ow. Them as can afford a Sunday joint o' meat tecks it down to Miss Bennett the baker; she roasts it in 'er big oven, an' then they tecks it back and keeps it warm in their own oven. I'll teck yourn down fer yer of a Sunday if yer likes. Only costs yer a penny.'

My mother thanked her but said she had seen an advertisement for a paraffin cooking stove, which had four burners, two of which could be used to heat an oven, and she proposed to buy one.

'Moight be best at that. Bit of a 'owdeyerdoo down at Bennett's sometimes. She 'erself allus knows 'oos tin is 'oos. But if she ain't abaht, some of 'em ain't above sneakin' off wi' someone else's. If it's bigger nor their own, that is.'

The Sunday morning procession of folk down to Bennett's bakery before midday carrying their joint in its roasting tin, covered by a white cloth in good weather and a piece of black waterproof American cloth in bad, was a feature of Overton life. Round about one o'clock they would process it back again to their homes.

Emma clashed a few pans together in the sink, 'If yer uses that there oven to dry yer sticks, which is abaht all it's good fer, you wants to watch aht fer yer cat . . . Yer'll need a cat to get rid of all them mice . . . Yer see, sticks dries quicker if yer leaves the oven door open to let the steam aht. An' if yer don't look out yer cat nips in fer a warm. We lost our ginger Tom one day. Couldn't find 'im anyweer. Then our Dad says, "Ey up! Someone's gone an' shut the oven door." Sure enough there's the cat sittin' on the 'ot sticks. 'E were a bit 'ot 'isself like. But 'e come out none the wuss.' She laughed. Her laugh was a succession of wheezing barks, like a sheep coughing, only quicker.

When at last our furniture arrived at Ashborough station it had to be unloaded into three vans each drawn by a pair of horses.

'My guy, Teacher,' Emma said. 'Yer ain't 'arf got a lot o' stoof.'

Not all of it would fit into the schoolhouse which was a good thing for Emma because she collected various odds and ends. 'No, no, Teacher,' she said. 'Yer don't want ter give it ter me. Yer wants ter sell it. It's good stoof!'

When she was told that she could have a small inlaid mahogany sideboard with a mirror above it, and a mirror in each of its three doors, and a white marble top which had been cracked during the removal, she was overcome. 'My guy!' she said, stroking it and with tears in her eyes, 'Fancy Emma Walton 'avin' one o' these. I wouldn't never o' dreamt it. Best thing I ever did cummin round 'ere ter 'elp yer a Toosday.'

But when my mother saw all the furniture, which she had bought and shared with my father, arranged in their new surroundings she wept a bit. Then she went out and made a bonfire at the end of the garden furthest from the thatched cottages, of all the rubbish which had been cleaned out of the house. She threw so much paraffin on the old mattresses that she singed half an apple tree.

She was due to re-open the school on the following Monday and decided that she better explore the village while she had the time.

'For 'eaven's sake, Teacher,' said Emma when she saw my mother setting forth with me in my push-chair one afternoon, 'don't yer be anyweer near Top Street come five o'clock becos of the 'osses.'

'Wot 'osses?' asked my mother who was beginning to come to terms with the dialect.

''Ibbert's 'osses, outta the farm this end o' Top Street beyond the Pump. 'Ookin' gret cart-osses wot they lets loose outta the yard come the end o' wuck. 'Arry 'e comes aht an' 'e shahts up the street "Ey up! Ere's the 'osses!" An yer 'as ter skip through the nearest garden gate as abaht twenty on 'em comes chargin' along, racin' each other ter the New Field wots up a lane off t'other end o' street. Fair thunder, they do. An they far . . .' Emma paused and thought a moment '. . . blows off outta their back-ends somethin' 'orrible.'

Seeing my mother laughing, she grinned and wheezed a bit while her shoulders shook. Emma didn't often find anything to laugh at and when she did it was quite a performance. ''Tain't no laughin' matter reelly. But we gets a bit of fun sometimes wen a stranger in 'is trap else dog-cart finds 'isself faced wi' the charge and 'is oss nips rahnd and bolts off back up the street wi' 'im ter get outta way. Yer should see their faces.'

'I'm surprised the police allow it,' said my mother.

'Well,' Emma shrugged, 'we ain't got no policeman in the village. An the 'osses 'as got so used ter the charge over the years that I reckon if they was ter try ter lead 'em they'd gallop up the street just the same, and teck the men wi' 'em.' She wheezed again, 'Eck an' 'ell. I'd jist loove ter see ole fat 'Arry a tryin' ter keep oop!'

The centre of the village is an oblong of thatched cottages, with their vegetable gardens behind them, sitting on top of the Green like a circus rider sitting on one of those one-wheeled cycles. A street runs round the Green, another runs up the east side of the oblong, another up the west side, and Top Street across the top. Each is about two hundred yards long.

The east street is the one which runs from the top of Oss Pond hill up past the school to the Pump where it joins Top Street at right-angles. The bit which forks off to the left past the gate of the playground runs on past the Stores to another fork. On the right is the way to the Home Farm and the lane which leads up to the Park. On the left is Pudden Bag, a cul-de-sac with cottages on either side of it. With its front gardens full of flowers it has always been the prettiest part of the village.

The west street also forks before it joins Top Street but to the right of course. It runs past more cottages and a farm to Plantham End where, as you would expect, the village stops. The road runs on over Brooks—a stream which runs across the south of the village out of the **Oss** Pond—up Brooks Hill and so away to the left past Cuckoo Spinney and Glebe Farm to Springwell and Plantham.

The wall of the Hall Grounds runs down Ashborough hill up past the Oss Pond then across to the end of Pudden Bag behind the allotments until it circles round to the Stables behind the Hall itself. With their lakes and woods and lawns the Grounds cover over a hundred acres. In those days for village folk to be caught trespassing in there spelt a heap of trouble; for adults a visit to the Earl to make a personal apology; for boys, if caught by a game-keeper, 'a good idin', which varied according to the temperament of the keeper from a real thrashing to a few clouts over the head and a kick up the backside.

The School Log Book, my mother found, showed that her predecessor had left in December 1918. A temporary, unqualified teacher had tried to keep classes going from January to March 1919. But she had not, it seemed, had much success since two of the only five entries for those months concerned letting the children off school early to watch the Hunt meet on the Green.

My mother's first entry, in her copybook writing, is 'April 28th 1919: school re-opened by Helen Buchan.' A new era of education had begun for the village.

Entries, as far back as 1882, when that particular Log Book was begun, show that the Family, its guests, and friends and their children were in the habit of visiting the school every fortnight or so 'to hear the children sing'. Indeed the Countess herself is recorded as having spent a whole morning 'teaching the children a new song'.

Unfortunately for her early relations with the Family, singing songs did not come high on my mother's list of priorities for her illiterate pupils. There were about forty of them; a dozen or so in the Infant Department under her assistant, and the rest under my mother in the senior one.

Two days after she had re-opened the school she was surprised when, in the middle of a lesson, two ladies wearing large hats and carrying rolled-up umbrellas swept into her classroom followed by a group of children.

'Good morning,' one of the ladies said, tilting her head back and studying my mother down rather a long nose, 'I am Lady Sarah. You must be the new headmistress. What is your name?' The words were uttered coldly as if a prelude to interrogation.

'I am Helen Buchan.'

'I believe you are from Scotland.' Then, without waiting for a reply, 'Will you kindly provide us with chairs. We wish to hear the children sing.' Her ladyship tapped gently on the floor with the ferrule of her umbrella.

Annoyed at this unwarranted interruption to her lesson my mother said, 'I will ask my assistant to arrange it,' and walked off through the curtain which separated the senior classroom from the infant one.

After the singing the beautifully turned out young gentry distributed one boiled sweet each to the suitably grateful, curtsying or bowing little peasants. The party then departed. My mother showed them out of the top door of the school.

Lady Sarah studied her again. 'Would you like to meet my cook?'

'No thank you,' my mother replied. 'Would you like to meet mine?'

The ladies gasped in unison, lifted their long skirts clear of the muddy playground and swept indignantly away.

Perhaps there were more guests at the Hall than usual, or perhaps the Family wished to look over the new headmistress and 'teach her her place', because they visited the school twice a week during the following month. Quite apart from the rage which she felt at being treated like a flunkey, my mother felt that the visits were undermining the ideas about the importance of education which she was trying to get into the heads of her pupils. So she decided that after the next session of singing and sweet distribution she would ask the Countess very politely to make her visits on a Friday morning when music was on the timetable authorised by the County Education Committee. She would point out that headmistresses were bound to adhere to this timetable.

The Countess was in her late fifties. She had a mass of fair hair gathered into a bun at the back, a strong rather than a beautiful face, and piercing blue eyes. She usually wore dark colours and a high crowned hat and drove herself round the village in a little open carriage drawn by two donkeys. She knew every man, woman, and child, by name, and woe betide any woman or girl who did not curtsy, or any man or boy who did not remove his headgear and stand to attention, as she, or any other member of the Family, went past. She frightened the life out of me and out of nearly everybody in the village except my mother and Gran.

When my mother made her extremely polite request her lady-ship was furious. 'I have never heard of such a thing. For over fifty years we have been visiting our school whenever we think fit and we shall continue to do so. I would point out to you that my husband owns not only the village but also the school itself.'

'I am sorry,' said my mother, 'but I am expressly forbidden to alter the timetable laid down by the Education Committee. The children are so backward as to be almost illiterate: a situation which I propose to correct. In future you will be welcome in school on Friday mornings, but the timetable will not be altered to permit singing on any other day.'

The Countess was pale and almost speechless with rage. She glared at my mother and may well have been surprised to meet a glare which matched her own. At last, 'You will be dismissed for impudence,' she said.

'I shall be very happy to leave this primitive place with a clear conscience. Only the sorry state of the children has caused me to remain in it. But I would point out that only my employers, the Education Committee, can dismiss me.'

'They will do as they are told,' snapped the Countess.

'Good,' snapped my mother. 'And the sooner the better.'

The local priest was chairman of the school management committee as well as chaplain to the Family—the church is attached to the Hall—and he called that evening with a demand that my mother apologise in writing to the Countess. This she refused to do. She pointed out that she had not yet signed a contract, and said that, after making a full report to the Education Committee, she would leave at the end of the month. He then ordered her, as her priest, to do no such thing. But she told him that they were no longer living in the Middle Ages and showed him out.

When, seething with emotion, she told Gran about this latest development, 'Ach I telt you not to come,' said her parent. 'Ye see they have the Feudal System here.'

My mother had only met the System in history books. The Scottish clan aristocracy were not superior beings from a superior world, and therefore as unknowable as God, but of the same name and the same blood as their clan. As fathers of their clan they were respected. But if the clan thought they needed advice they reserved the right to tell them so. Helen Buchan reserved the right to tell anybody anything she thought they ought to know.

Now she felt very much alone in a strange world. But next evening there was a knock on the door into the school from the sitting-room. A deputation of mothers was waiting for her. The efficient 'bush telegraph' had passed on the news that she too was about to leave the school. 'Please, Teacher,' one of them said. 'We don't want you to go. Our kids'll learn under you. They ain't never 'ad a chance these last few years.'

So, after promising not to tell anyone that they had been to see her, she said she would think it over and perhaps not leave after all if she received the support of the Education Committee. She did.

The report of His Majesty's Inspector of Schools, dated 20th June 1919 in the Log Book states: 'Since January 1917 there have been several changes of staff, including five Head Teachers. There have also been closures . . . The school is in a bad condition, in fact there is no subject in which the work can be called satisfactory. The stock is in a neglected condition, some of it mouldy and partly eaten by mice. The new headmistress has made a very good start.'

To the Countess my mother was now 'that Socialist woman from Glasgow'. And the feud between the middle-aged aristocrat and the young, athletic, university graduate smouldered on, with occasional bursts into flame, for the next four years.

But, although greatly interested in Christianity, my mother was never much interested in politics. She did become a Liberal for a time. But that was only a Declaration of Independence. On the evening of the first polling day after we arrived in the village the Estate Agent came and banged on the front door and demanded why she and Gran had not voted. 'You will go immediately,' he said, 'and vote Conservative.'

'How many candidates are there?' asked my mother meekly.

'Two. A Conservative and Liberal. You will, as I say, vote Conservative.'

'Wrong,' said my mother. 'You have just won two votes for the Liberals.'

CHAPTER THREE

Emma really had enough to do to look after her own family.
So after we had begun to settle down, she only came twice a
week to do the scrubbing and the washing. To do the other work,
and to look after me while my mother was in school, Mary joined
us. She was a tall, slim girl, aged sixteen, with hazel eyes, shining
rosy cheeks, and dark brown hair which hung down her back in a
long plait. When adults were about she was painfully shy and
never had much to say. But when we were on our own she was
great fun. She had a strong sense of humour, loved practical
jokes, loved the country-side, and was surprisingly well-informed
about it. Best of all she adored the sweet, golden-haired child
which used to be me.

For me life begins in Overton. I cannot remember a time before
there was my mother, and Gran, and Mary, and Emma, and me,
and the thatched village. My mother told me that my father used
to play with me on his knee; that the first steps which I ever took

were towards him. But of him I have no recollection. Although, I suppose, something of him may still exist in my subconscious without my knowing it. I wish I did know it.

The first thing I remember is a large bed. It had a high wrought-iron back with two rods about three foot long, which swivelled sideways, sticking out of the top of it. The rods and the high back were draped with filmy material with a pattern of small flowers with dark blue petals on a pale blue background. It hung down to the floor, but was gathered in at mattress level so that the bed looked as if it was protected by two huge angels' wings. I could stand on the pillow, grab the material, and make a wing flap in and out. But Mary disapproved of this, unclenched my fists from the stuff and plonked me back under the blankets.

At the bottom of the bed, among other decorations, were gleaming brass cones on rods. If I jumped up and down on the mattress these bounced and shivered and tinkled. But Mary didn't approve of that either. She would put up with it for a minute or two, then tell me to 'give over'. If I didn't she would whip my legs from under me and plonk me back on my behind again. This could develop into a good game because only in desperation would she kneel on the bed herself and I could jump up and down on the far side of it where she couldn't catch me. The first time I fell over the edge I accidentally grabbed a wing and slid down it to the floor. So after that I was careful to keep up near them. Mary got very cross if I didn't. 'Yer'll break yer silly neck,' she would hiss, 'an' I'll get into trouble.'

I had to have hold of her plait before I would go to sleep. So she used to sit on a chair close beside the bed, pull the plait over her shoulder, and lean forward so that I could have the end of it on the pillow beside me. Often it smelt of lavender. Sometimes she had to sit leaning forward for about half an hour which must have been painful for her. Sometimes I would pretend to be asleep and then, when she went to recover her plait, pull it. She was always very patient. 'All right clever Dick,' she would say, 'wait till tomorrow. I'll get me own back.'

Even when I lost my golden curls and ceased to be sweet, she rarely lost her temper with me, whatever the provocation. In a way she became like a big sister to me. But she was a much better friend than big sisters sometimes seem to be.

The next thing I remember is Brooks. Mr. Hibbert rented the first two fields through which the stream ran. He had two children in the school so my mother was able to get permission from him to take me along it in my push-chair. It was important to have the permission of a farmer to walk in a field because round about Overton gamekeepers would rudely order you out of them, or turn you back down any lane leading towards them. This was not because you were likely to damage livestock, crops, or fences, or to leave gates open. Nobody in the village was as daft as that. No, unless you were working in the fields, you had to keep out of them and out of the woods, and keep to the public roads, because the sacred pheasants, partridges, hares, and rabbits must not be disturbed. These were so much more important than mere people, that in the early 1920s there were no sports facilities for the village folk whatsoever. Not even the ancient common land which had been grabbed from them at the time of the Enclosures.

My mother bought a clockwork ship for me. It was black with three red funnels. We used to take it 'down Brooks' on Saturdays and Sundays. But it was designed to sail on ponds, not among the eddies and moss-covered stones of our one and only stream. It always overturned and floated upside down. So we got fed up with it and raced sticks—one each—downstream instead. When they were going well my mother picked me up and ran with me along the bank. When one or both stuck she put me down and we threw stones at them until we splashed them free, or, if it was a hot day, I paddled in and sent them on their way.

One afternoon we went further along the stream than usual and I came to a magic place. I had freed my stick from a piece of weed and had paddled round a bush when I saw it: a tall, glittering cave stretching away into the far distance. It had red, blue, and bright green lights flickering from its crystal walls. I was dazzled and screwed up my eyes. At the far end the water boiled and bubbled and chattered back to me. Then it came sliding into a black mirror which threw the flashing colours up to the rounded roof.

For a few moments I was spellbound. Then I called to my mother that I had found a fairy cave. She took off her shoes and stockings and we paddled into it hand-in-hand. 'Don't look back,' she said. 'You must never look back in a magic place.'

At the far end of the cave bushes bridged a deeper part of the stream. So she picked me up and took me out of fairyland. Then we had to go back and paddle through it again. But we could only go back to it on special days. The fairies didn't like it if you went too often, and you had never to look back.

My mother wrote a story for me which gave the names of the fairies who lived in the cave and of the elves who played tricks on them. It was published in a collection of children's stories. But the book was lost years ago and their names with it.

A year or so later I discovered why you could only go there on special days. It was only a stone bridge lined with grey cement over which perhaps, because it was too wide for just a farm track, the road to Plantham had run in days gone by. The sun made the magic when it shone into the far end of it.

Even to adults the countryside provides surprises. But to young people only three feet tall, to whom everything is new and full of mystery, it has a splendour which the years cannot destroy. Memory can make bolt-holes for us all. The snag is that you must not go back and expect to find, where you discovered it, what exists now only in yourself.

I can still remember some of the surprises which it gave me. My mother would never take me to a place where she might be turned back by the keepers, who were the Estate Agent's hatchet men. She was as unpopular with him as she was with the Family and could not expect to receive the preferential treatment given to the retired colonel and the retired bank-manager who lived in the village. But, when I was old enough to do without the push-chair, I would sometimes persuade Mary to take me into forbidden places.

The lane which led to the Park ran past the Home Farm and up past the cemetery. It was all right to go as far as there provided you didn't carry on beyond it into the scrubland or go into the long wood which ran towards it at an angle. In this wood Mary told me there was a gravel path under the beech trees called Lady Anne's Walk. Lady Anne had been well liked in the village, but had died in her early twenties. Mary said that she had often worn a blue dress and had taken two brown dogs with her on her walks.

For some reason, by the time I was five I had developed a strong ambition to walk where Lady Anne had walked. In my imagination I could see a tall girl with golden hair walking under beech trees with two brown and white spaniels. I probably built the picture out of something I had seen in a book. But that didn't make it any less real to me and, eventually, I talked Mary into taking me into the wood to see this path.

In order to stop me talking her into taking me into the woods she had described to me in detail all the nasty things which could happen to you in woods, from being scratched by briars, and bitten by foxes, to being chased by big men with red faces. To her descriptions I added my own elves, witches and fairies. I already knew these lived in woods. So, although I must have been very persuasive to get her to agree to take me, it was with decidedly mixed feelings that I climbed over the fence after her into the wood. I was wishing that I had never thought of the idea.

Mary whispered, 'Look weer yer put yer feet. Don't go crunchin' in the leaves, nor treadin' on sticks and snappin' 'em. Woods is quiet places and you can 'ear things for miles. Foller me. An' if I duck down, yer duck down, else a keeper will get us.' She was probably worrying about what my mother would say if we got caught.

Bushes grew on the outskirts of the wood and we had to crawl between them. But as we got in deeper there was less sunlight so there were fewer bushes and more ferns, some of which were as tall as me. We followed a rabbit-track winding through the huge grey pillars of the beech trees. It was a bright afternoon in early summer and golden light flickered among the millions of green leaves which danced overhead. Mary stood quite still for a time behind a tree and listened. In our world, where at this time we had no engines of any kind, sounds did carry for miles. Over the hammering of my heart I could hear sheep and cattle and a dog barking. There was a loud buzzing of insects up in the leaves. I could smell the damp, musty, earthy smell, which I had met first when Millie, the daughter of the head gardener at the Hall, had taken me into its long rows of hot-houses.

Mary moved out from behind the tree and signed to me to follow. We were moving towards the sun and every now and again a shaft of light glittered down through the leaves and dazzled me. The trees in the middle of the wood had been thinned when the path was made, so there were patches where the sun shone right down on to late daffodils and bluebells and primroses. It lit up the fronds of ferns and the bright new tops of the bushes.

Mary stopped, put her hand on my shoulder, then pointed ahead, 'There it is,' she whispered. And there it was. Lady Anne's path winding away through a huge space like a church under an arched shimmering roof of green light. Between the pillars along the path there were misty dark green shadows into which the bushes and ferns gradually vanished. In the distance the shadows closed in and took away the grey pillars. But, further away still, rays of light came down and brought some of them back again and lit the ferns with bright circles like those round the heads of saints in holy pictures.

I had imagined that woods would be full of black shadows. But there was no black anywhere, there was only green and yellow. Dark green, misty green, ordinary green, bright green, then a flaring, eye-hurting, dancing, yellow green which I had never seen before. Where the path went through a patch of light Lady Anne in her blue dress was bending to take a stick out of the mouth of one of her spaniels. She was patting the dog on the head. Now she would throw the stick for it again.

Mary whispered, 'Yer've seen it. Now let's get back.'

'Oh no,' I said. 'We must walk down Lady Anne's path.'

'Shush! We can't. We'll get caught.'

'No we won't,' I whispered. 'We'll keep stopping and listening.'

'Oh my guy!' sighed Mary.

I found that I liked woods. When we got back to the lane I looked up at Mary and said, 'We will walk there quite often.'

'Yes.' Mary sighed again. 'I specs we will.'

We did. It was Mary who taught me the basics of woodcraft: concealment, stillness, silence, patience; the use of eyes and ears and nose. It was surprising what you saw if you just obeyed the rules. A family of red-squirrels came and played for us, up and down, and round and round one of the giant beeches. Their tawny little bodies and fluffed out tails glowed against the smooth grey bark.

The next place I decided that we should explore was the Park. It took several weeks to persuade Mary to risk it. 'Wait until the bracken's higher,' she would say.

I had to look at it with longing and sigh and go all sad for about a week before it was time to say, 'The bracken's high now. So we'll go.'

'All roight. Let's get it over with,' said Mary.

The Park had a herd of deer in it. There was a high fence round it made of long slats of rough-sawn wood nailed upright to crossbars held up by thick posts. It looked like a long comb upside down. To go through the high white gate or climb the stile beside it, which was built like two ladders which met at the top, was too risky. But there was a draw-rail not far from the sea of bracken. The rail was free to move up and down in two slots. You lifted it, moved it aside, and squeezed through the gap.

From the gate the lane became a dusty white road running down between the East Wood and the West. Mary said it led to twin lakes about two miles away. The road was white because, like all the roads round Overton, it was made of crushed limestone.

We went through the draw-rail and, while Mary replaced it, I scuttled into the bracken which was taller than I was. It was like being in a green jungle. In places it was as tall as Mary so that she didn't have to crouch. We followed a path from the draw-rail to a cart track which led to an old quarry and wasn't much used. Grass and weeds had almost grown over it. The bracken was crowding in on it too.

It was all right to use the track because it had bends in it. All you had to do was peep round each bend to see that the next stretch was clear. If you saw or heard anybody you had to slip into the bracken, find a rabbit-track, crawl quickly along it for a bit, and then sit still. As long as you kept still, Mary said, a keeper wouldn't find you. But if you were soft and went and pushed through the bracken he would see the top of it moving and like as not come after you.

Nobody ever went through a jungle more carefully than I did through that bracken.

Soon we came to a place where trees and thorn-bushes pushed out into the bracken from the West Wood on our left. 'I've got a surprise fer yer,' said Mary. 'We crawls through these 'ere thorn bushes. Mind yer foller me close, else you'll get scratched an' tear yer clothes.'

She took off the belt of her dress, hitched her skirt up above her bare brown knees, put the belt back on again, and crawled into a sort of low tunnel between the thorns. I crawled after her. Sometimes we had to lie flat and push ourselves along with our toes and elbows. Sometimes her skirt wrinkled up. The backs of her thighs were rounded and brown and smooth like the shell of a brown egg, only a bit shinier.

Eventually she turned right and I found that we were crawling beside a curving stone wall. She kept looking up into the bushes. When we came to a gap in them she stood up, climbed on to the wall, and sat on top of it before helping me up beside her. Even on top of the wall we were hidden by the bushes. They were higher than it was.

I turned. I nearly fell off. I was so amazed. Inside the wall and the bushes was a small round pond. On it a moorhen was heading fast for the cover of green, sword-bladed reeds, which grew along the inside of the wall. Behind her, cheeping and paddling like mad, was a line of fluffy brown chicks, bobbing in their mother's shining wake, and weaving through the green circles of the lily-pads.

On the top of the crumbling wall, in the bits where the bushes didn't bend over it, wildflowers were growing, blue, and yellow, and pink. Small blue dragon-flies hovered over their mirrored selves or put their mouths against a flower or a stem while their wings flashed to hold the kiss. On the lily-pads were bigger yellow ones flexing their wings, while the water, wakened by the moorhen, rocked them gently in the sunshine.

There was a picture in a book of poems which had a green leather binding and pages edged with gold. My mother read one of the poems to me and showed me a picture on the page next to it. A lady in a long white dress was lying in a brown boat which floated on still water among green reeds with flowers between them. The lady had flowers too in her folded hands.

'Under tower and balcony,
By garden wall and gallery,
A gleaming shape, she floated by,
Pale between the houses high,
Silent into Camelot.'

The boat had gone now. But I remembered it.

We too were silent. I took Mary's hand. We watched all that was happening in that little, busy, world. We were so still that a yellow bird flew out from the bushes and hopped from pad to pad, disturbing the dragon-flies, until it found exactly the right place from which to take a drink.

When I looked at Mary she was watching me with a smug little smile on her face. 'Loike it?'

'Yes,' I said.

'Thought yer would.'

The bird flew away. 'Yellow-'ammer,' Mary said. 'The big flies with the shiny wings is dragon-flies. The little blue ones is all roight. But don't go swiping at the big ones. They sting.'

'How did the pond get here?'

'Folks made it for the cattle in days gone by. It's fed by springs. But there's a bigger one now, over yonder by the road. So they use that. It's fed by springs too.'

Then, of course, she had to explain to me what that kind of spring was.

I liked watching the pond. But Mary said, 'Come an' I'll show yer the rabbits.'

We crawled out from under the thorn bushes. 'Grown up folk can't get near that pond no more,' Mary said.

That made it even nicer.

We waited in the edge of the bracken until we were sure that no one was about. Then we went on down the track to the old quarry. We went so quietly that we were able to stand in the bracken and watch dozens of rabbits hopping about near their homes in a pile of rubble at the foot of the face of the quarry. Some of the young ones were chasing each other and a big one was chasing another big one.

'That's a buck chasing a doe,' Mary whispered.

'Are they playing?' I whispered back.

'Sort of.'

The doe ran into a corner between two blocks of stone. She was trapped. The buck jumped on to her, covering her back, and pressed her down. She threshed about a bit and then lay still. The buck went on trying to thrust her into the ground.

I was going to turn to Mary but she took me by the shoulders, held me back against her, and whispered 'Shush!' We watched until the buck got off the doe.

'Funny sort of game,' I whispered.

'Ain't it.' I could tell by the way her thighs and stomach quivered, warm against my shoulders, that she was laughing. It felt nice.

'Watch,' she said, and coughed.

Every rabbit froze. Not an ear quivered. Not a nose twitched. She coughed again. There were several double thumps on the ground and with a twinkling of white tails the rabbits shot back into their burrows among the rubble.

'Them thumps was made by the bucks with their 'ind legs. They're a warning of danger for the rabbits down in the burrows as well as ahtside. Boys wot's good with catapults sometimes creep up to weer we're standin' and bag a rabbit each.'

'Bag them?'

'Kill them.'

'What for?'

'To eat of course. Rabbits makes a good dinner fer 'ungry folk.'

It seemed a pity to me that people had to kill nice little rabbits for food.

On the way back down the lane we saw a green and yellow bird with a red top to its head fly out of a tree right in front of us. 'Woodpecker,' said Mary. 'See the silly way it flies, bobbing up and down . . . listen.'

I heard a high, laughing noise. 'Is that it, making that noise?'

'Ar . . . That's why some folks calls it a yaffle. Becos it laughs.'

That night, as I was holding her plait, I asked her, 'Do people kill dogs and cats for food?'

'Not us. But foreigners do. 'Osses an' all.'

'Does all meat come from killed animals?'

'O' course,' said Mary, 'weer else? Killed cattle, killed pigs, killed sheep, rabbits, 'ares, pheasants, cockerels, an' 'ens. Yer can't get it no other way.'

It made quite a lot to think about as the evening chorus of the birds helped me towards sleep. Thousands of birds singing. In Overton, in high summer, they wakened you in the morning and their song slid into your dreams.

And there was the Camelot pond too. And the funny games which rabbits played. And the nice feeling of a girl, laughing, pressed up warm against your back.

CHAPTER FOUR

Emma came to do the washing on Mondays. She did it in 'the copper' in the wash-house. First thing in the morning Mary would fill it with buckets of water and light a fire under it so that the water would be nearly boiling by the time Emma arrived at eleven.

Emma set about the washing with the same furious energy with which she set about most things. It was no wonder that she was little more than muscle and bone. First she sliced bits of yellow soap off a long bar. Then she plonked the clothes and the soap into the water, put the lid back on, and left them to simmer for a bit. She then spun them round with a 'dolly'. This was like a small wooden footstool. It had four little legs and a pole sticking up from the middle of it with a T-shaped handle at the top. You put the legs in among the clothes and spun the handle, first one way, and then the other to get the clothes off the legs. Emma seemed to enjoy this part of the job. She spun away like mad, half-hidden in clouds of steam, while the suds flew. Her cap used to slide over one ear and wisps of damp, sandy hair stuck out all round it.

The other bit she seemed to enjoy was slapping the clothes on to a washboard and then bashing away at them with the bar of soap. After this she rinsed them in a tub of cold water, then mangled them, whirling the handle regardless of fingers, sending water squirting out of the rollers into a zinc tub on the floor.

This was the tub in which I had my baths in front of the sitting-room fire. Mary filled it with pots of hot water heated on the stove. She then cooled it with jugs of cold water. I nearly always complained that it was too hot. But often my mother took a hand, felt the water, said, 'Get in, or I'll dump you in!' And that was that.

Baths in proper bathrooms are dull compared to those in front of a fire of blazing logs.

It was amazing how much time and energy folk put in to carrying water even if they had a piped supply in their homes. On washdays at least eight buckets would have to be carried into the wash-house for the copper and for rinsing, and eventually carried out again or mopped up. Jugs of hot and cold water had to go up to bedrooms, and pots of hot and jugs of cold into warm rooms for baths. And, since no cottages in the village had a piped supply, families had to fetch buckets of water from the taps on street corners. These could be over a hundred yards away. The yokes designed to help with water carrying were too big for children to wear. But by the time they were ten, both girls and boys in Overton had begun to develop splendid muscles just from the daily morning and evening chore of carrying water.

One Monday lunchtime, after she had pegged out the washing, Emma came into the kitchen and battled two buckets back under the sink and taught them their places. As the clatter died away, 'It's Overton Feast come Satterday, Teacher,' she said. 'The village will be full o' folk wot's come back to keep it wi' their famblies. We keeps opens 'ouse on Overton Feast yer see. 'Ole famblies goes rahnd the village to visit oothers. An' there's allus a bit of a "do" on The Green. Folks chips in wi' pies an' cakes an' sandwiches an' beer an' 'ome made wine. The wine's mostly rhubarb else tater wi' a 'andful or two o' corn chucked in. Yer wants to watch the wine. Overton wine is famous all rahnd abaht. 'Its yer straight between the eyes like the kick o' a 'oss.'

She scrubbed at her arms with a towel. 'All the villages keeps their Feast on their patron saint's day. Ahrs is in midsoommer so it's called "New Taters Feast". Springwell's is in the autumn so it's "Light Yer Candles Feast", an' Blackwell's is in December so it's "Icicles Feast". Course Ashborough an' Plantham, being bigger, don't call their'n Feasts; they calls 'em Fairs. Ashborough's ain't mooch. Plantham's is the best. The streets is full o' all sorts o' stalls and rahndabahts an' so on. We jist 'as ole Dodgie Wite. 'E goes rahnd all the village Feasts wi' 'is rahndabahts, swingboats, coconut shies, fortune-teller, an' a stall or two.'

'Ahr Dad's broother is goin' to walk over from Springwell wi' 'is fambly. An' me broother, not bein' married, is goin' to bike over from Ashborough. I 'ope the weather's good. We 'as the "do" in the barn back o' the Fox an' Geese if it's wet. But it's a pity for them wi' famblies walkin' in from Ashborough an' such like if it rains. All Overton folks likes to get back 'um fer the Feast, yer see.'

'Like at New Year in Scotland,' my mother said. 'Families always try to be together and friends visit friends.'

'That's it,' said Emma. 'An' in the evenin' we allus 'as a bit o' a dance. Jakey plays his melodeon and Fogabolla 'is fiddle.'

'Fogabolla?' my mother said. 'However did he get called that?'

Emma laughed and the peak of her cap went up and down like a bird pecking. 'As a little ole boy 'e 'ad the best belch in the school . . . It's foony 'ow our little ole boys gets their nicknames. They call ahr 'Enry "Wacca" becos, w'en 'e were little an' 'e saw a kid a wippin' of a top, 'e used to shaht "Goo on, wack 'er." So now 'e's Wacca Walton for evermore.'

'I thought an old boy was an old man.'

'Not in Overton, Teacher.' Emma laughed again. 'An ole feller is an "ole man" sure enough. But an "ole boy" is a kid. It moodles ahtsiders. Like the nicknames does. They was cahntin' oop in the poob the other night, an' they reckon there's over two 'undred nicknames in Overton. Yer see in the days afore there was any "Lloyd George"—the dole that is—if yer was sick or sacked yer got nowt. So sons tried to stay in the same village as their dads'.

Then if they fell outta wuck the fambly could 'elp. That's why we've go so many famblies wi' the same name, an' why we need nicknames to tell 'em apart.'

We knew that the next day was the Feast all right when on the Friday evening Dodgie's roundabout got going in the paddock behind the Fox and Geese. You could hear the blare of its steam organ for miles. On Feast afternoon my mother, Mary and I, went down to see it. It was fascinating. It stood in a gap in the centre of the roundabout which was driven by steam too. Lions and tigers were painted on the front of it in bright colours picked out in gold. At one end there was a Red Indian chief in a feather head-dress with a pair of cymbals one above the other on a rod in front of him. The bottom cymbal stayed still while the top one kept shooting up the rod and clashing down again on the other. When this happened steam seemed to puff out of the chief's eyes. At the other end there was a big negro holding a steel rod in one hand and a triangle in the other. The arm with the rod kept swinging up and down to make the rod bash the triangle. As it struck home steam seemed to snort from the negro's nose.

In our quiet little world the din and the quick untiring actions were unbelievable. It was the most exciting roundabout ever. The shiny black, brown and dapple grey horses squeaked and rattled as they went round and round. Belts driving this and that slapped and whirred. Everything else trembled and bounced and clanged, or hooted and whistled and boomed, while every now and again a piercing shriek from the engine made your head sing and sent clouds of steam whooshing round the riders.

'My guy, it's fit to bust,' shouted Mary.

Two small children whose parents were leading them towards the astonishing thing ran screaming. And another boy, at the first shriek after he had been put aboard, seemed to fly off his horse into the steam in sheer terror. He was neatly fielded by a grinning man with a coal-blackened face who pitched him on to the back of the first riderless horse with the practised skill of a cook tossing pancakes. There he clung round the neck of the horse with his eyes shut while half the children in the village jumped up and down and jeered at him every time he came round. He had not, it seemed, already collected his nickname. So from henceforth he was known as 'Steamer'.

My mother bent down and yelled in my ear, 'Would you like a ride?'

Hastily I shook my head. It was not yet for me. I much preferred the quiet places. So I had a few sedate rides in the swingboats with Mary and a bottle of lemonade before we went home.

Lemonade came in a pale green bottle. The neck was closed by a glass ball which was held in position by the fizz. To open it you had to thump the ball away with a round piece of wood which had a short peg sticking down from the middle of it. To stop the ball falling down it, the bottle was nipped in above the waist to make a slot for the ball to rest in. When the bottle was nearly empty you could put it to one eye and close the other as if looking through a telescope. Then if you tilted the bottle gently you found yourself looking into a green crystal cave where the lemonade flowed in and out. If you held it in sunlight all the colours of the rainbow flashed from the walls. It was like the magic place I had found down Brooks.

My horizons were widened further when, at the beginning of the summer holidays, my mother bought herself a bicycle. To keep her long skirts out of the spokes of the rear wheel it had a fan of green cords stretched from each rim of the rear mudguard to plates fixed on either side of the axle. It also had a pillion on the back for me and a basket in front shaped to fit the handlebars. When I was to go with her on the pillion she wore a leather belt with two hand-grips on it for me to hold on to.

We used the bicycle to visit nearby villages, and to explore the narrow little roads leading off the main ones. Even the main roads were only wide enough for two carriages or carts to pass one another. Like the roads in and around Overton no tar was used on them. They were just made with broken stone which got crushed by the steel shoes of the horses and by the rims of the wheels. In wet weather they were muddy and in dry they were dusty.

By then motor cars must have been running between Ashborough and Plantham along the main road which ran through

Blackwell and Springwell. But I can't remember one passing us
on it during our journeys. And we still had no motors or buses in
Overton. Apart from a few bicycles the village still depended on
the horse for its travel as it had always done.

Emma put it like this, 'We've got everythink we want in
Overton bar one o' these 'ere fish-mongrels. An' even then yer
can get bloaters an' kippers an' smoked 'addock from ahr butcher.
We've got three shops wots got, or can get, owt yer is likely ter
want. An' we've got a baker, a butcher, a tailor, a cobbler, a
plumber, a carpenter, a painter, an' a blacksmith. We used to 'ave
ahr own gas supply an' all, but the war put paid to that. 'Arry'll
(no nickname so you knew he was an incomer) meck yer man a
cradle fer yer wen yer born and yer widder a coffin wen yer die.
Wot more do yer want? I ain't never been beyond Ashborough
an' Plantham. Wot's at the back o' Overton, Teacher? Is it the
sea?'

Some women and most children had never even been to
Ashborough. Neither of the towns had a cinema. So, unless you
wanted to go to the Fair or the market, there was no point in
putting yourself out. To hire Kitty and the open trap from the
Stores, or Cob and the open waggonette from the Inn, to go
to Ashborough, cost four shillings. To hire the Inn's closed
brougham pulled by Captain, a big black gelding, cost five. This
was too much for folk whose income was thirty shillings a week.
Some men needed a bicycle to get to work in nearby farms or
villages, but most folk had to walk. They were used to walking
and five miles wasn't much. But there had to be a good reason for
doing it.

On one of our bicycle rides my mother stopped to talk to a
grey-haired man who was sitting at the side of the road on a piece
of American cloth to keep out the damp. On one side of him he
had lumps of limestone about the size of a football and on the
other side a heap of stones which he had broken down to the size
of a golf ball. To do this he used a hammer the head of which had
one end square and the other wedge shaped. It had a long, whippy
handle. He never seemed to take a swipe at the stone with it. He
just flicked his wrists and the lumps fell apart as the hammer hit
them.

'I would have thought you would have to hit harder than that,' my mother said.

He grinned. 'The trick is to know where to 'it 'em,' he said. 'If you swipes at 'em, they flies all over. You 'as to keep gettin' oop an' fetchin' 'em.'

It had been raining and his old patched coat was hanging on the hedge behind him to dry. There was a corn sack beside it which he wore over his head and shoulders to keep the rain off. You pushed one bottom corner into the other to make a hood. A lot of children wore them that way, because, I found out later, they had no coat. Corn sacks were most useful things. You could fold them up to sit on, or to wipe your muddy feet on, or to make beds for cats and dogs. And you could use them as rugs in cold weather.

'It's all roight this weather,' the old man told my mother. 'But it's bad fer yer roomatics in wet. Specially in winter.'

He seemed pleased that we had stopped to talk to him. My mother found out later that the job of stone-breaking was still looked down on as the last which old men could do before they had to stop work altogether and become a burden on their families, even though, since 1910, they got the Old Age Pension. This was probably because, at five shillings a week until 1919, it hadn't made all that much difference. Now it was ten shillings.

When we were out for a picnic one day we found a lake up a narrow, overgrown road near Blackwell. Bushes grew round most of it, but in the gaps between them you could see that the water was covered with lily-pads with their yellow flowers scattered among them. Where the lake ended there were two iron plates set in concrete. They had cog wheels above them and a metal handle. My mother said that they were sluice gates which could be raised or lowered to control the level of the water. 'Look,' she said, pointing to where the top of a wall showed above the grass round the bank, 'this lake has been made by people. It's an artificial one. I wonder why they put it here miles from anywhere.'

There was a little bridge of wooden planks beside the sluice gates. She decided that we would cross it and have our picnic on a level stretch of grass on the other side.

As we went over to the place, we found that the lake had tree-stumps all round it. 'It was once enclosed by trees,' my mother said. Then when we had reached the place, we found the remains of a pavement and flowerbeds. 'Those wild roses must once have been ramblers in a garden. Perhaps this lake was once in the grounds of a manor house. It's a lonely lake now.'

I didn't like the place. It was spoiled. Where the trees had been felled saplings had grown up and then been cut down and just left lying among the long grass. Like my mother said, it was a lonely and it was a sad place because it had once been beautiful.

As we were laying out our lunch a cracked bell began to toll from somewhere nearby. It had a trembling sound like the voice of a very old man.

'A funeral bell?' my mother shivered. 'Can't be.'

'Let's go,' I said. 'I don't like it.'

'No. Let's go and see where it's coming from.'

There was a ridge behind us. When we got to the top of it we saw below it, in what was now grazing land for sheep, a clock tower on a stone building. Between us and the building the grass went down in what looked like very long steps. 'Terraces,' said my mother. 'So the lake was once in the grounds of a manor house, or perhaps a castle. When we have finished our picnic we will go up that track to the clock tower and see if there is anyone there to tell us about it.'

When we got back to the lake we found a big, shiny rat with a long tail running off with one of our sandwiches. 'I don't like this place,' I said, 'something awful happened here.'

'Don't be silly!' While we ate our lunch my mother told me stories about how the children from the castle came to the lake for boating and fishing and games. 'It was a happy place,' she said, 'although it's a sad one now.'

When we got to the clock tower we found that it was part of a little church. An old couple were coming out of it. They told my mother that it was all that was left of Saxford Hall and village. A rich London baronet had bought the estate many years before. First he had the village pulled down to make himself a deer park. Then, when his wife took a dislike to the place, he had the Hall pulled down too.

'Folks reckon it were a grand place,' the old man said. ''Ouse parties in summer and at Christmas, wi' dozens o' extra carriages in the stables an' scores o' 'osses. An' the 'Unt used to meet 'ere an' all, wi' 'undreds o' riders.' He looked round the empty acres. 'Seems funny to think folks used ter live all round 'ere. I seed a picter o' the village once. It were a pretty place. But nah they gone an' chopped dahn all the trees it looks more like a blasted 'eath . . . It seems 'er Ladyship took a dislike to the place arter two o' 'er children got drowned in the lake. They went aht in a boat an' some'ow fell in.'

Now I knew why the place frightened me.

It was in that lake that I learned to fish. But I never liked to be there alone. It is now at the bottom of a huge reservoir. Five fathoms deep lie the ghosts of Saxford.

The longest rides we ever made together on the bicycle were to Ashborough. When my mother told her that I was going to go Gran objected. 'It's nae right to take that wee laddie a' that way. He'll fall off.'

'No he won't. He's got more sense.' And off we went.

Three-speed gears for bicycles came later. So we had to walk up the hills. But we could whizz down the other side. At first my mother took Barnswell Hill slowly with the brake on. But once she was sure that I wouldn't fall off, we flew down it. For the first time I felt the thrill of speed. I can still remember how the banks with their tall red wildflowers went whistling past.

Our rides to Ashborough were great treats for me. The main streets in the town were covered with tar and gravel and among all the horses, standing at the kerb between the shafts of broughams, carriages, and traps, were motor cars. Most had fawn coloured canvas hoods over them and flexible celluloid screens at the sides. But some were big slab-sided saloons, as high as a brougham and with glass windows. The drivers had to ask passers-by to hold the head of any horse near them before they could start up their engines. My mother said that on an earlier visit, she had seen a horse which had been standing quietly at the kerb munching oats out of its nosebag, go bolting off down the street nosebag and brougham and all when one of the engines went off with a bang. 'In a year or two I expect motors will come to Overton. And that will cause some fun.'

We went shopping and window-shopping and had lunch in the 'Olde Oak Tea-room'. Then we went round 'Piper's Penny Bazaar' where nothing cost more than sixpence and where I always got sixpence to spend.

A few months later, in the winter, when I no longer went with her, my mother came whizzing round the bottom bend at Barnswell to find a waggon drawn up in the middle of the road. When she slammed on her brakes the bicycle skidded sideways in the mud. She said the horse looked very surprised as she went under its nose. She skidded up the bank, landed in a thorn bush, scratched her face and ripped her skirt. The crash pushed the handlebars squint and bent one of the pedals. But the waggoner kindly straightened them for her and she carried on to Ashborough where she bought safety pins to mend the tears in her skirt.

Gran made a terrible fuss about the accident. 'You'll kill yourself and then what will your son and I do?'

My mother just laughed.

She gave Gran and me another fright during those same holidays in which she bought the bicycle.

She had decided that the walls of the school were bare and ugly. So, since she was an above-average artist with crayons and water-colours, she drew scenes from history on them on the back of old wall-paper which she pasted on to them. By the end of the Easter holidays she had completely covered the walls with murals up as far as she could reach by standing on a chair. These were so much admired by the children, parents, and visitors, that now she decided to cover the upper part of the walls as well.

She borrowed two planks and, using a step-ladder, made a platform for herself by putting the planks across the top of two blackboards. These were set in strong wooden frames with long feet sticking out at right-angles on each side with castors on them.

When Gran saw her up on this contraption she said, 'Come doon oot o' that! Mechty me! Is it no enough for you to be trying to kill yourself on yon bicycle? Come doon off yon perch. Whit do you think you are . . . a hen?'

My mother just laughed and went on working.

Gran looked at me and shook her head, 'She'll kill herself. I'm telling you. She'll kill herself.'

Then one morning when I was reading in the sitting-room and Gran was sewing, there was the most awful crash from the school.

'She's killed herself. She has. She's done it. I telt you she would. She's killed herself.'

Terrified, I ran into the school and found my mother picking herself up from the floor with her crayons scattered round her and one plank lying beside the blackboards. Limping and rubbing her behind with both hands she walked up and down muttering to herself while Gran and I watched in silence. At last she turned and saw us and laughed. 'Aren't I the biggest idiot. I stepped back for a better look.'

Soon the top half of the walls had knights in shining armour, and a King in a red velvet cloak, and sailing ships on them.

'Could you draw me the lady drifting silent into Camelot?' I asked.

When the mural was finished I took Mary in to see it. 'Does it remind you of anywhere?'

Mary took a closer look then shook her head.

'Our pond,' I said.

'Don't be soft. That's not a pond. It's a river.'

But whenever we went back to the pond I could still see the lady on it. I just didn't mention her to Mary.

My mother was pleased when His Majesty's Inspectors began to make good reports about the school. She read them to Gran and then stuck them in the Log Book. The one for 1922 says: 'The atmosphere in the school is friendly and the discipline good. The work in all subjects has reached a very satisfactory level; that in Arithmetic, English and Art is worthy of special praise . . . Art is of outstanding merit. The more capable children have acquired considerable skill in the use of pencil and water-colour.'

It was round about this time that I heard my mother telling Gran, 'It's heart-breaking. That girl Doris has the makings of a really good artist. She has got more talent than anyone I have ever taught. But she hasn't a hope of being able to develop it. She leaves school at Christmas. Such a waste.'

Doris was a big, untidy girl who came from one of the poorest families. That she should have such talent surprised me. I thought all artists should be neat and careful in their movements. Not all over the place like Doris.

For drawing I had no ability whatsoever. This was a big disappointment to my mother. And when she tried to teach me to play the piano I rebelled. But I liked reading. 'He has an ear for words. That's something,' she told Gran.

'Uh-huh!' said Gran. 'You'll remember that when his Grandma Buchan found he could talk before he could walk she said he'd either be a great preacher or a great leear.'

I grew up surrounded by books. A salesman used to cycle round the country houses, schools, and vicarages, with a case of books on the back of his bike and catalogues from publishers in the basket on the front. My mother soon became one of his best customers. She gave him tea while she looked through the catalogues. Then the books which she had ordered came by post.

The post was delivered each weekday by Bill. He wore a blue uniform and a cap peaked fore and aft like the railway porters. He cycled into Ashborough in all weathers to fetch the post. But when the village was snowed up he only walked the five miles each way every other day.

He had a big watch in his waistcoat pocket on a silver chain. 'Wot's Ashborough toime?' Mary used to ask him. And he would produce the watch and tell her. Then she would hurry back into the kitchen and put the alarm clock which ticked away there to the right time. To bring the village the right time from Ashborough Post Office was one of Bill's most important jobs. All Post Offices in the towns and villages had a big clock by which folks set their watches.

In every parcel of books there was always one or more for me. But I much preferred to listen to my mother reading than to read myself. So did the children in school. She could make the words come alive. I used to go in and sit round her desk with the others. She read us *Treasure Island*, *King Solomon's Mines*, *The Thirty-nine*

Steps, and *Kidnapped*, looking up sometimes from the book at us to see our eyes popping out of our heads.

She could make books really funny too. When she read *Brer Rabbit* to us, she had to stop every now and again while we all hooted with laughter. Sometimes she couldn't read for laughing.

One of the books I liked best was *The Lumberlost*. It was all about a boy who made himself a hut in the woods and used to go and live there among the birds and the animals. I decided that I would do that one day.

CHAPTER FIVE

FOR AN only child, unused to mixing with other children of the same age, going to school can be a painful experience. But I was lucky. I only had to step through a door into another world run by my mother. No bullying was allowed on the school premises. So even if anyone had thought that it was time the cosseted me was toughened up a bit, they had no chance to get at me until I was allowed to mix with the others after school hours. By then I had learned a thing or two and had made four firm friends who answered happily to the names of Leftie, Artie, Jippo, and Crum.

To begin with I was more than a little taken aback by the situations into which our friendship landed me. My friends were independent in outlook and adventurous in spirit. But in a year or two, as I grew from a delicate curly-haired darling into a pasty-faced boy with straight mousy hair and the biggest ears you ever saw, I was taken aback less and less. It is fair to say that I took to their harum-scarum ways as a duck takes to water.

My first clear memories of Christmas come from the year in which I first went to school. Until then I only remember pealing bells and crackers and paper-hats. But from that year I remember the excitement in school as the great day of The Party-At-The-Hall drew near. For children whose fathers were farmers or tradesmen, Christmas in our village was a wonderful time. But for those whose fathers were unskilled or out of work there wasn't a great deal of difference between Christmas Day and any other day, no matter how hard their parents tried to make it special. For them therefore The Party-At-The-Hall was the high-spot of the year.

The Family could have had presents distributed to the children, or they could have held the party in the barn at the Fox and Geese which stood in for a Village Hall. There was no need for us to be invited into their home, or for them to put themselves out to look after us personally. But they did. Their relationship with their villagers was certainly that of high-class persons with low-class persons. But at least it was personal.

By tradition the Party was held on the last day of term before the Christmas holidays. We formed up two by two in a crocodile with the youngest children at the front. Blanche, who had taken over as my mother's assistant, led the way with an electric torch and my mother was at the back with another. We went down Pudden Bag between the rows of thatched cottages, where lamps were already glowing behind the window curtains. The torches weren't needed yet because there was a powdering of snow and the stars were waking up in the clear, steel-blue, sky. But as we reached the wall of the Grounds the tall fir trees on the other side stuck up like spear points and cut away most of the light.

We went through the Nuns' Door. It was called this because the nuns had used it morning and evening on their way to church. As we filed through, Blanche switched on her torch and stood at one side to light the path for us.

It was dark among the trees. The lower branches seemed to be crushing down on the tunnel of light made by the torch.

Although there was a scent like Christmas trees, we didn't like the blackness and we all hurried up to get out under the sky again.

Beyond the trees the path ran down to a carriageway which cut across the middle of acres of lawns and went on past the front of the Hall itself. The lawns were white and Crum, walking beside me, said, 'Coo! Yer couldn't 'arf meck snowmen 'ere'.

The Hall had its own gas plant and, to help us to see our way, the curtains had not been drawn across the tall windows. We were used to a shadowy world of lamps and candles. So, to our eyes, the bright lights, throwing patterns across the glittering snow, were dazzling. It was like walking up to a fairy castle in a picture-book.

We put our coats and caps on trestle-tables in a corridor and then maids led us into a wide hall which had a shining staircase leading up from it to a balcony with pillars round it and a painted ceiling above it. But I only noticed these things later. At the entrance I was, like all the others, stopped in my tracks by the eye-opening sight of a Christmas tree so tall that it reached from the floor to above the rail of the balcony and which was brilliant with lighted candles and sparkling with silver and gold decorations.

We just stood and stared. Then we looked pop-eyed at each other and stared again. The maids had to come and take us by the hand and lead us across the polished floor into the open space round the tree.

In our wet boots the floor was hard to walk on. Overton, in those days, didn't go in for rubber soles. Crum slipped over and I fell on top of him. We weren't the only ones to fall either. Until we got used to the slippery floor we tiptoed about like cats on hot bricks.

First we played musical games during which, every now and again, another child hit the floor. Then we played blind-man's-buff and pass-the-parcel. Then we had tea sitting on benches at the usual long trestle-tables that used to be a feature of any community occasion.

During tea I noticed that two men with brass cone-shaped snuffers on long wooden sticks were keeping an eye on the tree and putting out any candles which were burning low. If a tree that size had gone up in flames it would have been a disaster.

Candles made better decorations than electric tree-lights do; they were brighter, and warmer, and alive. But you had to be very careful not to put them so near a higher branch that it caught fire. Quite often at Christmas parties someone would suddenly sniff the air and say, 'I smell the tree.' Then someone would quickly feel the branches near the candles to find out which was over-heating. The snag with candles was that even the thicker ones only lasted a couple of hours and after that there were no lights on the tree at all.

After tea the Countess gave us our presents. I can remember that mine was in a large coloured box. My mother had supplied names and ages and each present had a name written on it. The Earl was not there because he was an invalid at this time and hardly ever appeared in public.

The last of the candles on the Christmas tree were then snuffed out, and we sang carols along with the Family and its servants. Lady Sarah played the accompaniments on a grand piano. For years afterwards every time I heard 'O come all ye faithful' I could smell that huge tree and the smouldering wicks of its candles and see the shining staircase, and the balcony, and the painted ceiling. I expect most of my friends could do the same.

By the time we started back for school again the stars were bright in a blue velvet sky and the frost had stuck more sparklers in the snow. We could see that the terraced lawns swept down to a lake which was lined with tall, withered, reeds. Near it a big cedar tree had snow on its branches. Beyond it the huge white sheet of the lawns stretched away to another black, jagged, line of fir trees. Seen from our height it was a vast expanse; fit for giants.

Between the Party and Christmas Eve, children came round the houses singing carols. There was one which we used to sing in Overton which I haven't heard anywhere else.

> I 'ave a little whistle-bob made out o' 'olly tree,
> The finest little whistle-bob that ever yer did see,
> For it is a Christmas time an' we travel far an' near,
> An' we wish yer good 'ealth an' a 'Appy Noo Year.'

'Good missus an' good master if yer both do be in.
I 'ave a little pocket to put my money in,
For it is a Christmas time an' we travel far an' near,
An' we wish yer good 'ealth an' a 'Appy Noo Year.'

On Christmas Eve my mother always went to Midnight Mass because her voice was needed in the small choir. Gran used to read in an armchair beside the fire in our bedroom, while I kept waking up and asking her what the time was. Just before midnight the bells began to peal from the old church above the village. At the magic hour they clashed together three times and then went off into even greater merriment.

At this point Gran let me get up, put on slippers and dressing-gown, and find out what Father Christmas had put in my stockings hanging at the bottom of the bed. The sweets and small toys in these kept me occupied until my mother got back. One year he brought me a mouth-organ—harmonicas they call them now—and I drove Gran nearly mad with it.

This year Freddie and Frankie, two of the seniors, had helped my mother to get things ready after I had gone to bed, and she brought them back with her. Their nicknames were Duckie and Bongo. But my mother rarely used our nicknames out of school and never used them in school.

When I went downstairs into the sitting-room, I was so over-come by joy and surprise that like down at the hall, I could only stand and stare. A tree, so tall that it reached from floor to ceiling, was covered with candles, presents, and decorations, from which the flames of the candles and of the fire winked and smiled at me.

The main presents were my first leather football and a clock-work train set. It had two engines, three carriages and three goods trucks, a tunnel, a station, points, and signals. And it just fitted nicely on our dining-room table, brought through from the other room. I was in raptures as Duckie and Bongo condescended to play with it.

Later, my mother and I stood inside the curtains at the window to cut off the lamplight and looked out at the white garden with its frosted trees and rose-bushes lit by the stars. No Christmas card has ever been so beautiful.

When Duckie and Bongo had gone, she told me about the Christmas which she had spent with my father before he went off to war. I expect she didn't want him to feel that he was being left out of things.

The only thing which marred the magic night was that, the first time I bounced my football, it shot up and made my nose bleed.

Next morning, as we went to church, all down the street you could hear people calling 'Merry Christmas' to each other. And as we went down Pudden Bag people opened doors or windows and waved to us and called out 'Merry Christmas, Teacher!'

In the afternoon the hand-bell ringers came round and played carols on their bells. When they had finished my mother gave them mincepies and beer.

On the evening of Boxing Day there was to be a dance in the barn. I talked Mary into taking me down to see the decorations. The farm implements and lumber had been shifted to one end and folk had lent folding screens to hide them. The ladders on the racks on the walls had been draped with bunting and holly and mistletoe. And home-made paper-chains criss-crossed the dance floor. This was sections of floor-boards laid on the rough concrete and powdered with what Mary said was 'French chalk' to make them slippery. The powder was slightly perfumed but not enough to beat the smell of a pile of turnips behind the screens. But once the fun started who would worry about a good country smell?

While we watched, two waggons clattered up with the inevitable trestle-tables and benches. The shire-horses steamed in the frosty air.

'Are you going to the dance?' I asked Mary.

'Don't reckon so.'

'Why not?'

'Lot o' softness.' She kicked a pebble away from one of the wheels. 'Come on! Let's go and slide!'

Winter was a hard time in Overton and Christmas and sliding were, for the young, two of the few good things about it.

Mary said that, because of the snow and a week of heavy frosts, the slide down the little hill beside the Pump where West Street joined Top Street was better than usual this year.

You had to be careful where you put a slide because if grown-ups thought folk or horses might slip up on it they would scatter salt on it and melt it. But in snowy weather the steep little hill at the Pump wasn't used because it was easier to get on Top Street from East Street.

To make a slide, you got in line and stamped down the snow along a strip about a yard wide and twenty-five yards long. Then the seniors picked bits about a yard long and stood beside them on one foot while they polished the packed snow with the other. It was then time for everyone to get in line, run at it, and slide. This was tricky because some bits were not so polished as others and boys and girls went flying at all angles into the snow. But the whole strip was soon ice-slippery and, after the seniors had sprinkled water on it a couple of times and it had frozen overnight, it really was ice.

The senior boys fairly flew down it, their leather soles whirring on the ice. And the big girls weren't much slower. Of course we 'little-uns' got in the way of the 'big-uns'. But it didn't matter all that much, because if a big-un caught up with you he or she just put their hands on your shoulders and you leaned back against them and went whizzing down in front of them.

I soon found that, if you felt them begin to fall one way you had to turn sideways the other way. Then you either landed clear of them or on top of them. This was less painful than having them land on you. But to land on top of one of the big girls wasn't painful. It was quite nice.

To begin with Mary came behind me and took me down. Then a boy, who seemed to be a friend of hers, began coming behind her so that all three of us nearly reached the end of the slide.

As the sun began to set, our breath puffed out in longer plumes and the frost tingled our faces. When we got out of breath, Crum and I used to go and lean against the brick pillars of the Pump and watch the fun. We roared with laughter as boys and girls crashed into the snow and skidded along on their bottoms. We shouted 'Goo it Duckie!' . . . 'After 'im Bongo!' as our ace sliders raced towards the strip. And we joined in the chant of 'Keep the pot a-boiling!' as a never ending line of children circled on to the slide and then ran back up to the top again.

The big girls would try to dodge the boys who were out to catch them on the slide. They would run towards it and then side-step at the last minute so that the boy who had started after them went hurtling down by himself. If after several tries a boy did catch a girl, we always gave him a cheer.

The sliding would go on for hours. In a little world with no facilities for organised sport, it was the most exciting game which we could play. When a horse came clopping along Top Street we just stopped long enough to let it go by. In those days the streets belonged to everyone, not just to the traffic.

As the light faded the lamplight began to glow from the windows down the street and behind us the snow on the thatch of the cottages looked like thick icing on a cake. The three brown ruts in the snow on the street stood out clearly. The middle rut was wider than the other two because it was made by wheels going in both directions. Between the ruts were the two paths cut in the snow by the hooves of the horses. In snowy weather they had studs in their shoes for a better grip.

Now the young men who had finished work would come to the slide. Some brought their girl-friends, who squealed with delight as they were swept along. There was much shouting of 'Ey up!' . . . 'Catch 'er Tabbie!' . . . 'Goo it Speedie!' 'Look aht!' . . . 'Keep the pot a-boiling!' But it was no place for little-uns any more. We went home.

In Overton, and I expect in most villages, there were different seasons for the other street games which children played. Hoops, or tops, or marbles, would appear in the shops at the beginning of each season.

Most of the grown-ups realised that it was better for us to play in the streets than to get up to mischief. Some older children enjoyed playing cards, or draughts, or dominoes, but for the younger ones there was little to do. The only gramophones in the village were ancient things with big brass horns and most of the records were old and scratched. In most homes, until 'the wireless' arrived in a few years time, there was no music to listen to unless you made it yourself.

In the dark winter evenings after school, when there was no snow for sliding, we played 'fox and hounds'. This was a kind of hide-and-seek except that there was more than one seeker. When they were foxed the seekers used to sing a kind of old 'street-cry': ''Oller if yer far away an' whistle if yer nee-ar.' Those still hiding were then obliged to do one or the other.

Hoops, I think, came out in late spring and tops and marbles in the summer.

The streets running round the centre oblong of cottages made a good race-track for the hoops and the tops. We started from beside the Pump, raced down to the Green then up East Street and along Top Street and whoever got back to the Pump first was the winner.

We always knew, as we came up to a corner, whether a trap or a cart was coming the other way because we could hear the clop of hooves, the jingle of harness, and the crunching of the wheels. The drivers however couldn't hear us. Some got quite nasty if their horse reared or danced sideways into a tree when we popped up in front of it, racing neck and neck.

One incomer drove a young mare in a dog-cart—these were two-wheeled like a trap but had their bench seats back to back. He didn't just crack his whip at you or flick the lash past you. He aimed at your bare knees and sometimes he got them. In a week or two however it dawned on him that the frequency with which small boys had taken to dashing out from here and there and upsetting his mare was not accidental. And he kept his whip to himself from then on.

Grown-ups nearly always got the message in the end. It just took time.

You could buy posh wooden hoops in the Stores. But they weren't much good for Overton streets. They stuck in the mud, cow-pats, and piles of horse-muck. We preferred to use the rims of old bicycle wheels. They were heavier and cut through the muck.

Tops were about three inches high, T-shaped, and they spun on a round stud. You had a little whip with which to drive them. You wound the string round the upright, held the top near the ground and set it spinning by pulling the string away. Then you whipped it to send it spinning forward a few yards, ran after it, and whipped it again. Here again the cow-pats and the horse-muck got in the way. If you didn't look out your top stuck in them and had to be wiped in a clump of grass before you wound it up and set it going again. This could lose you the race. Some boys got expert at judging the strength of their lash in order to avoid these traps. They would probably have made good golfers. But this was a game of which we had never even heard.

CHAPTER SIX

THE SCHOOL was just one room about forty yards long. It had a high gabled roof supported by thick wooden beams. This looked nice but made the place almost impossible to heat in winter. It had two cylindrical iron stoves, with tortoises moulded on their tops. We stoked coke into them until they glowed red round the middle. But the place was still cold a few feet away from them.

An old curtain which had faded from red to pink divided the Infant Room from the Senior one. It was almost twelve feet high and ran across the room on a thick steel pole. At midday and in the evening a senior boy pushed it back with a long pole so that the whole school could join together for prayers. As the rings clattered back a pleasant, musty, spicy, smell came from the curtain and sometimes at midday the sun, streaming in at the tall window on the senior side, lit up the thousands of specks of dust which floated off it. For some strange reason I have always remembered the smell, the drone of the prayers, and the dust dancing in the sunshine.

When Crum and I were seven we joined Leftie, Artie, and Jippo in the Senior Room. They were a year older than we were. By then I no longer went for walks with Mary, who was 'a-courtin' with a boy-friend, but went exploring with my friends instead.

The urge to study wildlife had not yet smitten the nation and it had certainly not smitten us. We were just out to see interesting things and interesting places. But in our tiny world much of what was interesting was connected with wildlife in one way or another.

We didn't wander far afield in winter. This was partly because the gamekeepers could spot you more easily after the leaves fell, and partly because the sun went down quickly and you were liable to find yourselves caught out on the way back through a wood by the mists and the twilight. Many of the tales which parents told their children, when whiling away the winter evenings, were about the local ghosts. We knew all about them and had no wish to run the risk of meeting one.

On the southern edge of The Grounds are the ruins of the Old 'All, which burned down about 150 years ago. We knew that these ruins were haunted by the ghost of a girl wearing her white wedding-dress. During a party in that Hall to celebrate her wedding-day, there had been a game of hide-and-seek. The bride had found an old oak chest in a little-used store-room and hidden in it. But the heavy lid had snapped shut on her and nobody had heard her knocks and screams before either she fainted in terror or ran out of air.

Although both the building and the grounds were searched her disappearance stayed a mystery, until, months later, a new maid saw the chest, wondered what it was used for, and opened it. She found the eye-sockets of a blackened corpse in a wedding-dress staring up at her. She rushed screaming from the place and later, so folk said, went mad.

Several people had seen the bride's ghost near the ruins and also under the horse-chestnut tree, centuries old, which grows near them. Its branches grow out and down like the legs of a huge spider and where they touch the ground new trees have grown up to help support the bulk of the old one. Even in daylight it is an evil looking, crouching thing. At night, when the owls are screeching, folk hurry past it.

One New Year's Eve, when the bell-ringers were walking past this tree on their way to ring the midnight peals, the girl in the white dress had floated out from the blackness under the branches and chased them back to the village.

Old Jebra had been one of them and if you got him in a good mood he would tell you all about it. 'As we come up to the tree Charlie-Wagg 'e stopped dead. "Wot the 'ell were that?" 'e says. We listened. It were loike a dug wimpering quiet-loike. Then she came floatin' out clean through the fence, all woite with 'er arms stretched out at us. For a tick or two we was jist stook there a-starin' at 'er. Then we all took off a-runnin' loike 'ell.'

The old church, surrounded by its graveyard, is only a couple of hundred yards from the Old 'All and the tree. Opposite the graveyard is a house called The Beeches. It used to be haunted too.

It was built as poor-houses for destitute people. But it was converted into one house for a daughter of the Family on her marriage. She didn't live there long though because of the strange things that happened in it. Pictures fell off walls and pans clattered off shelves in the kitchen.

Twenty years or so earlier a tramp had battered a woman to death in the kitchen, and before that an old man had hanged himself in one of the bedrooms. But, since no ghost was ever seen, nobody knew which of them was bumping things about.

Then there was, and perhaps still is, the Ladylake ghost. Ladylake is the upper of the twin lakes down in the Park: a lonely place, two miles from any neighbour, and surrounded by woods. There was a gamekeeper's cottage beside it. The young wife of a keeper, driven mad by the solitude, and the silence, and the shadows, drowned herself in the lake. From then on the trees used to be shaken by gusts of wind that came from nowhere and went nowhere and folk could hear her laughing and screaming.

We knew that these things happened. And for all we knew there could be other ghosts in lonely places. So we kept well away from them after dark. We were more afraid of the ghosts than we were of the keepers.

There were four gamekeepers. The head one, whose name was Williams but who was known as Pinfinnigin, lived down at the Kennels near the walled vegetable gardens behind the Hall. Benson lived in the cottage down at Ladylake. Crowther lived in the Single Lodge at the top of Ashborough Hill. Moorhouse lived in the Double Lodge at the end of the avenue.

Williams may have got his nickname because at one time he had grown a straggly beard. There was a walking-song which went

'There was an old man named Michael Finnigin
'E grew whiskers on 'is chinnigin
The wind came up and blew 'em all innigin
Poor ole Michael Finnigin . . .
Beginnigin.'

You could sing the same verse over and over again.

One of the main jobs of the village bush-telegraph was to keep interested parties informed of just when each keeper was in the habit of patrolling where. The main scouts were small boys. But even grandmothers would pass on any information which they came across about the keepers' routine.

The fines for poaching rabbits were five shillings for a first offence, ten shillings or fourteen days in gaol for a second, and fifteen shillings or twenty-one days for a third. After that it was usually twenty-eight days without the option of a fine. For poaching pheasants the fines were doubled.

With wages at thirty shillings a week and the dole at one pound, these penalties were severe. Most men and boys were only driven to go after rabbits in order to help feed a hungry family. Only a handful went after pheasants to make a bit of extra money.

Poaching rabbits was looked upon as no crime by the community. No one could have foreseen that in forty years time the farmers would wake up to the fact that the thousands of rabbits were munching away at their profits and decide to exterminate them with the gruesome disease myxomatosis. But it did seem stupid that the fields and woods should be teeming with the little munchers while folk went hungry in the village.

No one could have foreseen either that, now, in an age so

permissive as to be unbelievable to us in the 1920s, Overton folk would no longer bother to poach. They no longer need to.

From the bush-telegraph we knew that just about the time we were coming out of school the keepers were heading home for their tea before setting out on their night patrols. So in summer this was the time when we used to slip off into the woods.

Pinfinnigin however was crafty. You never knew where he was going to pop up. He was grey-haired, red-faced, and usually wore riding breeches, a grey tweed jacket, and a hat which had a peak front and back like a Scottish deerstalker. Because he was no longer as spry as the other keepers he rode a brown horse from the back of which he cracked a long-lashed whip like the ones which Hunt servants use to control hounds.

He may only have meant to use the whip to frighten the boys he caught in or near the woods. But every now and again he did catch—and cut—a boy with the lash. To us he was Danger-Man Number One. We were certain that if his horse got near enough we would feel his whip. So, whenever possible, we kept near trees and bushes and we also took it in turns to keep a look-out for him. Leftie and Jippo were particularly proud of their woodcraft and they were liable to thump the rest of us if we got careless.

Because of the cover of its bracken and the protection of its trees and bushes, the area of scrubland near the East Wood was the safest place for us to go. It was as good as a circus to us, safely under cover, to watch other groups of boys on exploration bent, get interested in something out in the open, drop their guard, and find Pinfinnigin galloping out at them. We used to lie and chuckle as we watched the poor fools scatter in panic and zig-zag like rabbits away from the thundering hooves and the whip-cracks coming like gun-shots.

But one evening, when we were out to get a jackdaw for a pet, we were caught in the open ourselves and it was all my fault.

Bringing up a pet jackdaw is a tricky business. If you get it too young it will die. And if you wait too long you will find the nest empty and the birds flown. When you get one you have to let it out of its cage as soon as possible, partly to stop it pining away, and partly so that it can peck grit to digest its food. You have to

[71]

clip the feathers on one wing to stop it flying away. You do this for at least two years until it is completely tame. You then have a bird that will eat out of your hand, fly along the street to meet you and settle on your shoulder, and generally keep you amused by its antics.

That is the theory. But, because a bird which can't fly is only half a pet, you are liable to stop clipping its wing too soon. Then off it goes to rejoin its fellows in the wild. That is what Crum's had just done. At lunch-time it had been feeding out of his hand. In the evening it was gone.

Now Crum was one of a large family. His clothes were mostly hand-me-downs from his elder brother or bought in a jumble sale. His jackdaw had been one of the few things he could call his very own. So, although like most Overton youngsters he was used to hunching his shoulders against the slings and arrows of his poverty-stricken world, he was upset. Of course he didn't let on about it. But we could see that he was.

'Roight,' said Artie, 'Crum needs a noo jackdore. We'll git 'im one aht o' them there trees near the East Wood.'

Most of them there trees were old. Over the years gales had blown branches off them and the empty sockets had rotted and been pecked out to make holes for nests. You could spot them by the white streaks of droppings down the bark beside them. It wasn't unusual to spot three or four in the one branch. But to spot them was one thing. To reach them was quite another because they were often in smooth branches rising nearly vertically twenty or thirty feet from the ground.

Artie, however, was one of the best climbers in the village; better even than Jippo. Using his hands and knees and the sharp edges of his hob-nailed soles he could swarm up almost anything. He was a born acrobat and also a bit of a clown. He had a thin lop-sided sort of face and ears as big as mine. His hair was thick and stiff and stuck up like a brush from his head as it began to grow in from the close cropping which his dad gave it every three months or so. To hide it he wore a huge, grubby, peaked cap, which, although it had paper stuck inside the rim, was kept up by his ears. He wore it with the peak at the back so that he could see where he was going. His brother was much bigger than he was, so he was taking a fair time to grow into his latest hand-me-downs. Everything seemed to come down too far on Artie: his cap over his forehead: his shorts over his knees: his jersey over his shorts and his hands: and, to round things off, his stockings over the tops of his boots. But in spite of these handicaps he could squeeze through gaps none of the rest of us could get through and he could wriggle out of impossible situations. I think he must have been double-jointed.

We made an expedition to the scrubland and Artie, after swarming up one or two trees, marked his nest. 'This un,' he said. 'Too young now. But be ready in abaht a week.'

After school a week later he said, 'Toime to git Crum's jackdore, else they'll fly.'

Leftie said, 'I were goin' to see some colts brucken in.'

Artie and Crum just looked at him.

'Oh all roight. Wot's today?'

'Toosday,' I said.

'Weer's Benson Toosdays?' Leftie asked Jippo. The East Wood was in Benson's section and Jippo, two of whose brothers were out of work and poaching, was the authority on the whereabouts of the keepers.

''E's bin down West Wood lately last thing an' along dahn Brickles Spinneys as far as the Grounds.'

'An' Pinfinnigin?'

'Meets Benson in the spinneys soomtimes. But yer don't nivver know wi' 'im.'

'Right, Son,' said Leftie. 'It's yoor turn fer look-out. Fer 'Eaven's sake don't go off day-dreamin' agin. Yer won't 'arf cop it from Teacher if we get's caught.'

'All roight,' I said, 'no need to roob it in.' By now I was bi-lingual.

Artie chuckled, 'Yer'll need summat roobed on yer be'ind if Teacher gets to 'ear abaht this.'

He was right there. So I didn't argue.

We went up 'Ack's Cluss because it led on to Foive Acre and there was a thick hedge between it and Walnut Paddock running up almost to the deer fence.

In Overton a close had of course nothing to do with cathedrals or clergy. It meant a narrow enclosed entry or lane. I thought at first that a Mr. Hack must have been at one time the tenant of the nearby farm. But Crum laughed at this. 'Nar,' he said, 'At one toime the Fambly 'ad a lot o' 'acks wot used to graze in Foive Acre. To get there they was led up the cluss.'

'Wot's a 'ack?' I asked.

'A 'orse o' course. A ridin' 'orse wot ain't a thoroughbred or a 'unter.'

I expect he was right.

The draw-rail in the Foive Acre section of the deer fence was out in the open. But the bottom of two of the slats near where the hedge stopped had rotted away. So we always crawled through that gap. The Park at this point was still grazed by cattle. So we had to go crouching along an old drainage gully until we reached the bracken near the wood. After that it was a piece of cake until we got to the place where the trees and bushes began and the bracken ended.

The nest Artie had picked was in a tree about a hundred yards from the thick belt of thorn bushes which ran round this part of the wood. Between it and this cover there were a few bushes. But, if Pinfinnigin arrived, things could get tricky.

'Stop 'ere beside this bush, Son,' Leftie said. 'If 'e comes 'e'll be keepin' close in to the edge of the wood. 'E allus does. Keep yer eyes open an' if yer sees 'im whistle an' wave.'

The bush was a big one about half way between the wood and the tree. I kept watch right and left along the wood. When I took a quick look at the tree, Artie's knees, clipped round the branch where the nest was, seemed to be taking hours to get up it. I could only see his knees because of course he was keeping his body out of sight from the wood. My heart was hammering, so I was pleased when I saw that he was on the way down again.

It was at this point that a kestrel flew low past me. It settled on the dead branch of a tree where we knew there were jackdaws' nests. It had a mouse in the talons of one foot. As I watched, it took the mouse in its beak and flew into a crotch in the tree. A minute or so later it flew out without the mouse. Now that was interesting. Fancy jackdaws nesting in the same tree as a kestrel.

I looked back to see how Artie was getting on and saw him

jump down from the tree holding a bulge under his jersey with one hand. He'd got the jackdaw so now we could relax.

If Pinfinnigin's horse hadn't snorted he would have caught us for sure. At the dread sight of the brown horse, the whip, and the deerstalker hat, my lips froze and my mouth dried and all I could do was make a sort of whuff. I waved desperately to the others. But they had already seen the horse and were running back towards me and the wood.

Pinfinnigin saw them and put his horse into a canter 'Come 'ere, you lads!' he shouted. 'Come 'ere. I know 'oo yer are!'

But the others swerved away into some bushes and kept running for the wood. So he kneed his horse into a gallop.

He was going to pass between me and the wood. So I could have stayed behind my bush and let him go by. It would be nice to pretend that I drew him off the others on purpose. But the truth is that I was in such a panic that I ran out and headed behind him.

I heard him shout and crack his whip. Out of the corner of my eye I saw him wheel his horse and come after me. I could hear Leftie's voice telling me, as he had done over and over again. 'Dodge away from the 'orse. Dodge away. Use bushes to dodge rahnd an' owt else. 'Orses can't dodge all that sharp. Don't get into an open space wottiver yer do.'

'Dodge away from the 'orse! Dodge away from the 'orse!' The galloping hooves thundered the refrain at me. My knees felt numb and my feet pounded oh so slowly. I swear I could hear the creaking of the saddle between the cracks of the whip. Bushes came at me. Brambles tried to trip me. My chest was hot inside and wouldn't hold air. Then I saw clumps of saplings. Beautiful clumps of saplings, too close together for a horse to get through. No rabbit ever jinked through anything faster than I did through them.

Beyond them I could see the trees of the wood and the belt of thorn-bushes. Somewhere there had to be a gap to take a boy. I could hear the hooves coming at me again. Pinfinnigin was shouting. But I saw a gap, hoped it wasn't a dead end, plunged into it and crawled. Now I knew what a rabbit felt like when there was a crush at the entry to a burrow.

In the middle of the bushes, I lay on my side until I began to get

my breath back. I could hear Pinfinnigin shouting. 'Come out
you lads. I know 'oo yer are. It'll be the wuss fer yer if yer don't
come out.' But no wild animal ever skulked more tightly than we
did. So after a bit he gave up and, from under the bushes, I saw the
legs of his horse walking away.

When I met up with the others inside the wood Leftie was not
pleased. 'As a look-out, Son, yer a dead loss. I'm a good moind to
fetch yer one.'

'If it 'adn't bin fer 'im,' Jippo said, ''ole Pinfinnigin moight a
got us . . . My guy, Son! Yer can't 'arf shift.'

'Ar!' said Artie. 'Talk abaht go! Yer fair flew, Son.'

Crum didn't say anything. He was stroking his new jackdaw.

That was how I found out that I was going to be a sprinter.

When I was eleven my mother sent me off to a boarding school.
There I was introduced to a strange game called rugger. Like all
new boys I was shoved into the scrum. I couldn't see any sense at
all in being knocked about, kicked, and sat on.

Then one day somebody threw me the ball and said 'Run!'

I was playing for the Whites against the Reds. I was surrounded
by red jerseys, glaring eyes, and clutching hands. I dodged and
ducked. I swerved and jinked. I was clear. Feet thundered after
me. I ran. Behind the pitch was a row of trees. Thankfully I
headed for them. Voices shouted 'Touch it down!' But Buchan
could see trees and that was where he was going. When I ran over
the dead-ball line at the end of the pitch the thunder of feet
stopped. So I did too. Both teams roared with laughter.

At the end of the game, Munchie Collier, captain of the school
(God), who had been refereeing called me up to him. 'Surely you
have played rugger before?'

I looked up at him and shook my head.

'Then how did you learn to swerve and jink like that?'

'By being chased by a man with a whip on a horse.'

To a posh young man like him this was impossible and he
didn't know what to say. So he cuffed me and told me not to be
cheeky.

But my dash for the trees got me out of the scrum and on to the
wing where I began to enjoy myself.

Later still many of us found that being an Overton boy was

excellent training for the war which caught up with us. On things called 'Night Operations' we could teach the instructors a thing or two. And often we scared the lives out of 'the enemy': poor city chaps who blundered about in woods in the dark and crawled into streams which they had neither heard, nor smelt, nor felt cold on their faces. But that some day people would actually shoot at us was not in our minds at this time. Overton keepers drew the line at that.

But even Pinfinnigin had a sense of humour. A week or two later we went to an old sand-pit near my kestrel tree. Like the old quarry, it had become a big rabbit warren.

Jippo, as usual, was after a rabbit: a buck, he said, because at this time of year most of the does were feeding young. The flesh of a doe in milk tastes sour so that even a dog or cat has to be extra hungry to eat it.

He had his catapult with him and a pocketful of round pebbles from Brooks. But, before he was near enough to get a shot in, there was a thumping of hind legs and every rabbit hopped down a hole.

'Sod it!' said Jippo.

'A young buck could be down a dead-end,' said Artie 'Let's 'ave a look.'

Sometimes a burrow stops short two or three feet down against a boulder. If there was a crush of rabbits at nearby holes, a youngster might panic and dive down a short hole.

So we scrambled over the low, crumbling banks of the pit and stuck our arms down any small holes that didn't have tracks leading into them. We didn't bother with the big holes two feet or more wide which had burrows leading off inside them like rooms off a landing. So I was surprised to see Artie shoving his head into some of these and listening.

'Wot's 'e doin'?' I asked Crum.

'Reckon 'e wants a young un fer a pet.'

Just with that Jippo whistled. 'Ey up! Pinfinnigin!' said Crum.

We slipped away into some bushes.

But Artie hadn't heard the whistle. There he was wriggling his head and shoulders further down into a wide burrow. His old, patched, shorts which had somehow collected a rip in the seat were jack-knifed up in the air, and he was straddling his legs and pushing with his feet to get still further in.

We watched in horror as Pinfinnigin came round some bushes and walked his horse along the track that led into the pit. On the sandy soil its hooves made no sound. He saw Artie's wriggling behind and steered his horse up to it. The animal found this contorted human being most interesting. It pricked its ears, stretched its neck down, and watched, with its head on one side, the scuffling feet. Then it reached slowly and gingerly out, put its nose against Artie and blew up his crotch.

'Ooh ya!' said Crum.

Artie exploded out of the hole as if blown from a cannon. He was still in the jack-knifed position of a high-diver when he was four feet up in the air. Then he straightened, turned a back somersault, and sat down beside the hole. The horse shot backwards as he shot upwards. It reared and pawed the air in protest and Pinfinnigin was busy staying in the saddle. Meanwhile Artie stared like a mesmerised rabbit, his hair standing up straight in shock and his eyebrows curving up to join it.

When his mount had stopped pretending it was a war-horse, Pinfinnigin leant down and said something to Artie, who came out of his trance, replied, snatched up his precious cap and took off for cover like a bedraggled pigeon in full flight, his jersey flapping like wings over his hands.

Then, to our amazement, Pinfinnigin leant on his horse's neck and laughed until he nearly fell out of the saddle again.

When, as before, we met up in the wood, 'Wot did 'e say to yer?' asked Jippo.

Artie, still in a state of shock, blinked. 'Summat loike, "Wotcha doin' dahn there?" I think.'

'Wot did yer say?'

'Jackdorin'.'

'Wot, dahn a rabbit 'ole?'

'Well!' Artie shook his head to rid himself of the memory of such a horrible event. 'Wot would you 'ave said?'

It was a couple of months later when the nights were 'drawing in' that we got caught out again; this time by the mists and the shadows.

Antlers from the herd of fallow deer in the Park were prized possessions. A group of older boys had just come back with some from an expedition to the far end of the East Wood. So, one Friday evening after school, we decided to widen our horizons too by venturing thus far in search of antlers.

But although we saw a fox and some grey squirrels we had found no antlers by the time we reached the far end of the wood. We hadn't even seen any deer. This was disappointing. We had covered about two miles and seen nothing unusual except the fox.

From the edge of the wood we could see the dusty road leading to Ladylake and the wood round it. There the Family went for picnics and boating.

''Ow abaht 'avin' a go at Ladylake?' said Leftie. 'Dad sez it's noice.'

'Gerraway,' said Artie. 'Benson'll nab us fer sure.'

''E sometimes goes to the pub a Froiday noights,' said Jippo.

Leftie said, 'We could take it in turns to watch the road fer 'im while the rest look fer antlers.'

So that's what we did. But the sun was nearly level with the tops of the trees before the keeper came pedalling along the road on his bike with his labrador trotting beside him.

'Good!' said Leftie. ''E's only got that one dog.'

We nipped across the road and along a path through head-high bracken to the Ladylake deer fence. We couldn't find a way in until Jippo found a branch coming out over the fence from a beech tree on the inside. He jumped, caught it, and swarmed on to it. Leftie and Artie joined him and, with their weight bearing it down, Crum and I were able to get on to it too. We then shinned up the branch to the trunk and down it to the ground.

'Let's meck sure we can find it again. We might get split up.' Leftie pointed to a dead fir tree back along the way we had come. 'Remember it's opposite that there dead tree.'

Ladylake was certainly a nice place. The wood was mostly of pine trees and big firs like Christmas trees which reached right from the ground to level with the pine tops. They smelt like Christmas too. The rides were mown and rolled like lawns. We moved along them in single file under the shadow of the trees: five stealthy, pop-eyed little figures in shorts and jerseys, bare-headed, except for Jippo with his big floppy peaked cap the right way round and Artie with his one back to front as usual.

Our eyes popped even more when we came on a summer-house shaped like a Chinese pagoda. It had log tables and chairs on the lawn in front of it. We backed away and circled it in case anybody was inside.

When we got to the lake we found it was fringed by bullrushes taller than we were. We could hear water-fowl croaking but we had to go quite a way along the path before we found a gap through which we could get a clear view.

The clouds were aflame from the sunset behind us, mirrored in the patches of still water, dark green, between the lily-pads. So the water near us was warm and friendly, but out in the centre where no lilies grew it was black, and cold, and hostile, glinting and rippling away evilly towards a scowl of black trees at the far end.

Awe-smitten, we hunkered down on the bank and watched in silence. We had the scent of the fir trees behind us and the musty smell of the lake in front of us. Two swans came gently sailing by. Their breasts broke up the bright pattern of the clouds in the water. Their heads and the tops of their wings were edged with flame so that the white beneath looked pale and ghostly. They were aloof and disdainful in their beauty. Like that hand that held the sword which my mother had read to me about, they,

> 'Rose up from out the bosom of the lake
> Clothed in white samite, mystic, wonderful.'

then one of them turned its head, opened its yellow beak and hissed at us.

There was a scattering of small fish at the edge of the lily-pads. 'Pike gettin' 'is supper,' whispered Leftie.

The swans glided away round a cliff of rushes. Pigeon wings clattered against branches. A pheasant in the wood behind us got excited and shouted, 'Cor! Cock! Cock! Cock!' Then it took exception and whirred off screeching 'Cut-up! Cut-up! Cut-up! Cut-up!' A mist came curling along the water. An owl hooted.

'It'll soon be dark,' I whispered.

'Let's go,' Leftie whispered back.

We padded away towards the little pagoda. The dew was polishing the rides. Pausing to listen every now and again, we moved silently under the silent trees.

Then, right above us, came the most terrifying scream anyone could ever hear.

We froze. We were too stricken even to look at each other. Then 'Ladylake ghost!' sobbed Crum in a high trembling voice, which echoed each one's own despair. Death was upon us. Of that there was no doubt.

Another scream came from above us. It was answered by screams behind us. They shattered the grip of doom.

'Ooh 'eck!' wailed Jippo.

We rushed forward blindly. Artie and I collided and fell together in a tangle. He scrambled up and I ran after him, frantic at the thought of being left alone with this horror. After a few paces he stopped and I crashed into him.

'Wrong soddin' road!' he gasped. He had just begun to run back the way we had come when two more screams wrapped themselves round the pair of us. Artie seemed to take off and cover the next yard or so in mid-air. I took off after him into a nightmare of black trees, slashing branches, and crunching pine cones which did their best to slip my feet from under me. We found the fence by bouncing off it like a brace of hunted rabbits off wire-netting.

Artie crouched and looked through the fence. 'Dead tree.' He pointed to our right and we clawed our way through the Christmas trees along the fence until we caught up with the others as they were scrambling along the branch.

Crashing and stumbling through the bracken, regardless of the noise, we headed for the East Wood. In our desperate loneliness we would have welcomed any keeper, even Pinfinnigin.

Once inside the wood we had to stop to get our breath back.

'Oh my guy!' gasped Jippo, looking into the shadows under the trees, 'D'yer suppose, there's ghosts in 'ere an all?'

'Nivver 'eard o' none,' said Leftie.

'Up a tree!' said Artie.

'*Weer*?' We all ducked.

'Back there,' said Artie.

'Wot is?' asked Jippo.

'Ghosts! Two on 'em. Up a tree!'

'Gerraway! Ghosts don't climb trees!'

We didn't want our parents to find out that we had been where there was no excuse for our going. So it was several days before Leftie, by a series of casual, seemingly unrelated, questions to his dad, solved our terrifying mystery. It was not after all the Ladylake ghost which had chased us. No. The Family kept peacocks at Ladylake. And it seemed that peacocks scream like banshees and that they roost in trees.

CHAPTER SEVEN

WE HAD no resident doctor or nurse. The nearest nurse lived in Ashborough and the nearest doctor in Springwell three miles from Overton. Three miles is nothing much in these days of tar-macadam roads and motor cars, but our doctor trotted round several villages and their outlying farms and cottages on a horse. This gave him the advantage of being able to cut across country using bridle tracks. But he was getting a bit old for spending days in the saddle and he was beginning to use a brougham more and more.

In daytime when you could use the public telephone in the post office—or get one of the elderly spinsters who ran the office to do the phoning for you if you didn't know how—he could usually be contacted in an hour or so. But at night when the spinsters wouldn't open their door, and when the estate office which had the only other telephone in the village was shut, someone had to bike over to Springwell in an emergency to fetch him. What with the bike ride and the horse ride, it could be two hours or more before the doctor arrived.

My mother had done spare time nursing during the war. So, after she had given emergency treatment to one or two children, word went round that if one of your family chopped a bit off a hand, stuck a fork in a leg, or scythed a bit out of it, or developed a fever in the middle of the night, Teacher was the one to send for. The doctor fortunately was only too glad to have someone with nursing experience in the village, and over the years she developed a good working relationship with him.

Emergency medical treatment took her into people's homes and that led to her becoming involved in their problems. Soon, if a sick old person living alone had no one to sit up with them at night, or a family was in trouble with debts, or a man was forever getting drunk and beating his wife and kids, Teacher was the one to turn to.

Most people realise that there is more to Christianity than going to church. But, again, most people find reasons why loving their neighbour should involve the minimum of inconvenience to themselves. As I grew older I began to realise that my mother's ideas about Christianity were different from other people's.

When I asked Gran about this difference she said, 'When your Daddy was killed religion was a great comfort to your mother. She taks it seriously. But the thing is that many o' the folk in this village are in trouble most of the time. They've ower little money, ower little comfort, and, in winter, ower little food. Your mother will have to learn she canna put things right by hersel'. But she thinks it's her duty to do all she can.'

There were two things which made my mother hopping mad: snobbery and hypocrisy. And since there was a good deal of both around she had plenty on which to exercise her rapier tongue. She would come home raging about the poverty in the village. Some old woman hadn't had a proper meal all week; four children were sleeping in a room so damp that mould was growing down one wall; an unemployed man with a sick wife and three children had been fined half his dole money for snaring a rabbit.

When my mother paused for breath Gran would say, 'Aye! . . .

Uh huh!' now and again. And eventually, 'I'll mak you a cuppie o' tea.'

After the tea had calmed the storm she would look over the rim of her cup at her daughter and say things like 'Aye! God help the poor redskins. But you're nae God. The way you're giving away your money and running yoursel' off your feet it's just a question of which you do first—go bankrupt or kill yoursel'. Drink your tea!'

The Countess must have been hearing tales about the things my mother was doing and saying about the poverty in the village because she paid us a visit. Raging again, my mother told Gran about it.

The Countess had said, 'I would remind you that you are merely the schoolmistress. I am mistress of the village. Will you kindly stop behaving as if you owned the place.'

'And what did you say?' asked Gran.

'I said, "Own this rural slum? Heaven preserve me from such a fate!"'

Gran, who was sitting beside the sitting-room fire hugged her knees and chuckled. 'You better head for the Border afore the Sheriff comes.'

'It wasn't a nice thing to say. But I was so angry. I've had enough. I shall look for another post.'

'That's the first sensible thing I've heard you say in months.'

'There's a vacancy for an assistant headmistress at a big girls' school in Leicester. I'll apply for that.'

'Oh mechty! What's wrong wi' Scotland?' Gran sighed. 'I think I will away oot to Australia and bide wi' my sister Isie.'

My mother was asked to attend for an interview at the school in Leicester. But before she could do so a friend of hers came to Overton as chaplain to the Family and parish priest. He was a Benedictine monk who had, because of ill-health, been advised to leave his monastery at Fort Augustus on the shore of bleak Loch Ness.

Father Gregory was in his early sixties. He was bald with a fringe of white hair round his head which made him look as benevolent as Mr. Pickwick. He was beginning to go blind from cataract and looked benignly out on the world through the thick lenses of a pair of gold-rimmed spectacles. He was an international authority on Gregorian plain-chant, a composer of hymns, carols, and songs, and he was well-known in Scotland as a conductor of choirs and an adjudicator at choir festivals. My mother had first met him when he was training the college choir at Notre Dame in Glasgow. He was a quiet, kindly man. If there is such a thing as a saint, he was one.

Like my mother he suffered from the conviction that Christianity is by definition an active as well as a contemplative religion. Apart from his books and his piles of music manuscripts, he owned little but his clothes. His suits were shiny and patched at the elbows except for one which he kept for special occasions. He had a quite respectable overcoat, but, in order to preserve it, wore in winter an Inverness cape which Lord Lovat had given to him thirty years before and which had turned from black to green with age. He had no experience of running even a tiny parish like Overton and he begged my mother to stay and help him to run it, promising to act as a buffer between her and the Family. She thought about it, and prayed about it, decided in the end that his arrival in Overton must be part of God's plan, and agreed to stay on.

Gran got a lot of fun listening to her daughter lecturing Father Gregory on the folly of giving away nearly all the money which he received. She would get on my mother's nerves by chipping in with 'Aye! I've often said the same thing myself.' Or, 'You're right. Charity begins at home, that's what I say.'

Father Gregory would blink at my mother through his thick spectacles and puff away at his pipe. That pipe fascinated me. Although he kept puffing at it, it kept going out. When he left to go back to the Hall there was always a pile of spent matches in his ash-tray.

He had been given the old billiard-room at the Hall as a study and sitting-room and walked up from the Hall to have tea with us twice a week. He came through the Nuns' Door punctually at 4.30 pm and in summer I used to run down Pudden Bag to meet him.

I had a friend in the cottage garden at the end of the street nearest the Door. He was a jackdaw and he belonged to Blanche's youngest brother. As I got near their cottage I used to shout 'Jack...caa!' and he would fly on to the garden wall, flutter up and down, and send a volley of 'Caas' back up the street to me. We caaed away to each other until I arrived at the wall when he would fly on to my shoulder and gobble the bits of cheese which I had brought for him.

He guarded that wall against other birds and also against cats. Neighbours' cats had more sense than to take him on. They just pretended that he wasn't there. But now and again strange cats would get up on their hind legs on the wall and try to box as he fluttered round them and zoomed in to peck at the back of their heads. Jack screeched. The cats spat and spun and swiped at thin air. I saw a yellow and white cat take him on one day and it was more fun than Dodgie's roundabout.

When I introduced him to Father Gregory he was put off by the priest's black hat. But after a few days he got used to it and condescended to accept tit-bits sitting on the priest's shoulder.

Sometimes a member of the Family would walk up to the village with Father Gregory. Some approved of Jack and some didn't. I once saw Lady Sarah in a picture hat dancing round shooing at Jack, who was only trying to make a landing on the priest's shoulder. When shooing had no effect she swung her handbag. That was too much. Jack screeched and neatly shat all over her hat, whereupon her ladyship jumped up and down in rage and screeched louder than Jack. Father Gregory, shoulders shaking, had to walk away and study the roses in Blanche's front garden.

Kitty, Mr. Stanwell's pony, also got to be a friend of mine. He used to let me help groom and harness her. When he bought her she was, like many circus horses, a biter. But all the care and affection which he gave her cured her of that and in her middle-age she was a happy, friendly pony.

Her stable was up against our back garden wall and I used to neigh over it to her. To begin with I can't have got my neighs right because she ignored them. I was delighted when one evening she replied. After that we used to neigh over the wall to one another unless she was too tired after the day's work.

Most boys had a go at imitating the calls of animals and the song of birds. Jippo was really good at it. He could get calves to run to him by mooing and lambs to him by bleating. And he could get owls to follow him along spinneys by hooting back at them. In the dark you couldn't tell whether it was Jippo hooting or an owl. He tried to teach me to do it, but I never got it right.

Pets were important to us village children, partly because we lived in a community in which skill in the care of animals was respected, and partly because parents looked on pet-keeping as a nice safe hobby, which would keep boys out of trouble. The school playground was too small for playing cricket or football and if we were seen too often in the woods or in the Park our parents were bound to get a visit, or a nasty letter, from the Estate Agent. There was one pet, however, which was banned for children: a dog. Dogs could be a source of trouble and grief. If a dog strayed into the spinneys along the Ashborough Road or up the avenue it would be shot on sight by a keeper even if he could hear the owner calling and whistling after it. And there was always the danger that it would pick up one of the baits poisoned with strychnine which the keepers put down and die in convulsions.

These baits were sometimes pieces of rabbit and sometimes a whole one. Jippo told me about a family which had a narrow escape. The father was out of work and one of his sons thought he had been clever to find a dead rabbit hanging on a fence behind the Single Lodge. Unfortunately he pretended that he had found it in a snare.

Jippo said, 'It was Sago as took the rabbit. But when 'is sister Joan, bein' 'ungry, 'as the first mouthful o' the stew, she spits it aht on the floor beside 'er chair an' says, "Ooh mam! It tastes 'orrible!" An' she runs to the sink, scoops a cup of water outta the bucket an' washes 'er mouth out.

'"Wot yer mean tastes 'orrible?" sez 'er mam. "It's good stew." But the dad an' the other kids looks at Joan pullin' 'orrible faces an' spittin' in the sink. The dad sez, "'Old 'ard! Weer *did* yer get that rabbit, Sago? *War* it in a snare!"

'Before Sago can say 'owt, the poor ole cat under the table gives one 'ell o' a screech wot makes 'em all jump oop aht their chairs. It cooms aht from under rollin' over an' over, clawin' at a rug, an' screechin'. Sago sez it was a 'orrible sight an' 'e didn't blame 'is dad fer givin' 'im a good 'idin'. If it 'adn't bin for Joan 'avin' a quick go at 'er plate, they might all a bin poisoned like the poor ole cat. As it war they all 'ad to go to bed 'ungry.'

If Sago's dad had complained direct to the Countess about the poisoned rabbit she would have been horrified. But the village had accepted for years that poisoned baits were put down. And Sago had stolen one rabbit and his dad had poached the other. Under the circumstances to complain to the Estate Agent was likely to bring only trouble. People who depended on the estate for their jobs and cottages accepted that things were run as they had always been run and suffered in silence.

It was round about this time that my own first great pet came into my life. A pet which, over fifty years later, I still remember with love. She was a cat with some of the instincts of a dog. Her mother was a half-Persian stray which decided to have a litter of four kittens in our wood-shed.

As soon as the kittens were big enough to toddle I made a race-track for them using long stems from the snowberry bush beside the kitchen window tied to little pegs knocked into the ground to make the lanes. Since I had never seen a race-track this was quite a clever invention of mine.

When I had got the kittens in position and facing the right way I nipped to the other end of the lanes and called to them and scrabbled my fingers. The one with the black smut on her white nose nearly always won. I persuaded my mother to let me keep her and called her Smuttie. She began to grow into a beautiful cat with long silky black fur and a white shirt front and four white paws to go with her white nose.

When she moved into the house from the wood-shed she used to lie on my shoulder while I read lying on the rug in front of the fire or sitting in a chair. When I got up she hooked her claws into my jersey and came with me. Sometimes she didn't ever bother to wake up. At night she slept on my bed.

When she was nearly full-grown we played a game in which I swung a ball of paper, dangling on a string from a long stick, round the sitting-room. I trailed the ball along the backs of the sofas and the armchairs and along the tops of the bookcases. Smuttie was soon able to leap quite long distances and to land accurately on her target. I was proud of her jumping ability which, I claimed, was due to my training her.

She hated to let me out of her sight and, given the chance, would slip into school and join me. When I went out into the village she had to be shut up until I was well on my way. Even then she would sometimes track me along the streets and into the fields. Often, as I lay under the cover of a hedge watching out for keepers, I would look back and see her small black shape trotting along the way I had come, determined to catch up with me. It was several weeks before I could convince her that following me into the fields was not allowed.

At this time I was afraid of the great, dark, outside world. Even on a winter evening when the heavens were bright with stars like the way the Wise Men saw them at the first Christmas, I never, while hurrying home alone, saw in them hope and beauty, or heard the mysterious whisper of angels' wings. I saw only the shadows which were full, for me, of demons and witches and, strangely enough, black monkeys, with white circles round cruel yellow eyes. I had never seen, so far as I knew, even a picture of such animals. But I knew they were there. So I was careful not to be outside alone in the dark.

In Smuttie's first winter, however, Leftie managed to persuade his father, who rented the paddock near the Fox and Geese—the one Dodgie used for his roundabout—to let a few of us play football in it. This was such a great new thing that we went on playing until we couldn't see the ball. Then Jippo, Crum, and I set off across the Green for home. It was really dark under the trees. But that didn't bother me because I wasn't alone.

But they lived near the Green so that I had to run off up the West Street by myself. There was just enough light for me to pick my way along the ruts between the puddles and the horse-muck. Then, just as I reached the playground wall, what I dreaded would happen did happen. A black monkey got me. It came hurtling out of the darkness and grabbed me. A frozen hoof hit me in the stomach and iced up my whole body. My legs vanished and I would have fallen if the ghastly thing hadn't said 'Kerrim!' and nuzzled my neck. I had to lean on the wall until my legs and my breath came back again.

Smuttie, on my shoulder, objected to being pressed against the wall, said, 'Ey up! Clumsy!' and scrambled over my hair on to the other shoulder. There she rubbed her head against my ear and purred.

The following week we were allowed into the paddock again. This time I stopped before I got to the wall and called 'Smuttie?'

'Kerrim!' she said. 'Come on!' And when I did she sailed on to my shoulder.

I soon got used to her leaping out of the darkness at me. When there was a moon I used to walk up quietly in the shadows and watch her sitting patiently on top of the wall, just waiting for me. If I hadn't arrived she would probably have waited all night.

Then, having worked out that I always came from the same direction, she took to meeting me further down the street. The first time she leapt off the branch of a tree she had the decency to say 'Kerrim!' before she leapt. But a few nights later when the sky was clouded over so that it was black under the trees on the Green, Jippo suddenly took off in a buck-jump, shouted 'Oh yer! Ooh 'eck!' and seemed to be wrestling with himself. At almost the same moment Smuttie landed on my shoulder in an undignified scramble so that she had to dig her claws into my jacket. 'Huff,' she said 'Fuss!' And she swapped on to my right shoulder away from it.

'Wot's up?' asked Crum.

Jippo now wrestled with his breathing. I knew how he felt. 'Summat wi' big paws landed on my 'ead!' he gasped.

'Gerraway!' said Crum, 'bin a twig.'

'I knows twigs,' snapped Jippo. 'This warn't no twig. T'were 'airy, wi' paws.'

'Squirrel,' said Crum.

'Ain't none 'ere.'

'Panther,' I said, 'escaped from a circus.'

'They eat yer,' said Crum.

'Ooh yer!' said Jippo. Then, 'Gerraway, else I'll fetch yer one!'

We discussed the strange beast until I said goodnight to them on the other side of the Green. Neither of them had seen Smuttie.

A night or two later it was Crum's turn to do a war-dance as she used his head as a staging post to reach my shoulder.

'Aaah!' he yelled. And, when he had got his breath back, 'Ookin', soddin', gret thing wi' paws landed on me 'ead!'

'A black monkey, I bet,' I said. 'They strangle folks.'

'We ain't cummin' across 'ere in the dark no more,' said Crum.

Once more Smuttie swapped shoulders and neither of them saw her. But unfortunately, we were walking up the street in daylight soon afterwards when she sailed off a tree and landed on me.

'Ooh, Son!' said Jippo and turned on me with the light of violence aforethought in his eyes.

They chased me up the street while Smuttie clung on and spat back at them.

Next she began to develop a protective instinct towards me. Mary and I found this out when I went too far with my teasing and even this patient girl lost her temper and chased me round the garden. She finally trapped me behind the sofa in the sitting-room and was just going to give me the thumping which I deserved when a black ball of fury came bouncing in at the door spitting like a soda-syphon. Smuttie landed on the back of the sofa in front of me and crouched growling and tail lashing at Mary. I had to grab my cat as she tensed to spring.

Mary backed off. 'Coo! It woulda gone fer me.'

'It would an' all!' I said.

'Well it ain't fair. If yer a goin' to tease me, yer'll 'ave to shut it up fust, else it ain't roight.'

I had to agree. After that, when Mary began to get annoyed with me she would say 'Roight! Yer jist wait! Weer's that dratted cat?'

'That dratted cat' went on following me about in the house and garden for another year until she had her first litter of kittens and found other interests. We fed the hens together—my mother had a hen-run now—chopped sticks together, and fetched coal. I got so used to my cat being with me that I hardly noticed that she was there. But if she was missing for a time, I soon noticed and went to look for her.

She used to sit in the middle of the table and help me play with my train set. The tunnel fascinated her. She would watch the engine heading towards it, crouch, tail twitching, on the far side, then as it popped out of the hole, spring on it. It took some time to persuade her that the only time she was allowed to touch the train was when the clockwork motor ran down on the far side of the table from me. She would look at me and wait for me to nod and point to it, then she would mince up to it and give the engine—always the engine never the carriages or trucks—a gentle pat. If that didn't work she would move further up, dig her claws in its funnel and pull it forward. When it got going again she would say 'Kerrim!' and arch her back and look smug. But if it still wouldn't go she would sneer at it and turn her back on the useless thing.

Many cats look on humans as mere servants destined by fate to give them food and every comfort. But Smuttie would do things for me. She would lie on her side and paw things out from under bookcases. And she would bring me presents. Dead mice would be stroked against my cheek or dropped from my shoulder on to my book. A dead rat was once displayed attractively right in the centre of my pillow. She was very hurt at the way in which I spurned that gift and never put anything on my pillow again.

CHAPTER EIGHT

Plantham Fair was held on a Saturday in spring. It was the year after I got Smuttie that my mother first took me to it. So I must have been eight. A group of parents decided to hire the wagonette from the inn and they invited us to share it with them.

The wagonette was a high, open, four-wheeled vehicle with two bench seats running across it at the front and two more running along the sides at the back. The seats were padded and covered in the shiny black American cloth which was more water-proof than leather. A wagonette could take about ten people.

As usual Cob was pulling it. He was getting old so at most hills we had to get down and walk. I liked him. He would lower his head after you had given him a sugar lump and let you scratch him behind the ears. Captain, the inn's other horse was the big black which pulled the brougham. He would accept your gift, toss his head, and then sidle towards you and try to stand on your foot.

Boxer, the inn's handyman, used to say. 'Cob's a gentleman. But that there Captain is jist bad-tempered an' harrogant.'

Leftie, Crum, and two of the senior girls, Millie and Betty came with us. We were all highly excited. When we came to the very steep, tree-lined, hill which runs down past the Mill near Springwell, Boxer got down to put a wagon-lock under one of the rear wheels. This was a steel shoe which tobogganed along under the wheel, held to it by chains; we called it 'the sprag'. Its function was to help the hand-brake to stop the vehicle from going too fast.

Half-way down the hill we came to a sharp bend and the wagonette, which was already tilted forwards, now tilted sideways as well. We had to hang on to each other and to the seats.

Crum got so worked up that he shouted, 'I dunno wot weer a-cummin to. But weer cummin to summat!'

This my mother, at appropriate moments, used as a catchphrase for the rest of her life.

We had started out at midday and it took us two hours to cover the eight miles. When we arrived we found the streets packed with people. I had never seen so many.

The market square and a long, very broad, street were full of stalls, roundabouts, blaring organs, and other attractions. There was the Penny-on-the-Mat (later called the Helter Skelter); The Scenic Railway (Big Dipper); The Caterpillar (a train of cars covered by a green canvas hood); and Over the Falls where you climbed a tall structure and then sat on a seat of steel rollers. These suddenly collapsed and shot you on to a canvas conveyor belt which took you, in darkness, over some heart-stopping drops.

The first time I shot on to the belt I could see what I thought was a row of dolls in a patch of daylight, away down below me. I wondered if I was going to crash through them. But they turned out to be people, mostly men and boys, who had already had their turn and had stayed to watch as the girls came screaming down with their skirts—unless they knew the drill—up round their ears. I only found out about that added attraction in later years. But I did wonder why Betty and Millie were flustered and cross after they had had their go and why they wouldn't go Over the Falls again.

Leftie had been to the Fair before. He came snaking down the polished channel from the top of the Penny-on-the-Mat tower firmly seated on his mat. But, much to our annoyance, Crum and I could never leap on to our mats before they had shot away on their own. We came down on the seats of our shorts. My mother said she knew when we were coming because our empty mats always arrived ahead of us.

We screamed our way down the stomach-icing drops on the Scenic Railway; I, to my great shame, fell off one of the roundabout horses which were bigger and shinier than Dodgies; Leftie won glass jugs by knocking coconuts off posts with wooden balls; Crum and I won glass ash-trays by throwing rubber balls into bowls; we had a huge fish and chips supper (my first); and when we came out of the tea-room naphtha flares were burning among the stalls. I had never seen so many lights before. They turned green canvas to grey. And they made all the other colours different too. Those nearest the flares were paler and brighter. But those on the edge of the shadows were deeper and velvety; reds were toned down to the colour of port wine; yellow became orange; blue became almost black.

The flares made a different, flickering, world in which faces kept popping out at me from the shadows with bright, alert, eyes. I would have liked to sit quietly by myself and watch this new world. But the pubs were open now and our parents decided that it was time to leave.

After the bright flares the roads were dark. The brass paraffin lamps on the front of the wagonette did little more than light Cob's swaying flanks. But he wasn't going to do anything stupid and we met few other vehicles. Boxer only seemed to steer him when we came to crossroads.

Tucked up in a rug, I dozed leaning against my mother. I was only vaguely aware of the wagonette swaying as Cob swayed, of the jingling of his harness, the grinding of the wheels in the grit of the road, and of the scent of pine trees and of blossom in the hedgerows.

A spell of walking wakened me. Lamps behind the curtained windows of lonely farms and cottages sometimes glowed among the trees. The moon came out from behind clouds. Everyone started to sing. My mother sang 'Loch Lomond,' and 'The Skye Boat Song' as an encore, and the men sang 'The Lincolnshire

Poacher'. The chorus 'Oh it's my delight on a shiny night in the
season of the year,' seemed exactly right for a night like this. So
they sang all the verses again and we sang the choruses, while, in
the pauses, the steady rhythm of old Cob's hooves kept clopping
through.

When spring slipped into summer the 'top end' of the village
suddenly decided that the 'top farmer', from whom it bought its
milk, was watering same. It decided to join the 'bottom end' in
buying its milk from Green's farm beyond Cole's cottage up
Ashborough Hill. My mother had long suspected that the milk
was watered so she decided to buy her milk from Green's too,
and that I should fetch it, a walk of over a mile there and back,
morning and evening.

One evening on my way back through the farm buildings I
stopped to have my usual chat to a bay mare over the half-door of
her loose-box. I had given her a final scratch, picked up my milk
can, and turned away, when I saw that Mr. Green was watching
me.

'Didn't want to say nowt while yer was scratchin' 'er,' he said,
'but yer wants to watch Mollie, she bites.'

'Coo!' I said, 'I talk to 'er every evenin'!'

'Well now! That's surprisin'! She nips most folk she don't
know. Do you like animals?'

'Ar!' I said, 'specially cats, 'orses, and dogs. I were wonderin' if
I could 'elp Perce do a job or two, after school like.'

'Your mam wouldn't think much o' that.'

'I could ask 'er.'

'All right. Yer can 'elp if she says so.'

So most evenings and some Saturdays I helped Mr. Green's son
Perce with his chores. He had left school the year before and
looked on me as a nuisance at first, but changed his mind when he
found that I was useful.

One of the nice things about growing up is finding out that you
are good at things. I already knew I was hopeless at music and
drawing, and poor at arithmetic, but quite good at other subjects;
that I could run faster than anyone else my size in the village; that I
could toss up a pebble and hit it with a stick more often than not.

And I was especially pleased when I overheard Mr. Green telling his wife, 'That lad's got a way wi' animals.'

I suppose that, at this time, I was a bit lonely. I could see that even my friends were wary of me because I was 'Teacher's son'. The last thing they wanted to do was to bring her wrath down on them by giving me cause to complain of their behaviour towards me. They weren't to know that I wouldn't have complained; that I just wanted to be accepted as the same as everyone else and not to be the odd man out. They weren't to know either that even if I had complained my mother would just have told me not to be a baby.

As I grew older she was getting more and more reluctant to let me mix with the other boys. She said she didn't want me to learn their rough ways. But I suspect that she thought I was too young to know about sex, and was afraid that I would learn about it from them.

Since my relations with other children were now restricted, my relations with animals like Smuttie and birds like old Jack, and our garden robin, which fed out of my hand, became more important to me.

But, working with Perce, I soon found out that not all animals are nice friendly creatures; that some have become plain nasty, while others have a very peculiar sense of humour.

There was a horse called Scamp, which, ever since it was a colt had played tricks on people. He would take your sugar lump over his loose-box door, let you scratch his head, and then as you turned away nip you quickly and painfully in the shoulder. He would then toss his head up and down and do a little jig on his front feet: the nearest he could get to laughing.

Perce didn't warn me about Scamp. He and a couple of the men just laughed when I got nipped. 'Scamp don't mean no 'arm,' he said. 'It's jist 'is bit o' foon. Don't nivver go near 'im wen 'e's aht though, 'E'll jist flick 'is 'oof and fetch yer a rap on the leg. 'E knows if 'e does it to us 'e'll cop it. But you'd be fair game.'

But Perce did warn me about a brown and white cow called Daisy and about the bull.

Of Daisy he said, 'If that ole bitch so much as twitches 'er off 'ind 'oof, 'op it!'

And of the bull, which was chained to a manger in a stall, 'If, wen you're groomin' 'im, 'e starts to sidle over an' squash yer up agin the wall, kick 'im 'ard on the 'eel. Then 'e'll give over. It's jist a bit of 'is foon!'

I didn't like to admit that I didn't know where a bull kept his heel. So, when Perce went to fetch some straw, and the bull did begin to sidle over and squash me, I kicked him all up the back of his hock. But I was wearing gum boots, and I wasn't finding the right spot. About a ton of beef, bone, and muscle was crushing the breath out of me. Luckily he wasn't used to crushing anyone as small as me and I was able to wriggle into the curve between his belly and his rump, slip down, and crawl away.

Perce and the farm hands got a lot of fun out of watching the animals play their tricks on newcomers. They only warned you if you could get badly hurt. If for instance you went marching through the door of the milking-shed without first checking that the cows were not beginning to hurry out, you could get a horn through the chest. So you were warned about that. And you were warned about kickers. But a playful nip or thump was just good sport.

One evening during my first week of helping Perce, I wondered why I was being taken round to see his pigeons and why some of the men were hanging about. Not for nothing had I associated for a couple of years with Leftie, Artie, Jippo, and Crum. So when, as Perce was carefully drawing my attention to his white fan-tails on the roof of the barn, I heard the squeaking of hinges and the patter of tiny feet and at the same time he stepped quickly away from me, I stepped quickly away too.

A brown and white billy-goat with curved horns and head lowered in the charge glanced off my leg and sent me staggering. To let him out of his shed, when a stranger had his back to it, was, it seems, an established farm joke. On seeing an unsuspecting back Bill would charge out and butt the owner of it into a dungheap opposite his door. I had seemed such a sure thing that he was going flat out. With nothing to brake his progress he hurtled head-first into the dungheap himself, skidded over on his side, collected a heap of mucky straw as he went, and ended up buried in it.

Four white legs with flailing sharp hooves came out of the heap first. Then there was a heave and a devilish bearded face with glaring eyes and gleaming horns appeared. I had fallen, so the first moving thing the eyes saw was Perce, who was standing laughing. He didn't laugh for long.

Dung exploded in all directions as, mad with fury, Bill charged at Perce. 'Not me yer stoopid sod!' yelled Perce, leaping too late for the shed into which the men had already nipped. He was in full flight when the goat's head crashed into his backside and he seemed just to keep on going up. He landed in a wheelbarrow full of dung which overturned and smothered him.

Bill skidded to a halt and turned just as Perce got to his knees beside the barrow. Down went the horns again and the hooves did a couple of little jumps as the goat took aim.

Perce wiped sticky straw off his face, focussed Bill, and yelled 'Aah! Booger off yer bastard!'

The bastard did: straight at Perce who had to duck down beside the mucky wheelbarrow again. The goat fell over him after its head had glanced off his shoulder. So there was Perce, the goat, the wheelbarrow, and a pile of dung, all thrashing about together beside the shed. Its half-door was now firmly closed and over it a row of laughing faces beamed happily out on to the scene.

''Eave 'im off yer Perce!' said one.

'Ey up! 'E's a tryin' to kiss yer!' said another, as the goat side-swiped Perce with its head.

Perce started to crawl away presenting a plump backside to his pet, which promptly butted it not once but three times.

'One! . . . two! . . . three!' chanted the men. Then Perce got his mis-used bum behind the barrow again.

Next the goat which was kneeling on its owner's chest looked at me. It had the decency to get off him before it went into its aiming routine. My only refuge was up a short ladder which was leaning against the shed.

It must have been more than average bone-headed even for a goat because now it charged my ladder. There was nothing I could do except jump. It was in no way my fault that, as Perce got up, I landed on him.

'Aah! Shit!' screamed Perce, 'not you an' all.'

That evening, when Smuttie landed on my shoulder off the

playground wall, I stank so badly, that she screeched 'Yeow' and took off again without even a 'Kerrim'.

But the goat's rodeo act was not the best on the farm. Not by a long chalk it wasn't. The prize for this would have had to go to a big black shire-horse. It grazed in the Home Field which we had to cross to fetch the cows from Ten Acre. It would wait until you were in the middle of the field and then come at you in a mad gallop: a heaving, snorting, gleaming, mass of violence from under which plate-sized hooves crunched as the turves flew.

The first evening we went to get the cows Perce said, 'Yer wants to fill this 'ere bucket wi' stuns.' And he began to collect stones and pebbles from the farmyard. 'Yer see there's this 'ere young 'orse wot wasn't properly knackered. 'E don't mean no 'arm. But 'e loikes 'is bit o' foon. You'll see.'

I saw. 'Ey up! Run!' I said as the huge beast went into its charge.

'Nar, s'all roight!' said Perce, ''e don't like stuns.'

He then proceeded to take some out of the bucket and hurl them at the horse as it thundered down on us. I could feel the ground shaking.

When the animal was only about thirty yards away and my loyalty to Perce was about to snap and send me running for my life, one stone bounced in front of the horse and whistled past its nose. It wheeled then, and bucking and twisting and farting it went off back up the field.

'There y'are,' said Perce. 'Nowt to it. 'E jist likes 'is little bit o' carry-on.'

When I had got my breath back I asked him, 'Does this allus 'appen?'

'Ar! Meck sure yer 'as plenty stuns in yer bucket wen yer cooms on yer own.'

'I reckon I better practise a bit wile you're wimme.'

'Yer can 'ave a go tomorrer,' said Perce.

But, although I pelted away, the horse kept coming.

''Arder, Son! 'Arder!' said Perce. ''E won't turn till 'e 'ears the stuns whistle. Goo on! Yer won't 'urt 'im. 'E don't feel all that mooch!'

I wasn't worrying about the horse. I was worrying about me and throwing as hard as I could. At last—much too late I thought—Perce joined in and the horse sheered off and went into its rodeo act.

'Yer ain't a fat lot o' good, Son,' said Perce. 'I reckon I'll 'ave to keep cummin' wi' yer.'

What my mother and Gran would have said if they had known that I was being charged at, squashed, and nipped by animals I shudder to think. Luckily, being city folk, they had no idea what farm life was like.

Before the last war agricultural workers were looked down on as 'farm labourers'. They were supposed to be so gormless that unskilled work was all they were fit for. Unskilled? On the old-style farms an unskilled man, left to look after himself, would have been in hospital within a week. And by then he could have found that things like scything, loading a hay-cart, making a stack, let alone ploughing, which looked so easy, all called for skills as difficult to learn as they were hidden when the work was well done, and disastrously obvious when it was not.

CHAPTER NINE

SINCE WE had no electricity and no modern conveniences, the quality of life in our village depended very much on the weather.

In winter which was always damp and cold, when not actually freezing, folk went to bed early. They did this partly to save candles, paraffin, coal, and logs, partly because bed was the only really comfortable place in most of the cottages, partly because there was little else to do, and partly because most men had to be at work by six in the morning.

I heard old Moll, who lived alone in a tiny cottage on Top Secret, tell my mother, 'Oh, Teacher, ain't this 'ere winter a darvel? I wish I was one o' these 'ere 'edge-'ogs wot eyeberriates. I do an' all. But, there! We're inter Febooary an' we's gittin a quarter 'ahr extra dayloight ivvery wick. It'll soon be soomer, please God!'

In January the village did hibernate a bit. It was only half alive.

The daylight hours were so short and the muddy, cold, surrounding dark seemed to stifle us. On cloudy nights the glow from curtained windows scarcely reached the other side of the streets, and above us and all round us was the thick blanket of the dark. Sometimes I felt that if I went forward too quickly I would smother myself in its folds.

Inside the cottages people stuffed bits of paper and sacking into the cracks round windows and stretched long sausages of rolled-up sacks along the floor at the bottom of doors to reduce the fearsome draughts. The village was cold and drab and so were we. 'Let's get it over with,' was everybody's wish.

But by early summer Overton looked and felt a different place. When the first spell of warm weather came, folk seemed to open their eyes wide, throw off the black bindings, stretch themselves, and turn happily to the sun. We could understand why so many northern tribes used to hold festivals to celebrate its return.

In December it had been dark when we got out of school. By the end of January it was still daylight. On the evenings when I first noticed that the days were lengthening I used to feel that I was surrounded by a sort of glow which came not from the sky but from the ground and from things around me. Everything seemed to be heating up and about to explode into life.

But of course it didn't happen that way. Through February and into March flowers and trees gradually came awake.

In February the skylarks and a few thrushes and blackbirds began to try out their voices in short snatches of song. By the end of March they were all in full song again and it only needed the extra voices of the migrant songbirds in May to get the dawn and evening chorus back to the level at which, near trees, you had to raise your own voice to be heard above theirs: thousands upon thousands of birds singing. By then the countryside was brilliant with colour and music, full of life again. And so were we.

In February we remarked on the first snowdrops to pop up, gleaming white, among the withered leaves in sheltered corners. 'Ey up! Look! Snowdrops!' Later we admired what really were blue, green, and yellow, carpets of bluebells and primroses in the spinneys round the village. 'Cor! Look! Thahsands and thahsands on 'em!' We noticed the first bowls of primroses and the perfumed sweet violets which the girls picked from under the hedgerows for my mother's desk in school. As we went under the thorn trees, clouded with white blossom, we shook torrents of it down on one another and emerged powdered from the waist up. (But nobody ever plucked one of their gorgeous branches to take home, because to take one into your house would bring bad luck on the family for the rest of the year.) We said 'Coo! smell them jillivers,' as we went down Pudden Bag between the gardens glowing with wallflowers, daffodils and tulips. And we admired the foaming pink and white blossom of the apple and plum trees.

But as April gave way to May, and the dark, wet, thatch dried out to honey again, and the muddy, dun-coloured streets to chalk, and the bare-legged girls began to bounce along in bright cotton dresses, we no longer consciously revelled in the return of colour and comfort to our world. We took it all for granted as we settled down to enjoy the splendour of summer in Overton.

In that summer when first I began to help Perce on the farm, 'flaming June' lived up to its name. It got to be so hot in school that my mother decided that lessons would be out in the playground in the shade of the lime trees. So every morning before nine o'clock we lugged out desks and chairs and blackboards and every afternoon at four o'clock we lugged them back into school again. But the novelty of having lessons in the open air more than made up for the extra work.

It was difficult not to be distracted in the mornings. My mother would warn, 'Get on with your work or we will go back into school!' So we kept our heads down and only squinted at the drivers or riders of horses out of the corners of our eyes. The school is built on a mound so that, although the wall on the playground side is only three feet high, on the street side it is over six feet high. Sitting at the back of the playground therefore we couldn't see the horses themselves nor people walking.

We soon got used to Mr. Stanwell rattling past in his trap or Boxer in the wagonette. But sometimes groups of bowler-hatted toffs would canter past on their hunters. We found it hard not to look up at them. They, as was proper, ignored us. But some people in traps or dogcarts would rein back and stare at us, much to my mother's annoyance.

In the afternoons it wasn't distractions but sleep that was the trouble. The hush of an English afternoon in high summer settled on Overton in precisely the same way as it had settled, century after century, on the quiet places snuggled down at the end of their roads. The roads which lead nowhere except to them themselves.

The warmth from the playground would rub itself against my bare legs. The resinous smell of the warm varnish on my desktop, the scent of the blossoms, and the bee-drone coming from them, would push me gently towards the land of dreams.

A quarrel of sparrows screeching up from the street in a tumbling cloud, or a bucket clattering down under the tap at the Pump, would jerk me awake. Or a bit of chalk, thrown by my mother, would skitter off my exercise book or bounce off my forehead. When that happened you had to go and pick up the chalk, take it back to her, and collect a telling-off.

On Fridays we took the furniture back into school after the lunch break, for the afternoon was scheduled as 'Games' on the timetable.

Because there was nowhere we could go to play organised games, we had to make do with the playground. And because this was too small my mother included the street beside it in our rounders pitch. If a skittish-looking horse was coming along in a trap, or a group of riders, the fielders in front of the cottages just shouted a warning and my mother, who did all the bowling, waited until the street was clear again.

To protect nearby cottage windows, she also added a rule that if anyone hit the ball clean over the wall instead of hitting it down to bounce first on the playground side, the team was out. As added protection the tallest and best fielders were always placed in front of the cottages. But, in spite of these precautions, the ball did sometimes crack a pane.

Luckily the tenants of the cottages had children at the school. One dad said, 'It's all roight, Teacher. Ahr kids don't 'arf enjoy these 'ere games. So long as yer pays for noo panes, we ain't goin' to complain. T'ain't as if they gets bruck often.'

But the Estate Agent had other ideas. One day he marched into school with his hat on, 'These rounders,' he announced, 'must stop!'

My mother looked at his hat, then at him. When this had no effect she said quietly, 'Take off your hat. You are setting a bad example to these children to whom I am trying to teach the good manners which unfortunately nobody seems to have taught you.'

Since he had been in the habit for years of marching into cottages without knocking and with his hat on, he seemed a little taken aback. But he took it off and demanded once more that our rounders should cease.

'Give us the use of a piece of field where we can play organised games and we will be delighted to use it,' said my mother.

'Impossible!'

'Then I am sorry. The County Education Committee schedules "Games" on my time-table and I must abide by it.'

'You will stop this nonsense.'

'I will not. Now kindly go away. You are interrupting my lesson.'

When the children spread the news of Teacher's latest brush with the Powers-That-Be round the village it was highly delighted. But the Agent telephoned his complaint to the local policeman, who lived in Springwell, and that officer cycled over to investigate.

When I answered a pull at the back-door bell I found him mopping his face with a big red handkerchief. He was sweating, partly because cycling in his heavy uniform was hot work, and partly perhaps because he was going to have to face up to my mother. She was, by now, known for miles around as 'afeared o' nubbody nor nothink'.

When I told her that the policeman was at the door she put on her battle face and told me to show him in. The fine weather had already brought out the auburn in her hair and when I took him into the sitting-room she was standing bright-haired and bright-eyed in front of the fireplace. The glare which she gave the poor man frightened even me.

'Now Mrs. Bookin,' he said, fumbling with his helmet, 'Don't

you go an' teck on at me. I'm only doin' me job . . . It's abaht these
'ere rounders.'

'So I guessed.'

'These 'ere brucken winders.'

'Who is complaining?'

'Well the folks . . . I expect.'

'You *expect*?' The utter contempt for such an admission which
she put into that word nearly caused him to drop his helmet.

'I ain't spucken to 'em yit.'

'Oh! So it's only the Agent.' This casual brush-off of one of the
Great Powers set the helmet rotating again. 'You may tell him
that I have come to an arrangement with the parents who live in
the cottages. Provided I pay for the replacement of any cracked
panes, they are only too happy that, for the first time, their
children are able to enjoy organised sport like their more fortunate
contemporaries in the civilised parts of Britain. As you probably
know there is nowhere else for us to play in this primitive place
but in the school playground.'

'Oh well. If you've come to an arrangement an' they ain't
complainin', that's different.' He seemed relieved of a burden.

'You could take me to court. The story of how children who
are surrounded by green fields are deprived of anywhere to enjoy
organised sports, would make a good story for the *Leicester
Mercury*.'

'Oh! No need for that!'

'Then I am sorry that you have had to cycle all this way for
nothing. Would you like a cup of tea or a glass of cider?'

Later, as he shook hands, the policeman said, 'I 'eered as 'ow
you was a Tartar. But you ain't.'

'Oh, yes I am,' said my mother.

It was in the year of this wonderful summer that I started my
collection of birds' eggs. There were millions of birds and if there
was any law then against egg collecting we had never heard of it.
But Jippo and Leftie, who already had sizeable collections, told
me that no proper collector ever took more than one egg of any
bird.

Jippo was particularly strict about this. He knocked me aside one day when I had found a blackbird's nest in a hedge. 'Yer got a blackie's. Go proddin' them eggs wi' yer finger an' she'll loikely desert 'em.'

Leftie's collection was in a proper polished wooden collector's box which his uncle had given him. It had three trays, one on top of the other, divided into small squares in each of which an egg rested in fine sawdust.

Jippo's collection was in a biscuit tin and his trays were made of cardboard. He helped me to make trays for my tin.

It was Jippo too who introduced me to the way in which Overton brought up its children to look after themselves.

On one of our expeditions near the East Wood we came to an old thorn tree which had a likely looking hole in its trunk. ''Op up on that branch an' put yer 'and in,' said Jippo. 'Could be an owl's nest in there.'

I 'opped, put me 'and in, and got painfully pecked.

'Now yer know,' said Jippo. 'Next time yer'll 'ave more sense. Nivver put yer 'and in a 'ole wi'aht yer listens at it fust an' gi'es the tree a knock to meck the ole 'en fly if she's on. Yer wants to look under it, an all. See them bits o' mice an' gobbets o' stuff on the grahnd. That means she's 'atched. Chicks pecked yer I expect.'

I sucked my bloody fingers. 'Yer coulda tell't me.'

'Nar! Yer'd jist a forgotten. Yer won't nivver forgit nah. Yer'll allus 'ave more sense.'

Learning the hard way was painful. But it worked. We never did forget.

'Shoulda 'ad more sense!' was the village verdict on any thoughtless act. It covered a multitude of calamities big and small.

In the fine weather Emma left off her man's cap. The sun brought out glints of gold in her sandy hair and either the warmth or the breeze or both fluffed it up a bit. In an only slightly faded green cotton frock she looked more of a woman and less of a pirate.

'This 'ere weather's a treat, ain't it Teacher? If it keeps oop we'll 'ave a rare lot o' taters an' veggies outta the allotments. An' the farmers'll 'ave a good 'arvest an won't 'ave to goo a layin' men off coom winter.'

The fine weather brought the hay crop on early that year. In the evenings of school days and all day on Saturdays I went down to the farm to help harvest it. (However anxious a farmer was to get his crop safely in before the weather broke, no harvesting was done on Sundays.)

The horse-drawn mechanical hay-cutter had already replaced the scythe and every farmer owned one. Each had a long arm fitted with a comb of spikes to channel the crop on to a notched blade which clattered backwards and forwards behind the comb, and you could hear them all over the village.

The cutter began at the outside edge of the field and circled inwards round and round until only a ring of the crop was left in the middle. As it neared this stage a gamekeeper often arrived on his bicycle to make sure that the cutting stopped until any pheasant or partridge chicks which skulked in the ring had been flushed out of it. The blade could chop off wings or legs. Most farmers would stop the cutting at this stage anyway and flush out the birds because they wouldn't want to endanger their tenancy by chopping any. But some keepers could never resist a chance to exert their authority.

The swathes of mown hay were left to dry in the sun and had to be turned over each day and shaken up until they were dry right through. A stack with damp hay in it could catch fire through spontaneous combustion.

Horse-drawn swathe-turners which had revolving combs of steel spikes on them, to pick up the hay and turn it over, were probably in use on more prosperous farms. But round about Overton this work was still done by rows of men and women, and sometimes of boys and girls. We used two-tined forks with long handles. The tines were of thin steel, long and very sharp, and dangerous in unskilled hands. So boys and girls were only allowed to use them when they could be well spaced out along the swathes.

When the hay was thoroughly dry it was gathered into big mounds by a horse-drawn rake. This had a semi-circle of long iron teeth which the driver lowered on to the ground by pulling a lever and raised again when the semi-circle was full. By pulling the lever at exactly the right moment a skilled man could leave his mounds running in parallel lines across the field. This 'looked a treat' and showed the workers on other farms that yours took a pride in its work and knew what was what.

This was the kind of thing groups of men looked for when, careful in their only good suit, they made a tour of the village on Sunday mornings, before church, and compared the work on one farm with the next. A man didn't like to work for a careless farmer. He liked to take a pride in his farm just as he did in that aloof, close-knit, little community: his village.

Because nobody trusted that the fine weather would last, every possible minute of the fine days had to be worked. A wet June and July could mean that much of the hay crop rotted in the fields or lost most of its feeding value, even though it was put into temporary 'hay-cocks' when it rained and spread out to dry again on what fine days there were. A bad hay-crop was a disaster for a farmer because hay was the chief food for his livestock in winter.

The men worked in the fields from when the sun had dried the dew off the swathes until it set and the dew came down again. Women and girls brought breakfast, dinner, tea, and supper out to them and often joined in turning the swathes for an hour or so after they had brought a meal.

With their meals some men had beer at threepence for a bottle, some had cider at twopence, and some had lemonade at one penny. Tea or soup came in screw-top bottles wrapped round with a towel to keep it hot. Vacuum flasks at two shillings each were too expensive for folk to buy.

Once the hay was ready for carting there was nothing a small boy like me could do except fetch and carry for the men or hold a horse's head. But I liked just being there.

Loading a hay-cart was not just a matter of piling on as much as it would hold. Even though the loads were roped they would soon jolt apart on the way from the fields to the stack-yard and shift or fall off in bits on the steeper hills. Once again there was a hidden skill in the job.

I found this out one Saturday afternoon when Perce's brother-in-law came over from Plantham with his wife on a visit. He was a big, strong man who worked in a brewery, and he offered to unload one of the carts.

'Thanks!' said Perce. 'That'll be a 'elp.' And he winked at the carter.

The wink puzzled me. But not for long.

The brewer climbed up on to the load, which Perce and the carter had unroped, drove his fork into the corner nearest the stack and heaved. He looked surprised, spat on his hands, took another grip and heaved again. The handle of the fork bent as his eyes and his muscles bulged. The hay stayed put.

'Cor!' he said. ''Eavy stoof!'

His face was beetroot-red and the sweat was running off him by the time he had prised the corner off the load. After that he had no difficulty with that layer.

'I got the 'ang of it nah!' he puffed.

'Ar!' said Perce.

But the corner of the next layer once again refused to budge. 'Well, booger me!' he gasped. By now he had run out of spit.

'Stick at it!' said Perce.

Then his sister arrived. She took one look at her red-faced husband heaving again at the corner and then rounded on her brother.

'Oo!' she shouted. 'Yer deserves a good 'idin'! 'E could do isself an injury!'

'Wot's up?' asked her exhausted mate, leaning on his fork.

'Yer 'as to fork aht the centre o' each layer fust. It locks the ahtsides.'

''Eck an 'ell!' said the poor chap. 'I damn near ruptured meself . . . Coom 'ere you!' He slid down off the load. But Perce was already heading for the stables. The brewer clumped after him, but stopped quick when Perce nipped into Mollie's loose-box and the mare came to the half-door and bared her teeth.

'Shouldn't coom no nearer,' said Perce. 'She'll bite yer.'

'I can wait,' said the brewer. 'Yer gotta coom aht sometime.'

'Ah, don't teck on!' said Perce. 'That's the way I learnt about 'ay loadin' an stackin', an so did most other lads. Yer won't nivver forgit nah. . . . Not if yer lives to be a 'oondred, yer won't.'

Mollie gave Perce a nudge and he pushed her head away. Then he came out with that age-old Overton prophecy, 'Next toime yer'll 'ave more sense!'

CHAPTER TEN

THE SUMMER TREATS which the Family gave to the school were not such great occasions as the Christmas ones because of course there were no presents to look forward to. But the certainty of being able to eat an enormous tea, plus the possibility of winning a prize in the races and games, generated a lot of excitement in the last week of term, which was when the Treat usually happened.

As at Christmas our crocodile wiggled its way down Pudden Bag and through the Nuns' Door into the Grounds. We were allowed to go this way to church on Sundays. So there was nothing special for us to see until we had come out from under the belt of fir trees and turned left along a path which led to the drive-way across the front of the Hall. To get to the church door, which was at the back of the building, you took the right hand path.

On the left of the drive-way a terrace sloped sharply down to the lawns, which were patterned with flowers instead of sparkling with frost. Round the little lake sharp green swords had replaced the winter's withered reeds. In the gaps between the swords Canada geese swung on their paddles on the bright water, stretched their long black necks, and kah-honked at us.

The path down from the Beeches and the Old 'All divided the lawn in front of the little lake from a bigger one which ran right across the front of the Hall. Beyond it was a smaller lawn dotted with copper-beeches and beyond that a sunken garden where a wooden bridge crossed a stream. This stream ran out of the big Westlake, through the garden, then under the lawns to the little lake, then out under the wall of the Grounds into Oss Pond and out again to become Brooks.

My mother warned us not to go past the sunken garden to Westlake and told us that we could play round the copper-beeches until she rang the bell for the games and races. This year I got sixpence from the Countess for winning the race for the under-tens.

After the races we had tea outside on a paved terrace. If the weather had been bad we would have had it beside the big staircase where we had our Christmas tea.

We were seated on benches at the inevitable trestle-tables. But it was customary for the priest and the head-mistress to have tea at a separate table with the Family, which this year was represented by the Countess and her daughter-in-law, the Viscountess. The Countess never liked having tea at the same table as my 'socialist' mother. But tradition was tradition and it must be upheld.

My mother had not met the Viscountess before and was surprised to find that she was a friendly unassuming person who chatted away with no trace of the patronising manner so freely displayed by the other ladies of the Family when talking to 'one of the villagers'. This 'over-familiarity' towards a woman 'who did not know her place' infuriated the Countess. That evening I heard my mother telling Gran what had happened.

After simmering in silence for a while the Countess proceeded to give her daughter-in-law a dressing-down. She spoke in French so that a mere village schoolmistress would not understand. She told the Viscountess that this woman was impudent and that in any case a member of the Family must not be so familiar with the villagers.

Father Gregory saw that my mother's temper was about to explode. So he winked at her and asked her in French if I had enjoyed winning my race. She replied in French that I had but that I had given away my sixpence.

The Countess broke off in mid-sentence. She stared at Father Gregory with such a look of horror that the Viscountess had to put a hand to her forehead and bend over her plate to hide her laughter.

This was too much for her mother-in-law, who, white with rage, got up and marched into the Hall.

'Oh dear,' the Viscountess said, 'my mother-in-law is a very nice person really. But she has some very old-fashioned ideas.'

As the little peasants were crocodiling away back to the village, the Countess said to Father Gregory, 'Mrs. Buchan seems to be surprisingly well educated. Whatever is she doing, teaching in a village school?'

Father Gregory explained and from then on my mother's relations with the Family began to improve.

After the Treat came the summer holidays. Artie and Jippo got permission to dam up a bit of Brooks, where the banks ran high, to make a bathing-pool. The lakes were of course in forbidden territory. Even if they hadn't been the shallow ends were muddy and covered with lily-pads and, since we couldn't swim, we wouldn't have dared to dive into the deep bits.

To make our dam we used two old rusty sheets of corrugated iron held up by stakes hammered into the bed of the stream and supported by a wall of stones and clay dug out of the banks. Until we had made the wall strong enough, we let the water escape through a hole at one end. After a few days' work we had a pool about six feet wide, fifteen feet long, and four feet deep near the dam. In it we bathed naked and tried to figure out how people learned to swim. Every now and again we had to break off and throw pebbles at groups of girls who crept up to spy on us through the bushes of a nearby spinney.

No Overton boy of school age (up to fourteen) would be seen dead with a girl. To us they were soft, giggly, and silly. This was

most unfair. Thanks to the chores they had to do each day, most
of them were nearly as muscled as we were and nearly as tough.
Maidens they were. Gentle they were not. But we never even
thought of letting them have turns at using the pool. And even if
we had suggested such a thing they would not have accepted our
offer because they knew that we, in turn, would spy on them.
Bathing-costumes were unknown in Overton.

So, when we found three naked girls in our pool we were both
surprised and furious. We had always used it in the afternoons and
evenings. But then I read a book in which the hero went bathing
in a river before breakfast. Clearly this was a most manly pursuit
because the hero was a most manly man. I explained this to my
friends but only Jippo and Artie were impressed. They agreed to
'give it a try'.

The sun had just cleared the spinney and lit up the pool when
we arrived. We were moving quietly through the bushes along
the bank because we had seen a water-rat and Jippo was hoping to
get a shot at one with his catapult. We were about fifty yards from
the pool when we heard the splashing and the girlish laughter.

Jippo stared, thunderstruck, at Artie. 'Gels!' he said.

'Gerraway!' said Artie, as deeply shocked. 'Can't be!'

'Tis!' said Jippo. 'Coom on! Let's pelt 'em!' He began to collect
clods cut up earlier during the wet weather by the hooves of the
cattle.

When we had an armful each we crept forward. And there they
were: two girls of about our own age and a blonde one with long
hair who was much older, and on whose creamy back the sun was
glinting.

'Charge!' shouted Jippo. 'Pelt 'em!'

As the first clods splashed into the water the blonde whipped
round and stared at us in horror. 'Gerrout!' she shouted. 'Gerrout,
you boys!'

'Gerrout yerself,' shouted Jippo. 'It's ahr pool. We made it!'
And he threw another clod which she ducked.

Now, Jippo and Artie had at one time slept toe to toe in a big
bed with their two sisters. But I had never seen a naked girl before
except in books about the Old Masters.

This blonde was definitely a masterpiece. She had pointed

breasts tipped with red nipples which were circled by darker skin. Her whole body seemed to be made up of a beautiful design of gleaming curves. Even after she had raised her hands and flicked her hair forward over her breasts I was spellbound.

'Coom on, Son! Wot's up wi' yer? Pelt 'em!' shouted Jippo.

But I was never going to pelt anything so beautiful. While the two smaller girls climbed out of the pool and ran screaming, I just stared.

The blonde stood her ground and shouted at us until a clod hit the bank near her and spattered her with grit. Then she climbed out and, breasts quivering, made a rush at us. 'You wait till I get dressed,' she said, 'I'm goin' to come back and break your necks!' Then she stalked off towards the spinney where they had left their clothes.

The exit of my masterpiece was somewhat spoiled by a tread on a small thistle, a squeal, a leap, and a grab at a foot.

'We better 'op it,' said Artie. 'She's a big un. An' she will breck ahr necks.'

'Nar!' said Jippo. 'Not if we've got nowt on she won't. Strip off quick!'

He was right. They just threw clods at us from a distance. And girls could never throw straight.

What a pity that I never became a great artist like my mother wanted me to be. I could have made that girl immortal. I can see her now standing in the water. There was a mass of red willow-herb behind her, the sun was rim-lighting her golden hair, and the flickers from the water were stroking those gorgeous curves.

During the next week we sometimes saw their wet footprints on the dusty bank. But we never caught them in the pool again. No doubt they ''ad more sense' and kept a look-out. Then there were no more footprints. We found out that the girls had been on holiday at Glebe Farm.

After they had gone, bathing in the early morning no longer seemed worth the bother. So we bathed in the afternoons until we began to help with the corn harvest when we bathed in the evenings.

Every farmer owned a horse-drawn reaping machine. We called them 'binders' because not only did they cut the corn but gathered it into sheaves and bound them. It was a marvellous invention. Not only did it do away with the back-breaking work of cutting the crop, using a crook of wood to hold it together and a hooked sickle, but it also did away with the painful business of gathering up the bundles of cut corn and binding them into a sheaf by hand.

Like the hay-cutter, the binder had an arm which was lowered into the crop. It too had a comb of spikes to direct the corn on to the notched blade. It also had a separate circle of upright T-shaped arms which went round clockwise to press the corn down towards the blade. Once cut, the bundles were fed along a canvas belt into the machine where they were automatically tied with binder-twine into sheaves before being dropped back on to the stubble.

The binder-twine came in spools bigger than a football. 'A bit o' twoine' was used for hundreds of jobs on the farm, in the home, and in the garden. It could be found holding gates, fences, carts, and traps together, holding up trousers and skirts, belting old overcoats and sacks, and a doubled length held up many a washing.

Mr. Green's binder was pulled by three horses side by side. It was not as rusty and rickety as some. But it had off days when it was forever breaking down. The snarl up of corn and twine inside the machine, when this happened, had to be seen to be believed. Lovely harvesting weather could be wasted while he grappled with its innards or argued with sundry advisers as to what should be done.

'That there gear's come loose. Yer wants to toighten it! It's a movin' sidey-ways.'

'Nar! 'Tain't the gear! It's them claws. They ain't grippin' proper!'

'It's the tier! It's stickin'! Yer wants ter fetch it one, an' oil it.'

'That there rod's bent. Yer wants ter 'ammer it straight.'

Bent double, rummaging inside the machine, Mr. Green would hunch his shoulders under the torrent of advice until he got fed up. He would then uncoil, stick out a red, sweating face under a fringe of straggly brown hair, and shout 'Ah shurroop an' boogger off!'

One afternoon he grovelled inside the binder. It went for a few minutes and broke down again. This happened four times. The fourth time it happened he threw his felt hat at it, kicked a wheel several times, then grabbed a hammer and bashed it, saying, 'Yer rotten, bloody, bastardised boogger!'

I liked the sound of this. It had rhythm. I was quietly repeating it to myself that evening trotting into the house, when I ran into my mother, 'What were you saying?'

'Er . . . I was just describing a broken-down binder.'

'Well if I hear you describing anything in those terms just once more you will never go near that farm again!'

Amos fixed the binder and for the rest of the week it clattered away happily. I was quite sorry. Apart from when he set about it with a hammer, the best bit was when somebody leant against the machine and it moved forward a couple of feet and trapped Mr. Green's fingers in the tier. Roars and howls and oaths came from the innards while what we could see of his body writhed and twisted. The man who had leant on the machine didn't realise that he had caused the bother and it was a few minutes before Perce worked out how to release the parental paw.

Mr. Green sat in the stubble and put his misused fingers into his mouth. I was a bit disappointed. He seemed to have run out of cusses. But suddenly he took his fingers out of his mouth, turned his anguished face up to heaven and roared, 'Boh . . . oll . . . *lucks!*'

We stood around and stared at Mr. Green. Mr. Green sat and stared back at us. Nobody so much as twitched a face muscle. If they had he would have been after them with a pitchfork.

During the war a favourite piece of advice was, 'Get your finger out!' When I heard it, I often thought of Mr. Green.

As the binder whirled its arms, and snicked off the corn stalks, looped up the sheaves, and spewed them forth, teams of men and boys followed to pick up the sheaves and make the sloping stooks: usually ten sheaves set up on their ends with the ears of corn at the top and then leant together five to a side with a gap in the middle to let the air circulate and dry them out. We soon had our fields looking as if they were lined with miniature tents. Mr. Green liked to see these in proper straight lines. If you made a stook out of line he would holler, 'Wot's oop wi' yer? Are you squint-eyed or summat?'

Like the hay-cutter, the binder circled the field. As the area of standing corn got smaller and smaller, once again the wild-life skulking in it got packed closer and closer together.

The last piece of the standing crop was usually shaped like a witch's hat. As the bottom of it was cut away, the wildlife pressed together towards the point of the hat—the pike. Getting the animals packed together in this way made it easier to encircle them and kill them.

As the binder neared the centre of the field, unless the farmer was known to be 'a stroppy sod', packs of boys accompanied by packs of mongrel dogs would gather in the field eager for the explosion of the birds and animals and for the killing. Each boy hoped that he or his dog would kill more than one rabbit so that, with any luck, Mr. Green might let him take one proudly home.

The pike grew smaller and the explosion nearer. Boys waving sticks, and dogs waving tails, pressed in on the binder. Cries of 'Git back, else I'll boot yer arse!' were heard in the land. Boys yelled. Dogs yelped. The excitement was painful.

Mr. Green, Perce, and one or two friends, loaded twelve-bore double-barrelled shot-guns. They stood on the outer edge of the milling circle of hunters with their backs to it ready to shoot any hare or rabbit which broke out.

'Ey oop! This toime!' the boys shouted as the binder began to cut another swathe off the pike.

Then it happened. Pheasants, partridges, and pigeons, went screaming into the air. Rats, mice, rabbits, and hares, went racing and twisting over the ground. In trying to follow the twists of the hunted, the hunters as often as not fell over one another. Boy smote boy and dog bit dog. The binder crew nipped out beyond the seething, snarling, mass and clubbed away with their pitchfork handles. Beyond them the guns began to thunder.

For a couple of minutes there was howling, bloody, bedlam. Then boys, oblivious of the blood which ran down their shirts and the dog-fights which still raged round them, grabbed any rabbits which they had killed to their chests. With eyes popping they lashed out with their boots at any other boy who tried to take their spoils from them.

When the men had broken up the dog-fights and the boy-fights, Mr. Green let the more successful boys keep one rabbit each and then shared out the rest between the men and his friends and himself. The rabbitless boys trailed sadly home feeling that they had let their family down by not contributing to its supper.

The last stooks were put in line. The binder went clattering off to the next field that was ready for harvesting. What had been a rippling field of corn, a living home for scores of animals and birds, was soon silent and still. But not for long. In an hour or so the surviving scavengers were back, slinking through the stubble into the stooks, or flapping round them, pecking up the fallen grain.

For the next few days, until the stooks had dried out, they would have the field to themselves. Then the waggons would arrive, the sheaves would be forked up on to them, and taken off to the stack-yard at the farm. It would probably be spring before a threshing contractor worked his way to our village. So the stacks were carefully finished. Great attention to stack-yards was paid at this time of year on the Sunday morning tours of inspection. Votes were taken on which farm had the best-looking stacks. Angry words were exchanged and, but for the Sunday-suits, angry blows might well have been exchanged too, so strong was a farm's pride in the skill of its men.

At the end of the carting came the raking up of the corn which the binder had failed to tie. Until the raking was done one stook was left in the field as a sign to the gleaners to keep out.

In some villages the gleaning had to wait until all the farmers had finished their raking. A church bell was then rung as the signal for gleaning to start. But in Overton we didn't bother with that.

I used to go gleaning with Mary and her sister Margaret. Mary would say, 'Ahr Pip reckons 'Ibbert's Ten Acre'll be raked to-day. Shall yer coom gleanin' wimme tonoight?'

We each had a small sack and we crawled or stooped low among the lines of stubble, picking up every ear of corn which we could see. For a few days fields teemed not with rabbits but with crouching women and children, whose gleanings were added to the produce of the corn patch in the allotments, to feed the hens.

No committee meeting was held to decide which families should go into what field. As with many other events which could have led to quarrelling in the village, amicable arrangements just seemed to happen of their own accord. Eventually I realised that they happened because of years of tradition and habit.

Year after year the same families went to the same farmer for permission to glean in his fields. Provided nobody got greedy and tried to muscle in on extra fields, there was no trouble. Outsiders might think that in this and in other ways the village was stuck in a rut and needed shaking up. But we who lived in it ''ad more sense'.

The first time I went gleaning with Mary I came home with a sore back and knees all prickled by the stubble. I told my mother that I wasn't going again. She said that was a pity because the gleanings were important to Mary's family.

Then she told me the story of Ruth, and how a farmer in Bethlehem called Boaz let Ruth and her mother-in-law glean in his fields, and how he ordered his men to leave some corn for them to gather.

'Mary says Mr. 'Ibbert always leaves a bit o' corn special for the gleaners,' I interrupted.

My mother nodded. 'Later Boaz married Ruth. Their son was an ancestor of David of whose House Jesus of Nazareth was born. So you see gleaning has been important to people for thousands of years.'

This gave me a lot to think about and of course I went gleaning whenever Mary asked me. Somehow it seemed to be a link between me and the villagers of Bethlehem, as my mother, I expect, had guessed that it would.

With an extra five pounds in the offing—equal to three weeks' wages—men got careless with beer, cider and lemonade bottles and left them lying under hedge-bottoms without bothering about the refund of the one penny deposit on them. So Artie and Jippo talked me into doing gleaning of a different kind. We took a sack and rooted about among thorns and nettles and cow-parsley and in one evening collected thirty bottles.

In the course of being stung and scratched in the pursuit of pennies I heard a horse snort and saw Pinfinnigin coming along the hedge towards us. Restraining a strong desire to bolt, I said, 'Ey, oop! Pinfinnigin!'

'S'alroight,' said Jippo casually, ''e'll know wot we're abaht. 'E won't moind.'

When Pinfinnigin arrived and reined up, 'Wot you lads doin'?' he asked.

'Bottlin',' said Jippo.

'All roight. But moind that's all. An' keep aht o' them spinneys.' He looked at Artie. 'An' no Jackdorin dahn rabbit-'oles neither.'

When he'd gone. 'Soft ole fool,' said Artie, 'oo'd go Jackdorin' this toime o' year?'

When the last sheaf was safely carted there were no great feasts or fuss in Overton. Perhaps our farmers were too poor or too mean or both. The only celebration in our village was a Harvest Dance in the barn towards the middle of September.

But of course, after all the hard work, and the long hours of overtime, when the men got their harvest money they felt they were due for a few celebrations of their own in the pub.

On the Monday night, when what was likely to be the last of the celebrations was going strong, Watto had to work late on one of the farms up the Avenue. He was none too pleased about this. So to 'Meck it oop to 'im loike' the farmer gave him a billy-goat to go with the nanny which he already had down on his allotment.

The gift of the goat seemed a good idea to Watto at the time. After all he could always sell it. So he set out walking, with the goat tethered to the back of his bike. The goat didn't much like the bike and at the end of the Avenue it decided enough was enough and it was going home. When Watto objected, the goat went for him and he had to dodge it round the bike, which the goat set about because it couldn't reach Watto.

The bike fell over, and in the course of trying to butt it to death, the goat got its tether tangled in the handlebars. It dragged the bike up the bank with Watto hauling on the frame behind the saddle, the goat hauling backwards at the front, and pausing every now and again to side-swipe the front wheel.

It was Watto himself who told Jippo and me about it. 'I were fair wooried,' he said, 'me ole boike was worth more than the damn goat. But jist wi' that the goat 'e fell backards inter ditch and the bike fell on top of 'im. So there's boike and goat all tangled oop in keck [cow-parsley] and nettles. 'E lies still a glarin' at me. So I goes and cuts a forked stick off a tree to fend 'im off wen I set 'im free, an' goes back an' sets abaht untanglin' 'im. Wen I got 'im arf aht I remembered the farmer's missus 'ad gie me a few lettuces so I gie one ter goat. Wot wi' the stick an' the lettuces I got 'im dahn Ashborough road and oop Oss Pond 'Ill. Boot by the toime I got ter poob it were gittin' on an' it looked as if I woren't goin' to git more'n one drink, if that. So I tied 'im to outside o' fence near bar door an' went in to sink a few points quick loike.

'They were 'avin' a real ole sing-song an' bar were fullish. Soon Chuckie, the barman, shahts "Toime!" But 'e 'as a job ter git anybody ter goo. Then 'e says, "I ain't servin' no more else I'll lose me job." So Bogo an' Footie goes aht singin'. In a tick they're back, lookin' wooried loike an' poozled. They wispers to one another but don't say owt.

'Then Jebra 'e goes aht swayin' a bit. 'E comes back in a roosh a fallin' over 'isself. "Oh my God, Chuckie," 'e says. "Gie's a drink fer pity's sake. I jist seen ole Nick. 'E's a glarin' through a gap in fence. Yer can see 'im clear in loight from door . . ." "Is that wot it is?" says Bogo, "me an' Footie seen it an' all!"

'Chuckie 'e looks at me, "It's Watto!", 'e says . . . Jebra says "'Ow the 'ell can it be Watto wen e's 'ere an 'e ain't got a black beard an 'orns an' bloody great starin' red eyes . . ." "'E's oop to 'is tricks again," says Chuckie . . . "'Oh 'is 'e?" says Romeo-Jack wot gets nasty wen 'e's 'ad a few. 'E scowls at me an' 'e's a big boogger. So I thought I better 'op it. "I ain't up to no tricks I says. Boot I'll goo an' see wot's there."

'Footie an' Bogo an' Jebra follers me to door. An' be'ind them cooms Romeo-Jack.

'I goes aht an' wen it smells me the damn goat bleats . . .

'"It's a bloody goat," says Romeo-Jack. "Let me get at 'im . . ." Boot 'e 'as to push past Jebra. I get goat untethered. Then Romeo grabs me arm an' I thinks I'm fer it. Boot goat 'e makes a ram at Romeo an' gits 'im roight in the belly. Dahn they both goes in a 'eap. Romeo 'e rolls abaht 'uggin' 'issell an' goat butts 'im again in the back. I pulls 'im away 'an the rope slips out me 'ands an' off shoots goat back 'ome. I 'ops on me boike an' gits away afore the rest can git 'old o' me. Me bein' the only one that were sober.'

Next day Romeo-Jack went looking for Watto. But when his hang-over was gone he saw the joke.

'Did yer get the goat back, Watto?' I asked.

'Ar!' he said. 'Mecks a good watch-dog. Nobbudy dare go near the damn thing, 'cept me. Now I know why I were give it in the fust place.'

CHAPTER ELEVEN

After the corn harvest came the fruit harvest. Any boy whose family had fruit trees in its garden suddenly became extra popular, and some owners patrolled their orchards at dusk with a stick and a dog.

With only a quick grab at one or two plums or apples in mind and your escape route carefully planned, you were unlikely to be caught 'scroompin', but if you were caught you got thumped and that was the end of the matter. It was a risk which you all accepted. Anyone who got caught, 'shoulda 'ad more sense!' But folk with only one or two trees rarely had them raided because any boy seen doing so got his 'good 'idin'' from his parents.

By tradition there was mischief which children could get up to at their own risk and nobody thought much about it. And there was mischief which, by common consent, was banned: interfering with livestock, hay-cocks, stooks, stacks, allotments: damaging trees, hedges, fences, or gates: vandalism of all kinds and theft.

Offenders brought down on themselves not just the wrath of the sufferer but the wrath of the whole village. So the Springwell policeman rarely had to be called in. The community—although it never gave itself such a fancy name—punished its own offenders, and the Estate too took a hand if its interests were involved.

Within the prescribed limits we children were surprisingly well behaved. We had no playing field, no radio or telly, no discos, but we made our own fun. The village did the same. It loved a good laugh. So to children and to practical jokers much was forgiven.

As autumn advanced most of my friends were fully occupied on Saturdays, and on weekdays for a couple of hours after school, in helping to harvest the produce of the family allotment. The corn had already been scythed and stacked but the potatoes had to be lifted and put into clamps—long tent-shaped heaps covered with soil—to protect them against the winter frosts. And spring cabbages had to be planted. But as the days shortened and the leaves turned to red and gold and the bonfires in the allotments signalled that the main work on them was ending, the gloaming brought another season of fun for us children.

In high summer we went to bed in daylight. On our expeditions only the cover of the bushes, hedges and bracken stopped us from being seen and recognised. But in the evenings now there was enough light to see our way about, but, with floppy cap pulled well down and jersey collar pulled well up, not enough for anyone to see who we were. My mother couldn't understand why I made a fuss all of a sudden to get a cap. Or perhaps she did understand. Anyway I got one.

In the early evening the favourite game was 'kick the can'. It was a form of hide-and-seek. One of you kicked the tin-can as hard as he could and the searcher had to go and collect it and put it back on the base while the rest rushed off to hide. Tin-cans were so scarce that even battered, rusty old things were treasured. If you were the searcher and a farmer or gamekeeper broke up the game, it was a disgrace not to collect the tin before you ''opped it'.

The lane leading up to the cemetery had a farm wall about ten feet high running along it for about a hundred yards. The wall was of blocks of stone and had a flat coping on top about three feet wide. We raced two at a time along it. If the 'chaser' behind you touched you before you got to the building at the end you were 'out'. If he didn't he was 'out'. The last boy 'in' was the winner.

It was as well to make sure your cap didn't slip over your eyes during the race because there was a bed of nettles ready to receive you on the outside of the wall, and, as often as not, a raging farmer and his raging dog on the inside of it. It would have taken a tank to make a dent in that medieval wall. But, for some reason, our races along it nearly gave him apoplexy. He was an incomer of course.

Another autumn pursuit was the gentle art of tip-tap. Two of you crept up in the dark to a window where you could see a light through the curtains. Standing on the other's shoulders one of you pushed the point of a safety-pin into the wooden frame above the window. Beforehand you had threaded a piece of black cotton with a black button on the end of it through the ring of the pin. You then retired into the shadows and tied the end of the cotton to a fence, tree, or bush, so that, if you had to run, it would be there when you got back. When you jerked the cotton the button swung and tapped insistently on the window.

Most Overton families had the sense to ignore the ghostly tappings. So the trick was usually played on incomers. But one bad-tempered man, known as Bolshie, was always good for a laugh. He would stand it for a few minutes then rush out shouting 'Yer young darvels . . . I'll belt yer . . . I'll skin yer alive . . . Gerraht of it!'

He was a short man so eventually he would be driven to bringing out a chair and putting it in the flower-bed under the window so that he could grope about feeling for the cotton. The time he fell into a rose bush had the village laughing for a week.

One year an artist and his wife, who had decided that 'quaint' Overton was just the place for them, provided several days of entertainment. They decided that their cottage must be haunted. Then someone explained 'the phenomenon' to them and they went into a huff.

As for most people who fancied a 'quaint' life in our village, one winter was more than enough for them. They departed in the spring. 'Good riddance,' said Jebra. 'Yer 'as ter 'ave a sense o' 'oomer ter live in Overton. Folks wi' no 'oomer jist mecks trooble. An' that fancy feller were madder nor Watto's goat!'

At this time of year the girls had a practical joke of their own. Strangely enough it was rarely practised by boys. Perhaps because they hadn't the patience to lie in wait.

The pan lavatories, the 'roosts' we called them, stood together in a row in the yards at the back of the terraced cottages. Each lavatory was numbered so that the families knew which was whose. Big families had two or more. Only the inn had a whole row of seats with several holes and several pans in the same lavatory. There was one big hole for men, two smaller ones for women, and two tiny ones for kids. They were not of course meant to be used at the same time. It was just that, since the full pans were only taken away and replaced by empty ones once a week, if there had only been one or two, they would have overflowed.

The pans were taken in and out through wooden flaps at the back of the rows. And it was these flaps which gave the girls a chance to get their own back on some of the boys. They would wait in the dark until their victim had bolted himself in, then creep up to the flap, lift it quickly but quietly, and shove a bunch of thorn twigs over the top of the pan and into his bare behind. The result was said to be spectacular.

A more crafty method was to tickle him with a long piece of grass which could be mistaken for a large spider.

Among the men Watto was the chief joker. He had two cronies in crime, Jockey and Rhubarb.

There was a little balding chap who had a wizened sort of face like an elf, and who often got drunk on Saturday nights. Until winter set in, he used to sleep it off for an hour or two propped against a tree on the Green rather than face his irate wife who was bigger than he was. He was so short that he was known as Three-Foot.

One night when he was snoring away against his tree Watto tripped over Three-Foot. Jockey lived near the Green so Watto sent him home to fetch a wheelbarrow. With Rhubarb helping too, they wheeled the still-snoring Three-Foot half a mile through the village and up the drive leading to the house of a retired colonel. There they propped Three-Foot against the front door, rang the bell, and ''opped it'.

Watto told us, 'We 'eard the Colonel uppen the door an' ole Three-Foot slitherin' in. "Good God!" says the Colonel, "wots got inter the silly bugger nah?" Then 'e looks up an' dahn but o' course 'e can't see nubbody. "Ah well!" 'e says, "I expect straw's as good fer yer as a tree." An 'e drags Three-Foot across to a shed an' doomps 'im in. Fancy 'im knowin' Three-Foot slept agin a tree. Mebbe 'e's fell over 'im 'issell.'

Next day Three-Foot was worried. He told Jippo, 'There's no knowin' weer I'm a gonna end oop next. I'll 'ave ter goo on water-waggon. An' that'll kill me fer sure.'

By the beginning of November the wind had swirled the fallen leaves into waves several feet deep up against the walls in some places. You could dive into them and roll about in them and pile them on top of yourselves. When you shuffled your feet through them their brittle chafing sounded like the sea breaking on the sands at Skegness where my mother had taken me during the summer holidays.

Dunkie was the roadman whose job it was to sweep the leaves into heaps for carting. If you kicked about in one of his heaps he would chase you waving his besom. He was a bit simple was Dunkie. If a wind blew up and started to toss his heaps about he would shake his fist at the sky and shout, 'Give over . . . damn yer!' Then he would chase after the chuckling leaves.

The first nip of the frosts reminded everyone that food would be scarce for the next five months. The potatoes were in clamps, the winter greens in rows in the allotments ready for cutting, the corn in sacks in the shed, ready for feeding the hens and the pig. But parents would not be easy in their minds until the pig was safely killed and salted and its meat hanging from the kitchen beams. For most families, boiled bacon and vegetables was the main supper through the winter. And a lump of pork fat in a potato roasted in its jacket was all the midday meal some children got.

The killing of the pigs would begin in late November and carry on into January. As the killing time drew near mothers were said to worry more about the pig's health than their husband's. If dad got bad like as not he'd get better. But if the pig got bad like as not it would be a disaster. Pigs rarely fought against illness but just lay down and died. A pig which got erysipelas and came out in purple spots was usually a goner even if you promptly buried it up to its neck in its own muck which was the best cure.

Because pig muck was a bit strong for gardens, folk liked to mix it with horse and cow muck. Boys went round with shovels and boxes, with long wooden handles nailed on to them, and screwed on to a pair of old pram wheels, to collect the droppings in the roads and lanes. In the summer evenings they set off after school to fill their boxes. Now, at the approach of winter there was extra shovelling of 'mook' and trundling of boxes to finish getting the necessary ingredients for the manure heaps which would ripen on the allotments until the spring.

I saw one boy whose box was nearly full of lovely squelchy stuff being pursued by his little sister who was bawling her head off. ''Old on me duck,' he said. ''Old on a tick wile I gits this last lot then yer can 'ave yer roide.'

Sure enough he shovelled up a line of horse muck, dumped her on top, and trundled her, beaming happily, home.

Now a new dimension was added to the assortment of smells in the village shops. All the year round except at Christmas—when the smells of holly and small fir trees were thrown in—the mixture was paraffin, spices, hams, cheeses, candles, ironmongery and leather. It was topped off by the smell of corduroy and sweat, human, bovine, equine and canine, provided not by the management but by the customers. But now, for two weeks before Bonfire Night, the pungent, exciting smell of gunpowder thrust through the humble, peaceful, smells.

Like most houses in Overton our three shops were all on the damp side. So to stock the fireworks for more than a couple of weeks led to a lot of complaints about duds. Only one, the Stores at the top of Pudden Bag had been built as a shop. It had a big plate-glass window at the front and three smaller ones along the side. But except at Christmas time, when toys were on display in the front window, there was never any point in looking in at them because they were just used to store items not in regular demand: things like zinc tubs, wash-boards, coal scuttles, creosote, pick-axes, wire-netting, and so on.

The other two shops were Choc-Eye Bottomley's on Top Street and Bennett's next to the bakers. These were just the front rooms of cottages with a counter opposite the door, and with shelves of sweetie-jars behind it and overflowing shelves of this and that along the rest of the walls. Piles of clothes flopped about on tables and all sorts and sizes of gleaming metal objects hung from hooks on beams. In either shop a tall man could play quite a tune with his head.

Apart from tins of syrup, cocoa, and bully-beef few things came pre-packaged. Sweets, tea, flour, dried peas and beans, and even sugar and salt, had to be tipped into scales, weighed, and put into paper bags. And of course things like bacon, butter and cheese, had to be cut up before weighing. The shops would make up your orders for you into cardboard boxes and deliver them. But many women preferred to go to the shop in person, sit on the seats provided, and have a leisurely chat while other people were being served. If strangers came in they would often let them be served first, more out of curiosity about what they wanted and who they were, than out of politeness. Besides they would be enjoying their chats while waiting.

Because of the wide variety of the stock even the Stores, which had three times as much space as the other two shops, had outer reaches of shelves which were not well charted.

One day, while Crum and I were waiting to buy sweets, a man asked, 'A' yer got any 'air-clippers, Mrs. Stanwell?'

'Yes,' she said. 'I know we have. Sid ordered some more at Christmas. But he's aht. I reckon they're on one o' them four shelves over there. Shall you send yer little ole boy for them later or would yer loike ter have a rummage now?'

'I'll rummage,' the man said.

'Good,' she said. 'You'll most likely find a box of fish 'ooks as well. We've lost 'em. Give them to me will yer if yer do?'

Of the fireworks 'Jumping-Jacks' were our favourites. They cost a penny and hopped about fizzing and banging away round people's ankles. Tossed into a 'roost' under the door in the dark they were always good for a laugh. Tossing them anywhere near horses, ponies, or cattle, was however banned.

Small rockets and roman-candles were threepence, medium ones sixpence, and large ones a shilling. But unless you lived well away from cottages or farms your parents wouldn't let you have rockets because the stick might come down smouldering and set fire to thatch or to stacks.

Armistice Day was held on the eleventh of November. The First World War ended at eleven o'clock on the eleventh day of the eleventh month. So each year at that hour on that day the whole nation went silent and still for two minutes. We knew from the newspapers that the members of the Royal Family and the members of Parliament went to a ceremony at the Cenotaph as the traffic in all our towns and cities stopped completely. In school we stood to attention for the two minutes remembering the dead. Then we said the age-old prayer of David the King:

> 'Out of the depths I cry to thee O Lord,
> Lord hear my voice.
> Let thine ear be attentive
> To the voice of my supplication . . .'

On these Armistice Days and on the anniversaries of the killing of my father in France, my mother was always sad, and quiet, and moody. On one of them the village War Memorial was unveiled. I heard my mother telling Gran that she just couldn't bear to take the school down to the little ceremony in which a bugler would play Last Post. But she went.

It was about a week after Armistice Day that Leftie got the idea that we should visit the dovecote down beside Westlake. The lake was on the edge of the Grounds with one bank in a field and the other in the Grounds themselves. It was dangerous territory. Particularly since Pinfinnigin lived near its shallow end. The dovecote was in the field. It was circular and built of stone like a small tower, and underneath it was a shelter for cattle.

We had heard some of the older boys talking about how, if one of you stood on a manger, the rest could climb up over him through a trap-door into the cote, then pull him up. According to them there was a seat suspended on pulleys from a beam pivoted in the centre of the roof. On the seat you could use your hands to push yourself round the nesting-boxes in the walls and you could raise and lower yourself up and down the rows of them.

Rooks, they said, shared the nesting boxes and, because they were vermin, in the spring you could collect dozens of their eggs and have an egg fight, throwing them at one another. In early summer you would have been able to get fledgling pigeons, if Pinfinnigin hadn't kept a special watch on the place at that time.

Leftie, who usually planned our more daring operations, argued that the keeper wouldn't be bothering about the place in autumn and so this was the time to find out if there really were these rows of nesting boxes and this seat.

So, after tea, we went down Oss Pond Hill, up the lane through the spinney on the south edge of the Grounds, past the old spider tree, the Beeches, and the old church, and into the dovecote field.

As we approached the lake water-fowl went skittering and screeching among the mists and the lily-pads. They set up such a racket that we had to hide under an old fallen tree for several minutes before we were sure that they hadn't given us away. While we were under the tree we wondered whether the older boys had been having us on so that we were wasting our time.

But everything was as they had described it and we each had to have several goes at swinging ourselves round and round the nesting places from which of course the occupants had exploded, through the holes in the walls, at our entry. If anybody had been watching this would have been a dead give-away. But we were lucky.

What with one thing and another the moon was up by the time we passed the church on our way home. Beyond the grave-yard wall there was an iron gate opening on to a path which led down to the Hall. For the first two hundred yards or so it wound its way beside, and sometimes between, the evergreen shrubs which surrounded the ruins of the Old 'All. They made a wild tangle about fifteen feet high and, even in the moonlight, as black as sin. It was no wonder, that, what with them and the ghost, not to mention the graveyard, few people went down that path at night.

Leftie pointed to the gate. 'Dahn there is a thing called a "ram".
It pumps water by itself wi' nothin' drivin' it. In a stone sort of
cellar it is, dahn steps along by the path.'

'Gerraway,' said Jippo. 'Nowt goos by itsel'. 'As to be driven
by a windmill, else a water-weel.'

'Goes by itself,' repeated Leftie. 'Went there last wick wi' Felix.
'E was checkin' it.'

Felix was the village plumber called—because he was forever
walking about at a smart pace—after the newspaper cartoon *Felix
the Cat*, which '*went on walking . . . went on walking still.*'

'Git aht,' said Artie.

'It does!' said Leftie, annoyed.

'Can't,' said Crum.

'Roight! Coom on an' I'll show yer!' Leftie headed for the
path.

''Old 'ard,' said Artie. 'Not past the Old 'All an' inter the
Grounds?'

'Wot's up? . . . Scared?' sneered Leftie.

'No I ain't!' said Artie, 'Boot . . .'

'So it goes by itself . . . yes?' said Leftie, angry now.

'Can't,' said Crum.

'Roight . . . coom on!' Leftie went through the gate while the
rest of us looked at one another and shuffled our feet.

'Yeller!' taunted Leftie. So we went.

Where the shrubs overhung the path we ran. Then in the clear
bits when we came out into the moonlight again we kept in their
shadow. Eventually ''Ere's the steps,' said Leftie and disappeared
down them. It was dark down there but we heard him striking a
match and, as it flared, we followed.

Sure enough there was the ram, a round black thing which
popped up and down with a thump in a trough of water. 'Every
time it thumps,' said Leftie, 'it pumps water up that pipe leadin'
from the trough.'

'My guy!' said Jippo, ''ows it wuck?'

'Dunno,' said Leftie.

We marvelled over the ram while he struck matches. Then he
pointed to a wall, glinting with water and slimy with moss, of the
underground building. 'Through there is a way into the secret

passage wot leads from the Old 'All to the new un, wot used to be a farm-'ouse.'

'Oo yer!' said Crum.

The match went out. 'That's me last,' said Leftie. We didn't exactly run up the steps. But we were quick.

As we reached the overgrown shrubs again Artie said, 'Ain't nivver seen the Old 'All.'

'Coom on then,' said Leftie, who had (of course) and who (of course) knew a way under the shrubs.

We crawled down what had once been a path and came out on cracked overgrown paving between a pattern of beds in what had once been a terraced garden. Facing us was, at right angles, the remaining gable of the building. As we approached I saw in the broken front wall a tracery of fluted stone with the remains of tall leaded windows. Beyond them was a coat of arms. The moonlight made the white stone glow with what, to me, was a ghostly light.

I no longer felt black monkeys waiting for me in the shadows. But the story of the bridal ghost which haunted this place appalled me; on the one hand the girl scrabbling inside the chest and on the other the maid looking down at the skeleton in the white dress and screaming and screaming. The eye-sockets of the wizened face stared at me from out of the white stone. So I just stood and looked while the others scrambled over fallen stones and two owls drifted silently through the tracery. Perhaps my fear spread to the others because, after a minute or two, even Leftie turned back.

After we had crawled back to the main path we heard voices, mens' and girls', so we crawled under the shrubs again. Two couples came out arm-in-arm into the moonlight. 'Grooms and maids from the 'All,' whispered Leftie, 'let's give 'em a froight!' But before we could do anything one of the maids snatched her arm from under her companion's, pointed, and screamed—a high-pitched wailing scream of terror. Immediately the other girl screamed too. I looked under the bushes along the path and there pacing slowly from the shadows and into the moonlight was a tall black figure in a huge black cloak and with a black hood framing its ghastly white face.

There was a drumming of feet on the path as the couples ran and an explosion from the shrubs as Leftie, Artie and Jippo followed them. But Crum and I were paralysed with fear. An ice-cold pain burst in my stomach and went tingling through my whole body.

The figure came on and then looked up startled. 'Oh dear!' it said, and I recognised Father Gregory in his Benedictine cowl.

When Crum and I had crawled out on the path, 'What was that about? . . . and what are you doing here?' he asked.

I explained that he had looked just like the ghosts in pictures.

'Oh dear!' he said again. 'I don't usually wear my habit but there was a nip in the air tonight and I put the hood up to keep my head warm.'

'Huh!' we said when we caught up with the others, 'fancy running from Father Gregory . . . Yeller! Yeller!'

They chased us back to the village where next day everybody knew that the white ghost at the Old 'All now had a black one for company.

In school we all boasted that we had been there when the couples saw the new ghost. 'It's true,' Jippo said, ''orrible it was . . . 'orrible . . . I ain't nivver run as fast afore.'

We were heroes for a week. Then the truth leaked out.

CHAPTER TWELVE

O N SATURDAYS now, the village began to echo to the screaming
of the pigs. Some families favoured a November killing,
some a December one, and some big families saved the killing of
their second pig until the end of January. In most winters over a
hundred pigs were 'stuck' in Overton.

My mother had never let me go with my friends to watch the
killings. She said that all the screaming and the blood brought out
the worst in people. But, one Saturday afternoon, we were playing
football in the paddock when the screaming started up in a nearby
allotment and we all ran to watch.

An owner and the 'pig-sticker' were about to drag a second pig
out of its sty when we arrived. The owner was forcing the animal
against a side wall and the sticker was trying to slip a loop of rope
over its snout. When the noose was in position and tightened, he
hauled, the owner pushed the pig from behind, and it screeched
worse than peacocks, bag-pipes, or banshees.

I was surprised at the number of people, both men and women, who had come to the sties. Jippo said, 'There's allus a lot o' folks coom to fust stickin's. Mecks summat to look at. But they soon gets used to 'em an' then only them as is goin' to 'elp cooms.'

As soon as the pig was dragged out of its sty, sundry helpers pounced on it and half carried it to 'the scratch'. This was a sort of stretcher on legs. It was made of heavy wood. It probably got its name from being the place where the carcase was scraped clean.

The animal was lifted on to the scratch and tied quickly down to it. At least that was the idea. If the noose slipped from the snout however things could get tricky. A pig-bite is an extremely nasty wound because it crunches right through into the bone. A big screaming pig slashing its fangs from side to side was apt to turn brave enthusiastic helpers into refugees in no time at all. Then men bearing long-handled rakes, to fend it off with, had to chase the animal round the cabbages and brussel-sprouts, and force it back into its sty to be looped up all over again. Meanwhile it continued to yell its head off.

The pig stuck out over the front of the scratch so that the sticker could slit its throat and slide an enamel basin under it to catch the torrent of blood.

At this point the business was usually all over bar the cleaning, scraping, and gutting, as the screams grew weaker and then stopped. But knots tied in bloody ropes by bloody fingers can slip. That afternoon, an extra big pig gave such a heave as it felt the knife that it burst clean off the scratch. With mouth gaping in rage and pain it made such a ram at the sticker that it knocked aside the owner's rake. Women screeched as loud as the pig as they tucked up their skirts and ran. Men cursed. The sticker fended the animal off with the basin before he slipped down in the pools of blood and was rescued just in time by two men with rakes.

I was a bit sorry that the pig hadn't managed to get a bite into the sticker because I had taken a strong dislike to him. He was a big, bearded, red-faced, man who wore an old flat-topped, greasy, felt hat and a sacking apron over an equally greasy overall coat tied round with twine. The ends of his moustache were waxed into points and his little watery eyes peered piggishly around. He used to put the knife into his mouth as he slipped the basin under the slit throat, so that, after he had stuck a few pigs, his beard was clotted with blood, some of which still dripped on to the sacking apron.

He fancied himself as a comedian. To the 'horrified' squawks of the women he would cup the warm gushing blood in his hands and drink it. And he would push his finger up a dying pig's backside and then lick it.

One of his favourite sadistic tricks, was, after he had cut out the gall-bladder, to say casually to some lone child, 'Stand on that fer me, will yer?' If the boy didn't know any better and did so, a jet of stinking liquid shot up his legs. It went on stinking for days no matter how often the legs were washed.

I couldn't see anything funny in the death of any animal even one as unlovely as a pig. So to me the whole business was undignified and revolting. It didn't occur to me until years later that many of the people in our village would have thought the same; that 'the bit o' foon' was one way of helping to face up to the nastiness of what had to be done whatever anyone might think about it. In a city it was easy to escape from the ugly realities of the natural life. In a village it was almost impossible to do so.

Before the killings started, a big fire had been lit near the sties. It had a metal grid across it so that pans of water could be boiled for scalding off the remains of the bristles after the tops of them had been burnt off with torches of flaming straw. After the scalding the scraping of the carcase began.

Then came the ritual of the 'first meat'. The sticker sliced out the piece under the stomach, shouted 'Belly-bit's aht, moother!' and held it aloft in both hands. The woman of the house had to be ready to go forward with a dish to receive it while well-wishers applauded.

The day the family pig was killed was especially important for the wife. Every bit of the carcase must be used. The feet became boiled trotters, the head became brawn. The larger intestine became the skin of the sausages made from the scraps, and the smaller intestine became chitterlings. Even the bladder, when cleaned and blown up, made a toy for the children.

Young wives were anxious about 'meckin' a moodle o' things'

and letting their husbands and their families down. Mothers, mothers-in-law, sisters and friends, would go along the day before the killing to make sure that she had been able to borrow all the necessary utensils, and to help clean them. Then, after the killing, they would help to cut up and prepare 'the fries'. These were made up of the bits of meat which could not be salted. Since there were no refrigerators, only an exceptionally big family could eat them all before they went off. So they were distributed round a circle of friends and relations who would, in their turn, distribute fries round the circle when their own pig was killed. By staggering the killings each circle made sure that, for a few weeks anyway, its members ate well.

The sticker gutted the carcase out on the scratch and cut off the meat which could not be salted. The wife and her helpers carried these and the guts home on dishes. The husband and his helpers carried home on a stretcher the rest of the carcase, which had to drain before it could be salted.

Sometimes the only place where the carcase, complete with head, was safe from dogs, cats, rats and mice, was the big cupboard which most cottages had under the stairs. There it sat up, leaning slightly forward, in the big zinc tub in which the family had its baths.

An unfortunate sister-in-law from Ashborough once opened the door of one of these cupboards by mistake. The sight of a disembowelled pig sitting up grinning at her in the light of her candle was too much for a townswoman. She dropped the candle 'an' went off in a fit o' the screamin' ab-dabs'.

This event appealed greatly to Overton's macabre sense of humour. For years afterwards, preceded by, 'D'yer remember wen ole Soapie's sister-in-law . . .?' it had the village in stitches all over again when pig-killing time came round.

The salting of the main carcase was a job for an expert. He had to press out every drop of blood from the veins. If any were left in, the piece would rot and an extra hungry family result.

When the hams and flitches were safely hanging on the beams, and the brawn, trotters, chitterlings, and fries dealt with, in a good year, a wife could relax a bit and begin to look forward to Christmas. She had already made her jams of perhaps plum, apple, gooseberry, rhubarb or bramble. She might still have some pickles and chutney to make, and she would have to keep an eye on the home-made wine fermenting away in jars above the kitchen range. But, provided it had been a good summer, and there were plenty of 'taters an' veg' on the allotment, the food for the family was now stored. If it had been a bad summer, or the pig had went and died, and food was going to be scarce, well there was nothing she could do about it except pray that the Lord God would provide.

I learned about the importance of the pig, and of the storage of food in general from a woman's point of view, from old Lucy. She came to do our washing for a few weeks while Emma was ill. Not only did Lucy visit homes to wash the clothes, she also visited them to wash and lay-out the dead.

She was a tiny, thin woman, with grey hair scraped into a bun at the back. For washing clothes she wore a sacking apron over an old blue serge skirt and, like Emma, a man's cap. Like Artie she wore it with the peak at the back so that she could see what she was doing. In cold weather she used to sniff a lot and twitch her little nose so that, under the cap, she looked like a rabbit with its ears laid back.

For the washing and laying out of the dead, however, Lucy was posh. She wore a high black velour hat, shaped like an old-fashioned beehive, a stiff black skirt, and a spotless white starched apron. The effect was only slightly spoiled by the enormous pair of men's boots which peeped out from under either skirt.

Her posh 'official' dress sometimes had a quite magical effect on the sick. If Lucy went to see them wearing it, folk who had been laid-up in bed for days were known suddenly to be cured and get up and about again. They knew she had a habit of 'eyin' yer oop'.

She was always hopeful about her posh job. When a woman died she would say 'Uppen grave fer she . . . Uppen grave fer three!' And, 'The bells tolled that 'oller a Soonday. There'll be a death in village. Mark my words.' The end of the year was a likely time for business too. 'A green Christmas mecks a full church yard!' She had strong likes and dislikes did Lucy. Of a woman she hated she told me, 'Ah well! I've ahlasted 'er any road. She's bin an' died o' the dropsy. An' there she is, swelled 'og-size, lyin' arse-uppards in the cemingtery.'

If the weather was too bad to go into the playground at the mid-morning break, I used to go into the wash-house and chat to her while I turned the mangle.

One week she was very happy and singing to herself in a high, reedy, sort of voice.

> 'Oh Genevieve, sweet Genevieve,
> The days may come,
> The days may go,
> But la la la
> Da, da, da, da,
> Sweet memories of long ago.'

She never could remember all the words.

'A' yer seen me froont door, Son?' she asked.

'Ar!' I said, 'looks noice! A noice shade o' green.'

'Int it! Me nephew coom uvver from Plantham an' painted it fer me. Better nor that there sh . . ., mooky brahn coolour all cottage doors is painted in Overton.'

Lucy swore like a trooper. But because she was afraid that I might repeat her cuss-words in front of my mother she often corrected herself in mid-cuss, so to speak.

The following week she was in a rage, muttering to herself and banging buckets about. Her eyes were all narrowed under her glowering brows so that she looked more like a tetchy little stoat than a friendly rabbit.

'Don't mind me, Son!' she said. 'I'm that mad! I could kill that bloody Agent. I only 'opes as 'ow I 'as the job o' washin' an' layin'-aht the boogger! I'll enjoy it! I will! I'll enjoy it.'

She glared at me, 'An' don't yer goo a bloodyin' an' a booggerin' in front o' yer mam neither!'

I thought I better try to cheer her up a bit. 'She once caught me a' callin' a brucken-dahn boinder a "bloody, bastardised, boogger!" So I ain't loikely to do that agin.'

For a tick or two it cheered her up in admiration. 'Oo did yer 'ear a callin' it that?'

'Mr. Green.'

'Ooh ar! Ole Bill allus could stick a few together. 'E went to school wi' me.'

But then her troubles caught up with her again. 'D'yer know wot that bloody, stook-up, iggerant, snobbish, son-o'-a-cross-eyed-bitch, went an' said ter me today?' She put on a posh accent. "'Oo give yer permission ter paint yer door that 'orrible bildous coolour?" 'E was a lookin' at me dahn is soddin' gret long conk. 'Good 'eavens, we'd 'ave a village lookin' like Joseph's coat o' many coolours in Bible if we let ivverybody paint their doors any 'orrible coolour they fancied. Yer will jist 'ave it painted the proper brahn agin!"

'I were goin' ter say my green were bettern shit-brown. Boot then I thinks better on it. Don't want ter git put aht. An' I don't want ter lose me job as layer-aht neither. Nah me nephew'll 'ave to buy a tin o' . . . Ooh! I'm that mad! . . . An' don't yer goo sayin' shit neither, else Lucy'll cop it. By guy I will!'

'S'allroight,' I said. 'I'll only tell me mam that yer called the Agent a bloody son-o'-a-cross-eyed-bitch wi' a soddin' gret conk.'

'Ooh, yer wouldn't!' she gasped. Then she saw me grinning and splashed suds over me.

Lucy being older could remember farther back than Emma to the days when Overton had been entirely self-supporting, and had its own little gas-plant down at the end of Bennetts' yard. 'We 'ad a gas-lamp ahtsoide Stores; another at Green weer West Street joins it; anoother ahtside poob; anoother in Bennetts' yard; anoother at Choc-Eye's; an' anoother ahtsoide Estate Office. 'Tween't mooch. Boot yer could mostly see 'em shinin' in the poodles an' cow-shit. Nah them's went, yer can't see owt. I don't moind the 'oss-muck that mooch. It cooms off easy. Boot cow-shit is that *sticky*!

'We used to 'ave a miller. 'E's gone. We used to 'ave a tailor till Mr. Newey went an' died. So 'e's gone. Course most folks mecks their own clothes. Boot it they wants 'owt special now they 'as to ask Ricker, the carrier, ter git it fer 'em. They gies 'im the soize an' the kind o' thing they wants, an' 'e brings 'em a few to choose from. On apperer they calls it. Boot t'ain't the same as seein' the stoof in the shop.'

Ricker went off in his van, drawn by a big skewbald gelding, to Melton on Tuesdays, to Plantham on Wednesdays, and to Ashborough on Saturdays.

Lucy also told me more about the Lloyd George. 'The in-stewrance they calls it. Wen a man's in wuck 'e buys a stamp at Post Office fer ninepence an' sticks it on a special card. If 'e falls aht o' wuck the noomber o' wicks 'e draws the Lloyd George depends on 'ow many stamps is on 'is card. Arter that 'e 'as to apply fer the P.L.I.'

'Wot's that stand fer?' I asked.

Lucy stopped soaping a pillow-case, blinked a bit, and frowned. 'Well, the "P.L." stands fer Poor Law that I do know. Boot wot the 'ell the "I" stands fer, I dunno . . . I reckon it could be Instertoot . . . Any road if 'e passes for the P.L.I. 'e gits seven-an-sixpence a wick if 'e's single an' fifteen bob if 'e's married. Boot 'e 'as ter be in 'is 'ouse by nine o'clock at noight, an' 'e moostn't be seen goin' ter poob nor buyin' fags. If 'e is, 'e's stroock off an' gets nowt. Same rules as Sick an' Dividin'.'

'Wot's Sick an' Dividin'?'

'It's a Cloob. Men pays in threepence a wick. Then if they gets bad an is off wuck they draws five bob a wick out o' foond. That's the Sick bit. The Dividin' bit 'appens each year at Easter. Wot's left in foond arter the sick benefit 'as bin paid aht is divided among all the members . . . Afore the Lloyd George an' the P.L.I. started oop, if it weren't fer the Sick an' Dividin' an' 'elp from their famblies folks would a starved. Damn near did soomtoimes. In the bad winters durin' Great War the Fambly used to give 'arf a deer ter nuns each wick an' they ran a soup kitchen in the school wi Lady Anne an' Lady Sarah 'elpin' dish aht. Dunno wot we would a done wi'out that theer soup kitchen . . . The village ain't nivver bin the same since that damn war. Booggered us oop proper it did.

'The winter o' 1916 was the wust. Ricker took 'is son Tabbie ter Melton market an' they got stuck in an 'oller fer three days an' two noights. It jist kep' blizzerin an' blizzerin'. The snow were oop ter top o' weels. They 'ad to dig a 'ole rahnd back o' van ter shelter the 'oss . . . I arst 'im wot they ate. Soft question to arst a carrier. O' course the van were full o' food they'd bought fer folk at market. But Ricker said it weren't 'arf cold, even under a taprawlin' wi' parcels an' stoof on top.

'Ooh, it were a darvel o' a winter that were. Couldn't git aht me door fer two days. An' wen I did the cart-roots were damn near knee-deep on me. Everythink frez. Water in boockets. Milk in cans. Even the piss-pot oonder bed. I 'ad ter use a tin o' that there consented milk wot me sister give me at Christmas . . . Good job nubbody died in them two days . . . Boot theer, they'd a frez, coom ter think on it, loike everythink else . . . Talkin' o' carriers, a yer seen that theer steam thing?'

That there steam thing was the first lorry to visit Overton. It came round our shops from Roberts and Roberts the wholesalers in Leicester. It had a tall, shiny, black funnel at the front with a brass rim round the top. Underneath that was a squat vertical boiler over a coke fire which was in a kind of brazier. Behind the fire two chains led from the steering gear to the front wheels. These, like the rear ones, were about two feet high and had solid rubber tyres about eight inches wide.

In good weather the lorry could go as fast on the flat as a horse could gallop with a trap. And it could keep it up for a couple of hours, which of course a horse couldn't. But on hills in thick mud, snow, or ice it often got stuck and had to be towed up by horses. Before they would go near it, the driver had to douse the fire to stop steam billowing out of the escape valve on the funnel and from sundry places underneath as well.

When it was going full-out along Ashborough road it was an exciting thing to see. The smoke from the funnel blew back in a long plume and in dry weather the dust blew back in a long cloud. The engine hissed 'Chuffa . . . chuffa . . . chuffa . . .' to itself very quickly non-stop, like a squirrel chattering. And the rest of the machine rocked and bounced and clanged over the rough roads.

The first time we saw it ranting and rolling along, Jippo said, 'My guy! It's a goin' loike one o'clock!'

This was a favourite expression in our village. It described rapid progress. But what one o'clock in particular had to do with speed I never found out.

The steam lorry was an awful warning to horse drivers and

riders of the shape of things to come. Soon the motorcar would arrive in the village. It would begin as a joke and end as a tyrant. And life would never be the same again.

Now, if a chuffing, chuntering, and clanking, were heard on the breeze, folk connected in one way or another to a horse would say, ''Ark! Is it that damn steam thing? It is! Weer's a gate?' They would quickly lead their horse into the nearest field and keep its head turned away from the monster to stop it driving the poor animal into a fit.

The day the monster was going full-steam down the avenue and met the Hunt in full-cry coming up it was a never-to-be-forgotten one for those who were privileged to witness this collision of ancient and modern.

Hounds were running through one of the spinneys and the field was galloping up the road. Since the Hunt took priority over everything else it was not expecting a check. When they heard the tongue of the pack or the huntsman's horn, or glimpsed flashes of red through trees and hedges, and realised the Hunt was coming their way, people reined in and got down and held their horses heads. Even so the animals would probably buck and rear and do their best to join the torrent of high-bred gleaming horse-flesh topped by high-bred gleaming humanity which surged past them. It could all be extremely inconvenient. But the Hunt didn't give a damn about that.

The monster however was different. It could stop of course. And it did. But it couldn't get off the road and it couldn't stop steam hissing out of its escape valve or fizzing out in white clouds all round it.

The Hunt split before this apparition like loam before a plough-share. The leading riders had some warning of the hazard ahead. They saw the monster shudder to a halt and were able to swing their horses off the road and into the spinneys. But riders further back down the galloping column got less and less warning as scores of horses checked at the awful sight.

At first the animals didn't believe their eyes. There was no such thing so it couldn't be there. Then, when they realised that their worst fears were justified, they simply took off in whichever direction offered the best line of escape.

Ladies and gentlemen went flying into saplings and bushes. Some went the right way up; some upside-down, and some flat-out as in diving. Others clung on anyhow as their horses bolted hell-for-leather for the fields.

One Baronet, having extracted himself from a tangle of brambles, limped over to the driver who, according to himself in the pub that evening, was studying the tree-tops from the safety of his cab. The Baronet was stuttering with rage. If the driver's story was true the gentleman said, 'You . . . you . . . bloody s-stupid . . . s-sodding . . . s-steaming . . . s-stinking . . . s-snake! Do this again and by God I'll shoot you!'

'Wot did 'e think I was goin' to do,' the driver asked the public bar, where his story was going down a treat in more ways than one, 'disappear in a cloud of me own steam?'

The next evening the accounts of one or two grooms, who had been fortunate enough to see the fun from the back of the field, had the pub, and later the village, in stitches again.

It wasn't that our village held anything against the Hunt. It didn't. It was just that, as winter approached, it didn't often find much to laugh at.

The Overton meets were usually held during the school terms. But my mother always adjusted her timetable so that we could go down to the Green and watch them. We stared spellbound at the splendid horses and their splendid riders. We were particularly taken by the gorgeous and occasionally beautiful ladies perched on their side-saddles, with the flowing skirts of their black riding habits draped over the flanks of their horses, their spotless white stocks and gloves, and their veils stretched round the rim of their black silk top-hats and covering their faces in a filmy little curtain. The young ones looked wonderfully cool and aloof. I was sure that butter wouldn't melt in their pure mouths.

When we got to the Green grooms were already walking blanketed horses round to keep them warm. Sometimes one groom could be leading four horses: two on each side of him. These were from the stables of wealthy owners who provided two horses for each member of its family and of its guests. Grooms brought the spare horses along at a modest pace at the back of the field to take over from the first horses when they were blown. Some hard riders would have more than one spare. Grooms often left their stables at dawn to walk the horses to the meet.

Most of the Hunt members still arrived in carriages. But a few had begun to use motorcars. These too were of great interest to us because nobody in the village owned one yet.

The carriages and the motorcars followed the Hunt by the nearest road so that they were on hand when the members decided to call it a day and head for home leaving the horses to the grooms. One of the reasons why many members preferred still to come in carriages was that they could negotiate fields and muddy lanes which were impassable for motors.

As the time of the meet approached the grooms began to put the members up on their horses. The men members of course wore hunting-pink and black toppers. Those in the field who were not members wore black coats and black bowlers instead of toppers.

While they waited for the pack to arrive, the riders walked their horses round in small groups chatting to one another. The scarlet and white of the men was bright among the black and white of the ladies. Soon the Green itself and the open space in front of the inn looked like a scene from a pageant of England. Gentry and yeomen, grooms and villagers, we had changed little. The bright eyes, pricked ears, tossing heads, and shining coats of roans and chestnuts, blacks and greys, were changed not at all. And the thatched roofs, the old stone walls, and the great trees, which made such a perfect setting for this piece of country history seemed to glow with pride.

The pack itself came surging on to the Green led by the huntsman and surrounded by the hunt servants, the whips, who wore scarlet coats and black jockey caps. The hounds were cream and brown and kept together, tails high and waving. If one strayed from the pack a whip would call it by name and send a long lash flicking above its back.

Knowing ones like Speedie, would say, 'Ah! They've got the bitch-pack aht terday. So we should see soomat!' Why the bitch-pack was better than the dog-pack I never found out.

Speedie, as one of his many odd-jobs, helped the keepers to

stop earths and the hunt servants to dig out foxes which had gone to ground. When meets happened in the school holidays and we were able to follow on foot, Speedie 'kep' us roight' and made sure we didn't make a nuisance of ourselves.

When we had seen the pack arrive we ran back to school and sat on the wall of the playground. The Hunt always moved off up West Street, past the school and the Stores, and then up the lane past the cemetery to the woods in the Park. Sitting on the wall we were on a level with the riders.

When the pack, followed by the toppers four abreast and filling the whole street, had passed us, the bowlers had still not left the Green. The whole village seemed to be full of colour and chattering hooves.

Most of the toppers ignored the line of scruffy little peasants. We might simply not have existed. Usually only a few of the men would nod and smile at us or raise a gloved hand. But once a beautiful brunette turned in her saddle and gave us a long, lovely, smile from under her veil. We were smitten instantly into silence. I was so enchanted that I nearly fell off the wall.

Although Overton was in the recognised hunting shires, ours was not of the best. The woods were too close together and sometimes linked by spinneys, so that crafty foxes, instead of instinctively running down wind to let it take their scent away from the pack, would veer into a spinney, run up wind through it and round in a circle. When, in the holidays, therefore, we were allowed to trot along behind the field, if we stayed in the Park, there was usually plenty to see.

Speedie warned us of the terrible things that would happen to us if we 'headed' the fox. This was the most dastardly of crimes; second only to shooting one. If, after hounds had worked a fox out of a wood, you frightened it back in again, or if, when hounds were running in the open, the fox saw you ahead of it and swerved off line, perhaps causing the pack to overshoot the scent, then you had headed it, and may the Lord have mercy on your soul.

When hounds were drawing a covert you were safe if you stayed with Speedie, watching where the field gathered and where the carriages, traps and gigs stayed. Even then on a day when there wasn't much wind you had to keep your wits about you and be ready to make yourself scarce.

One day a distinguished looking lady and a girl descended from a carriage and walked into a field on the edge of the West wood. At least the girl walked; the lady limped along using a stick.

'That's the Marchioness,' said Speedie. 'She broke 'er ankle in a fall earlier on an' it ain't better yit.'

We could just hear the pack crashing about in the middle of the wood. Then a hound gave tongue and one or two others joined in. At this point a rider posted at the far corner of the wood, to watch for the fox breaking out, made a signal to a group of riders in the field. They came cantering towards us. The lady too turned and began limping out of the field.

Soon we could hear that the pack was drawing nearer through the wood.

''Urry oop, mam, for God's sake!' muttered Speedie.

The Marchioness was doing her best. But the pack was winning.

Speedie was so overcome that he grabbed my shoulder and squeezed it painfully.

'Stan' still, mam . . . stan' still',' he said, ''e's in the 'edge-bottom! Oh my guy, the Master'll eat 'er!'

'Wot an' 'er a Marchioness?' asked Jippo.

'Wouldn't matter if she were a duchess! . . . Stan' still mam!'

But suddenly a fox, like a red streak, flashed into the field, saw the couple, turned, ran along the edge of the wood, then darted back in again. A minute or so later the pack came roaring out into the field in a burst of cream and brown, all baying mouths, and leaping haunches, only to check and split and circle, noses down, tails waving, as they overshot the scent. Then they turned at sixes and sevens and wandered silently back into the wood again.

''Ere 'e comes,' said Speedie.

He pointed to a big red-faced man, riding a big white horse which was thundering down on the couple from a gate at the side of the wood.

As he approached the Marchioness raised her voice. 'All right,

Master,' she called, 'we are extremely sorry. But you needn't come any further, we know that we are silly shits!'

I could scarcely believe my ears.

The Master reined up, glared, shook his fist at her, and galloped back into the wood.

'That's wot 'e allus calls ladies wot 'eads the fox,' explained Speedie. 'An' 'e allus calls men soddin', stoopid booggers. Bin doin' it fer years 'e 'as.'

We found that some riders, both men and ladies, tried to keep as straight a line as possible after the pack, jumping fences, hedges, and ditches, unless a board painted red and stuck up on a pole in a hedge warned them of danger on the other side of it. Other, more timid souls, went a roundabout way using gates and never, if they could possibly avoid it, jumped anything.

Groups of us boys used to compete to take over the gates which would be most in use. Usually, after we had opened our gate, a lone rider or the last of a group would toss a sixpence at our feet. But some would lean down from the saddle and put it, or even a shilling, into our hands, and say 'Thank you'. We found that these nice riders were usually those who were resting their muddied, blowing horses.

Some riders, however, went through with neither a coin nor a 'Thank you'. The thing to do then was for all of you to bay like hounds and crash the gate closed behind them. Since they were usually not too safe on a horse, if a buck or a rear or two resulted, you got a bit of fun. And if they approached your gate again you ignored their shouts of 'Hey you . . . open the gate!' and got more fun as they tried to get their horses alongside it and hook it open themselves with a hunting crop. All the gates had latches which could easily be hooked open in this way. But many city ladies and gents couldn't manage it. 'Proper toffs' who could, would sometimes, hang back and watch the fun with us.

Some riders were embarrassed when they came off at a jump. But most were just plain furious. The mount of one gorgeous young lady slipped at a muddy take-off, fell at the fence, landed her on her face, then cantered off. She got up plastered with mud, her bashed topper hanging by its cord down her back, and brushed mud and hair out of her eyes. When she saw her horse disappearing she stamped her foot in rage, cracked her crop against the fence and shouted to another rider, 'Catch that big stupid bugger for me, will you please?' Then she added, 'Daft, bloody thing!'

I was appalled. She was so beautiful. 'Cor! Young ladies swear too!' I said.

'Not 'arf!' said Artie. 'Good as ahr dad, some on 'em!'

Mary's elder brother Johnnie, who was a groom at the stables of a wealthy man who lived near Ashborough, told me that his boss always went hell-for-leather. If anyone tried to follow him over a difficult jump and fell, he used to turn in his saddle and roar with laughter at them.

Johnnie said that although the grooms enjoyed the hunting season it involved very hard work. They had to be up at four in the morning to prepare the horses and get them to the meet. Then, after the Hunt, the animals had to be walked back to the stables, rubbed down well, and then checked every half hour. The more excitable ones often broke out into a sweat again. That meant that they had to be rubbed down all over again. Sometimes the grooms didn't get to bed until ten o'clock at night.

Once after a hunt we found a dead fox crouching in a deep, partly overgrown, wheel-rut on a track in the Park. Its belly and brush were caked with mud.

'Got away from 'ounds,' said Jippo. 'But it were so done-up, it died.'

At that moment I hated the Hunt. I hated the way it had earths stopped; how it hunted bewildered young cubs in the autumn to train its hounds; how it dug out foxes which had outwitted the pack. It seemed a funny kind of sport to me.

I said all this to Speedie. 'Ar!' he said, 'Boot remember foxes is vermin. They'll git among 'ens an' ducks, an' they won't jist teck one. They'll goo mad wi' killin' and chop the 'eads offen the lot. I've seen forty 'ens all copped by a fox wot dug inter their pen. Foxes ain't no teddy-bears. They're killers. Yer goo along the soide o' a wood in the snow an' see the bloody mess weer they've killed rabbits an' birds. So if it weren't fer the 'Unt, an' the compensation it pays ter farmers, foxes would'a gone the way o' wolves. There wouldn't be none.'

'Besides,' he chuckled, 'soom foxes is so dead crafty yer can almost 'ear 'em laughin' at the 'ounds. 'Untsmen git to reckernise a fox's tricks. They gies 'em names. There's one round 'ere they calls "Rupert". 'E's led 'em a dance these last foive year. An' there's a vixen they calls "Mabel". They nearly 'ad 'er once. She'd gie 'em a three moile roon rahnd in a circle. Then she nipped dahn a big rabbit-ole an' got stuck. The 'untsman put 'is arm dahn an' 'e could feel 'er brush. "Dig 'er aht, Speedie," 'e says ter me, "it's Mabel. Put 'er in yer sack an' let 'er goo in yon field. I'll 'old 'ounds round back ter gie 'er a start."

'They 'ad a good chase fer uvver a moile. Then they lost 'er. Clean vanished she did. Next day, a farmer wot 'ad bin aht wi' us, says ter me, "Yer knows that Mabel wot we lost? Well ahr mam went aht ter feed 'ens fust thing s'mornin' an' she sees a vixen joomp dahn outta that thick oivy on top o' that ole cow-shed wall o' moine. I bet it were Mabel. No wonder we lost 'er, wot wi' smell o' cattle an' smell o' the oivy."'

Speedie went on. 'Sometimes a fox uses special escape places fer years afore they're fahnd. Sometoimes they ain't nivver fahnd.'

I think he was right. Six years or so later I was fishing for pike in a punt in the middle of the lower of the twin lakes. I could just hear hounds drawing the East wood about a mile away. Then I heard the huntsman's horn. So, since what breeze there was blew towards me from the wood, I turned and faced it, cast out on that side, and kept a look-out for the fox.

It had been a clear January day. But it wanted only a couple of hours or so to sunset and the sun had gone in behind a bank of cloud low on the horizon, although the rest of the sky was palest blue like a thrush's egg.

I didn't see any sign of the fox until the wide fringe of withered reeds under the bank began to twitch as something pushed through it. Then an arrow-head wake began to cut the water. At first I thought it was a moorhen. But then I picked out the ears.

The fox swam round towards the boathouse which had a line of duckboards on poles leading out to it over weeds and mud at the shallow end. I watched the wake disappear into the open end of the shed and a minute or so later I saw the white patches on the fox's mask peeping out through a broken plank in the gable above the same end. He must have been sitting on the beam supporting the gable. I realised that the breeze would be blowing his scent towards me down the length of the lake.

I could hear the pack coming in full cry up the far side of the hill which stood between the lake and the wood.

The light had that luminous quality which you get on a clear day when there is a nip of frost in the air. All the colours were muted; the pale grey of the leafless trees and bushes blended into the bleached yellow of the grass and the reeds. The land, like the lake, was sleeping.

Then the pack came racing over the rim of this quiet, pastel, world. It came rushing round the patches of bracken, pouring relentlessly on. Next the scarlet of the huntsman and the whips galloped into the scene; glowing figures on chestnut horses pounding down the hill; then the rest of the field burst in waves of colour into my view. So charging cavalry must have looked. I was glad that I was not a foot-soldier waiting for the screaming shock of their arrival.

The pack crashed through the reeds. Hounds swam round in circles, then went back to the reeds again and floundered among them in the shallow water.

I turned my back, cast my bait out on the other side again and hunched my shoulders deeper into the turned-up collar of my coat. The field had enjoyed a splendid gallop. Let that be enough. I was on the side of the fox.

Out of the corner of my eye I saw the huntsman and whips arrive and the field rein in and begin to line the hill which was now as vivid with scarlet and black and white and every shade of gleaming, sidling, brown as it had been pale before.

I heard the huntsman and the whips lifting the hounds and soon I saw them casting along the far bank ahead of me. At one point I could see a rider shouting to me, but I couldn't hear him.

And all the time their little quarry sat quietly on his beam.

Eventually they gave up. The light was fading and they cantered back into the sunset.

Soon the lake grew grey and misty. The trees at the top of the hill became a black frieze against the flame of the sky. Not a fish moved and neither did the fox.

I got fed up waiting for him, hauled in my anchor and began to pole back to the boathouse. I was half-way back to it when he jumped down on to the duckboards, took a long look at me, shook himself, trotted casually along them, and vanished behind the reeds.

I bet he'd done it all before.

CHAPTER THIRTEEN

A NY TIME after the middle of December the first hard frosts bit into us. The wind chilled our homes through every nook and cranny. And the village battened itself down again for the three miserable months of winter.

On freezing mornings my mother opened the school half an hour early so that children could huddle along the square metal railings which guarded the two coke stoves. Some were warmly dressed. Others were still wearing the darned jerseys and dresses which they wore in spring and autumn.

Christmas was a good time for my mother, with the help of better-off parents, to find spare jackets and cardigans, so that we all had them. It didn't much matter in wintry Overton whether girls wore boys' jackets and vice versa, just so long as they had them. The same thing applied to overcoats. But these were harder to find and some children came to school in snowy weather with a sack, hooded over their heads and shoulders, and tied round their jackets with twine.

Because few parents could afford, or had the time to knit, gloves, it was cissy to wear them. After they left school girls might wear them. But not men; to this day those of us who grew up in our village in the 1920s and 1930s hardly ever wear gloves. Although I know it's daft; not to wear them is, for me, a kind of tribute to the men, women and children whose sense of humour saw them undefeated through those tough times.

Round the stoves in the mornings little-uns would sometimes cry with the ''ot-aches'. These were the sharp pains in frozen fingers and toes which came on as they warmed up and the blood began to circulate properly through them again. The older children got the pains as well. But once Overton boys and girls reached seven or so it took a lot more than the 'ot-aches to make them cry.

One morning, just before Christmas, the little-uns of one big family were crying for a different reason. When my mother asked them what was the matter they just went on sniffling. But when the eldest son arrived he said, 'Please, miss, the pig's jist went an ate the cockerel wot ahr dad were fattenin' for Christmas. It were abaht roight an' all.' The bird, it seemed, had flown into the sty, landed in a pile of muck, and stuck.

We were all looking forward to our Christmas dinner and could see just what a disaster had hit the family.

My mother said, 'Never mind. Let's ask Father Christmas to bring you another one.'

''E won't,' sobbed one little boy, ''E don't nivver listen.'

My mother got one of the pile of hankies, which she kept in her desk for such pain-wracked moments, and helped him and the others to blow their noses. 'Perhaps he wouldn't always,' she said, 'but if we all ask him hard enough I'm sure he will this time.'

Since we all had great faith in her, this cheered us up. If she said it would happen, then it would.

At tea-time I heard her telling Father Gregory about the pig that went an' ate the cockerel. 'When they say things like that, you could cry or you could laugh. You end up blowing noses.'

'Will they really get another?' I asked.

'Of course,' said Father Gregory. 'Father Christmas will get one. Not alive though in case the pig eats it too.'

I was glad. Although of course, being nearly nine, I knew there wasn't any Father Christmas.

When next I went to chat to her, Lucy was cussing the winter. 'These 'ere dark evenin's is a darvel. I does 'ate 'em. I went an' dropped me key ahtsoide me door last noight. *Could* I foind it! Me pessocks (feet) were frez, an' I grovelled all rahnd me doorstep. An' it were rainin' an' all. I 'ad to knock on next door an' borrer a box o' matches. Mecks yer look a fool. I'll 'ave to buy a new battery fer me torch.'

'It were still rainin' wen I 'ad ter nip aht ter me roost. There's four in a row in ahr backyard. I pops in, in dark, loike I allus does, bolts door, an' I'm jist uppin' me skirt wen ole Dunkie says,"yer in the wrong un, missus!" Soft ole fool! I damn near sat on 'im! T'weren't me as were in the wrong un. T'were 'im! An' 'e lets me bolt the door an' all. I screamed. An' 'e laughed. An' I 'opped aht that smart I damn near fell. 'E's a daft ole sod.'

She spun the dolly in the clothes, spun them off it, and bashed it on the side of the copper to get the water off. It was clear 'she were mad'.

But then she laughed, 'Ah boot t'other day 'e got in trouble wi' Agent wot cooms ridin' oop street on 'is 'oss. Dunkie wips 'is cap off that smart 'e sets 'oss a-rearin'. Agent shahts, "Good God, man, ain't yer got more sense nor wave yer 'at at me 'oss?" Dunkie says to me "If yer don't teck yer cap off yer in trooble. An' nah, if yer does yer in trooble. Wot the 'ell are yer ter do? If I wasn't bald, I'd leave boogger at 'ome." Served 'im glad it did.

'Boot I were in trooble wi' Countess missel' a Satterday. She uppens me kitchen door and gies me sooch a froight I damn near dropped me basin.' Lucy put on her posh accent again. "That's a good smell comin' from yer pot," says 'er ladyship. An' she goos an' lifts lid. "That's a 'are," she says, "weer did yer git it?" I tells 'er Mr. Green give it me, wot's the truth. "Oh did 'e?" she says. "I'll git Agent ter arst 'im abaht it. There's far too mooch poachin' a gooin' on."

'As she's leavin' an I'm givin' 'er a curstey on me doorstep, she sees the littlest un next door a kickin' a lilyburnum tree in their garden. So she rattles 'er stick on fence an' shahts "Mrs. Taylor, coom 'ere at once!", An wen Gert cooms an' cursties she says,

"Since yer can't git yer choild ter stop a kickin' that there tree, tell yer 'usband 'e must put woire-nettin' rahnd it." She's a proper Tartar is 'er ladyship.'

The shooting season was now in full bang. Every Saturday we could hear guns going in the woods round the village. On these days my friends went beating. This was an important job for them as well as an exciting one because they got two shillings and a rabbit for the day's work.

The beaters, both men and boys, met at the Green at four in the morning. They had to be in position at the first wood by five. Some of the boys had a coat. Most had a woollen scarf over their cap to cover their ears. It was pinned at the neck and tucked inside the collar of their jacket. They all carried their sandwiches and a mug for cocoa.

The keepers met them at the wood and put the boys in position round it. Their job was to keep the game inside by tapping gently with their sticks on fences or trees on its fringes, while the men built fires on three sides. They lit these, partly to provide warmth and light, and partly because the smoke helped keep the pheasants in the wood. The boys took turns to go to the fires for a warm and a mug of hot cocoa.

The toffs wouldn't come of course until it got light enough for them to see what they were shooting at. They would arrive either in the saddle or in traps or dog-carts. Even if they could get to the wood, motors were noisy brutes. Then the men would form up in a half-moon formation in the wood, with Speedie and Muncher on each end of it. Their job would be to see that the formation kept its shape and didn't go forward too fast and panic the pheasants into exploding out in all directions. They would drive the birds slowly to the edge of the wood from which the boys would have been cleared. There the guns would be waiting.

The flames flickering on fences, bushes, trees, and on shadowy figures coming in from the freezing dark. Quiet voices. The wind moaning quietly to itself in the trees. The crackle of the fires. The gentle, eerie tapping.

Misty light creeping in as if from the ground. Grey grass. Grey trees. Grey bushes. Grey people.

The flames paling as the sun fired the sky on the rim of the wood. The greys warming into greens and browns; into frost-pinched faces and white breath-plumes.

The thud of hooves on grass. The rattle of wheels, the creak of springs, and the clink of harness. Silent gun-dogs on leads. Loaders carrying guns. Men and boys crouching at the fires for a last warm. The guns taking up their positions. Speedie and Muncher lining up their men in the wood. Always the eerie, encircling, tapping.

The whistle. The swish and crunch of feet in formation treading forward. The birds, crouching, puzzled, muttering to each other, moving away from the fearful feet, until there was nothing in the world for them but to take wing on the fatal side. The warning shout. The screaming of the wings and the crash of the guns.

Eventually I and some of the others would see more dawns like these. But they were in other countries. The fires came from shell-bursts. And the game was different.

While the shooting season swung noisily into its stride, the poaching season slipped softly on its way. Dads, laid-off because of the bad weather, and trying to exist on the Lloyd George or the P.L.I., went after rabbits. A nice big rabbit, stewed with dumplings and plenty of veggies from the allotment made two free meals for all but the biggest families.

Most had learned as boys how and where to set snares. These were little nooses of braided wire attached to pegs which you pushed well down into the ground beside rabbit-tracks under hedges, bushes, and bracken. The noose, arranged over the track, tightened as a rabbit's head went through it and broke the animal's neck or strangled it.

The trouble with snares was that, if a farmer or one of his sons or a keeper spotted one, they might, instead of lifting it, hide near it at dusk and catch whoever came to check it. Boys therefore often did the checking.

Crum and I met Jippo late one Saturday afternoon. He was walking along near Cuckoo Spinney admiring the scenery. 'A yer seen anybody?' he asked.

'Courtin' couple dahn road,' said Crum, 'nubbody else.'

'Sure?'

'Course,' said Crum.

''ang on then an' keep yer eyes uppen.'

He nipped into the spinney and in a couple of minutes nipped back. 'Got un! An' I've reset snare!'

'Weer's rabbit?' I asked.

'Up me sleeve.' He was wearing an old, cut-down coat of his dad's.

Because you could get caught checking your snares some men preferred to work together in twos and threes and use nets. You could bag more rabbits that way and, provided you kept a good look-out, you were less likely to walk into trouble.

Speedie was one of the best men in the village with the nets. Many a family or an old person living alone got a free meal from Speedie.

'Do yer use a dug to drive rabbits inter nets?' I asked him.

'Nar, Son! Fer Pete's sake don't nivver use a dug. If a keeper cooms along 'e'll shoot it an trace yer by yer dead dug. Besides dugs is too noisy, crashin' an' bashin' abaht.

'Tunnip else cabbage fields is best fer rabbits. Yer wants a noight with a bit o' clahd an' a bit o' moon boot not too mooch o' either. Yer moves wile moon's be'ind clahds an yer uses yer eyes ter see if anybody's abaht wile its aht. Wen yer sure the coast's clear yer moves inter field, sits dahn, an' waits fer a bit o' moon so yer can see ter set the nets. Then wen moon cooms aht yer lies dahn an wen its in yer goos back ter end o' field an begins ter push the rabbits towards the nets. Yer goos bent double loike an pats yer 'ands on yer thoighs. That's all yer got to do, lyin' still in the bright bits. The rabbits runs inter nets an' gits tangled in 'em. Gooin' abaht the job that road I only bin nabbed the once. An' that were me own softness.'

Speedie sighed and shook his head. 'There were this 'ere tunnip field near Springwell. It were fair 'otchin' wi' rabbits. I goes there wi' me ole mate Muncher. It were jist the roight kind a noight. But wot do we do? We're thirsty arter ahr boike roide. So as we're passin' the Dog an' Duck we decides to 'ave a point. Softest thing we ivver did.

'In bar a bloke cooms oop to us an' sez "Yer from Overton ain't yer? Wot yer doin' in Springwell? Yer ain't boiked uvver 'ere jist

fer a pint." I says we're on ahr way to see their 'ead-keeper Mr.
Tyler abaht a beatin' job.

'We goos aht an' Muncher says 'e don't loike the look o' that
there bloke an' we better jist goo 'ome. Boot I tells 'im not to be so
soft. We leaves ahr boikes be'ind 'edge an bags nineteen rabbits.
Wen we gits back to boikes there's this bloke an' anoother 'idin'
near 'em. They turns aht to be sons o' the farmer. They tecks us to
Mr. Tyler wot tecks the nets an' the rabbits, wot 'e gives to the
blokes. Bein' a noice feller—not loike ahr bloody keepers—'e's
willin' to let it goo at that. But these two won't 'ave it. We gotta
goo ter Court.

'We cooms up in front o' Sir Arthur. We explains weer outta
wuck an' Muncher 'as a loine from doctor abaht 'is missis bein'
very ill. "I'll give yer a chance then," says Sir Arthur; "foined ten
shillin' each, else fourteen days!"

'That weren't givin' us no chance. Shoulda bin foive shillin'
else seven days fer a first offence. Any roads we ain't got ten
shillin' so it looks loike fourteen days in gaol. Boot Mr. Tyler
sez 'e needs us next Satterday fer the beatin'. So 'e pays the foines
an' we does the beatin' for nowt. A roight noice feller is Mr.
Tyler.

'We ain't nivver bin nabbed since. Were aht last noight. Boot all
we netted was ole cat. Got a fox once. Wot a mess o' the net 'e
made.'

'When I git a bit bigger could I coom aht wi' yer one noight?' I
asked.

Speedie's eyes nearly popped out of his head. 'Not bloody
loikely! Yer mam'd 'ave me 'ead off!'

As the winter dragged on some of the little-uns round the
stoves began crying with the chilblains as well as the 'ot-aches.
Some of the older children had them too. Their fingers were
swollen up like sausages. They itched and itched until some of the
sufferers scratched them raw.

Crum was upset one day. His mam's chilblains were terrible
and she hadn't been able to get the kitchen fire to go first thing in
the morning. His dad had been mad at her because he could only
have a mug of skimmed milk and slices of bread and marge for his
breakfast. Crum said it was all his fault because he hadn't put the

sticks in the oven the night before until too late. So they were still wet.

My friends didn't like to talk about their homes. But because he was so upset I did get Crum to tell me about life in his cottage in winter. Like most others it was 'two oop an' two dahn'. On the ground floor was the kitchen-cum-living-room and the parlour. Upstairs were two bedrooms. All the rooms were about twelve feet square. Between the bedrooms was a small boxroom. The wash-house was a lean-to outbuilding and their roost was on its own down the garden.

The parlour was only used on Sundays and on special occasions. Like the kitchen it had a flagstone floor covered with peg rugs which his mam had made and a square of coco-matting.

His mam and dad slept in one bedroom, and he and his brother in a big bed in the other. His sister slept in the boxroom.

In winter his father had to be at the ironstone workings by seven o'clock. In summer at six. At about half-past five his mother would knock on their doors as she went downstairs with her candle. Then she lit the lamp in the kitchen, raked out the ashes from the range, re-lit the fire, and put the small kettle on it. It was filled the night before. After a heavy frost you didn't want to have to go breaking the ice on the buckets under the sink. The big kettle would have taken too long to heat. It went on later and simmered all day.

The family washed in the kitchen in the evenings when you could have a little hot water to take the chill off the basin. Dad, like most Overton men, only shaved after the week's work on Saturdays. The children had to go out while he did it because he used a cut-throat razor and could cut himself if disturbed.

Breakfast for the children was most likely a mug of cocoa and a couple of slices of bread and dripping. Dad got fried bread and bacon. Then Dad would set off to work on his bicycle and the children would set off to do their daily errands.

Crum's sister, being the eldest at thirteen, would set off for a farm on the Avenue to fetch a quart can of the skimmed milk left over after the butter-making. It cost tuppence. There and back she walked nearly three miles. So, in deep snow, they had to pay for proper milk.

His brother, aged eleven, went off to the Hall with a bowl to get scraps or a big lump of dripping at the door to the kitchens. Either cost fourpence. This was a 'cook's perk' about which the Family knew nothing. When the Family supplied food to needy folk it did it free. He had to be sure he got there early to take his turn at the door. Sometimes he went on to Pinfinnigin's to see if there was any 'broken rabbits'. These were the ones riddled with pellets at point-blank range by stupid toffs during the shoots, and cost sixpence each.

Crum himself went off to run errands for the butcher. For these he was paid threepence a week out of which he was allowed to keep a penny.

His mam made a football-sized suet pudding every week with raisins in it. At midday each day the children got a slice of this with home-made jam on it. Now and again they got a big potato roasted in the wood fire with a lump of bacon fat in it as well.

The main meal was at six in the evening after dad got home from work. It could be rabbit stew, or boiled bacon, or, provided dad was in work, sixpenny worth of liver, or a shilling's worth of brisket. As long as he was working they could sometimes afford a Sunday roast, price three-and-sixpence. When he was out of work they, like other families, lived mostly on rabbits, bacon, dumplings and veggies.

Crum's mam got most of their clothes at jumble sales or made them herself. His dad mended their shoes, cut their hair, and did what carpentry and cement jobs were needed round the cottage.

At breakfast one day, I told my mother that I had been talking to Crum about his home. 'It must be rotten to be poor,' I said.

My mother looked at me for what seemed a long time before she spoke. 'So you've begun to notice,' she said. 'I'm glad. Go on noticing. Most people never do.'

It was in March that year that the big blizzard hit us. Some folk said it 'were the wust in livin' memory'.

'Roobish!' said Lucy. ''Tain't nowt ter 1916!'

But it was the worst I ever saw. The snow drifted deep against the playground and allotment walls in West Street. It was so deep that not even with three trace horses could the old V-shaped wooden snowplough get through. Men had to dig a way for the horses through the middle of the drifts. Then, what with the digging and the ploughing, the snow-piles reached the bottom of the windows on one side of the street and the tops of the walls on the other. Everybody tipped their ashes into the street because, even with studs in their shoes, the horses could hardly get up it.

The frosts were so hard that we could walk over the tops of hedges, where the snowdrifts covered them, and not sink in at all.

Icicles four feet long hung from thatch and had to be snapped off before their weight damaged it. But you had to be careful not to break off the edge of the thatch with them.

Dead birds lay under trees and bushes. I saw the corpse of a jackdaw dangling by one frozen foot from a telegraph wire. Its feathers were ruffled by the wind which swung it to and fro.

No vehicles could get through to Ashborough for over a week. Bill the postman said, 'I expect I could get through on a 'oss. Boot I ain't got un. An' even if I 'ad, I couldn't roide it.'

Apart from those who had indoor jobs or were looking after animals, most men in Overton were laid-off. Work on the iron-stone quarrying was literally drifted to a halt.

In the Park and in the other acres of scrubland, the weight of the snow bent the withered bracken down and formed long tunnels which looked like white waves in a white sea. In the tunnels rabbits skulked. After school we sneaked in groups of six or so into this winter world. When we tapped on the roofs of the tunnels the rabbits ran out and floundered in the snow where they were easy to kill with sticks. We could bag a couple each in no time. Sometimes we could have taken more but there is a limit to the number of rabbits a boy can hide on his person. We tied the hind-legs of the rabbits together with a 'bit o' twoine' and then tied them to a larger bit which we put round one shoulder like a sash. Then we put our coats back on. We looked distinctly odd. So we went back to the village by devious ways.

In the white wilderness, after sunset, the light came up from the snow. Anybody moving out in the open stood out black like a bruise. So the keepers, who couldn't cover all the bracken, had no chance of creeping up on us. Even if they saw us, they couldn't get near enough to recognise us. It is surprising how fast a boy can go, even at a crouch and with rabbit heads banging on his knees.

I enjoyed those evenings. The hunting was exciting and so was dodging the keepers. And I felt that, for once, I was doing something useful. I could never keep my rabbits of course. Artie or Jippo would take them for ole Moll or Lucy.

One evening when I was late for supper my mother asked me where I had been. When I told her she asked what happened to any rabbits which I caught. Then she thought for a bit before pointing out that if I were caught the Agent would enjoy demanding an apology from her. She finished with, 'So don't get caught. Don't take silly risks.'

I said, 'Fat chance o' them catchin' me. I shift too quick.'

'Don't use village talk to me,' she said. 'With me you will continue to speak properly.'

So I went on being bilingual.

For me, the beauty of the woods and of the open spaces under snow in moonlight or starlight added to the excitement. I doubt if I thought of them as beautiful at the time. I just knew that I liked being among them; liked looking at them.

I found that snow lengthens distances between faraway things and shortens them between close ones. It makes even well-known places look different as I found one day when I lost the others and nearly lost myself.

Sometimes before the daylight faded I would let them go on and stand alone on the edge of a spinney looking for movement out in the white wilderness. There was none. The trunks of the trees stood out black against white. But their branches merged into the black line of the wood beyond. The trunks were black pillars sometimes arranged in circles, sometimes in lines which led my eyes towards the wood. Out there was silence. If I stood for a time listening and only hearing the sound of my own breathing, I found that it was not an empty silence. It seemed as solid as glass. It pressed down on me and round me, squeezing me in. Time had stopped. I was a statue under a glass cover and I would be staring out at this same frozen scene for ever.

It isn't a good thing to go on listening at silence for too long. It's as risky as really getting down to thinking exactly what you are, what you are doing where you are, and whether you are really there at all. 'That road,' Jebra would have said, 'a feller could droive isself offen 'is choomp.'

Once when I set off after the others, I came to the edge of West Wood. I could see that the blizzard had whitened the undergrowth near the fence. But beyond, the brown of withered bracken, ferns, and leaves still showed. Through this dark inner world of the wood an open ride ran untrodden and sparkling white. As I stood at the end of it, it looked like an aisle sloping upwards lined with black pillars. From my height it seemed endless. The snow-light killed the shadows in which danger lurked. Everything was clean and clear; frozen in time. Surely this was a way leading to eternity and to God?

On one of the anniversaries of my father's death my mother had told me the legend behind the song *Loch Lomond*; how the Low Road is the way by which the spirits of her dead warriors return immediately to Scotland.

A Jacobite officer was captured at the battle of Culloden and taken to London. A friend visited him the day before his execution. To comfort his friend, the prisoner said:

> 'Ye'll tak the high road
> An' I'll tak the Low Road
> An' I'll be in Scotland
> Afore ye.'

Was the Low Road white? And was it lined with pillars clothed in black samite? Had my father gone along a road like this, my white way? And was there a brilliant light at the end of it?

I could see him, in his uniform, moving quickly along. He was going away from a small boy in a grey overcoat, who had a scarf over his floppy peaked cap and round his ears, and who was ankle-deep in snow in his dubbined boots.

We had arranged, one day, to go sliding after school. But three of us landed in a heap on the 'Oss Pond slide at lunch-time and my left arm was painful. So I decided to go up to the Park to get rabbits with Jippo instead.

We went up Lady Anne's walk through the spinney following the path Benson had made along the edge of this his beat. This was risky. But it was better than getting snow over the sides of your boots. There was still enough light from the sunset clouds to splash pink over the mounds of white beside the path and to turn black shadows into brown.

We went in silence as usual. We wanted to see or hear squirrels or foxes or woodpeckers or hawks, before they saw or heard us. Especially we wanted to see Benson from as far off as possible.

Jippo whispered, 'We'll slip along by spinney ter West Wood. We can git the rabbits on way back.'

A gale had brought down several beeches on the edge of the wood. The trunks and splintered branches were still lying where they had fallen. So we found ourselves a perch among the branches of one of them, where we were hidden by the trunk, and settled down to see what turned up.

A hare came towards us. It was using the path because that saved it having to do hops, skips, and jumps over the lumpy snow. The wind was blowing towards us and it came close enough for me to see its eyes, bright and alert, never still. It sat up on its hind legs, its enormous ears pricked and swivelling, its nose twitching as it tested for hostile scents. Perhaps some sixth sense warned it of danger or perhaps it heard our breathing. Suddenly its ears went back and it took a great leap off the path and a series of leaps over the snow to cut a corner, get back on the path again, and race away.

'Damn!' whispered Jippo. 'Shoulda brought me catapult.'

I turned towards him and then turned back again as he nudged me and nodded to the path.

A fox was trotting along it, lowering its head now and again over the scent of the hare. It too came close so that its coat changed from dark brown to tawny-red and I could see the white patches on its mask and the white tag to its brush. It stopped and noted where the hare had left the path. Then it trotted on along it and disappeared behind us.

'Ain't arter the 'are,' whispered Jippo. 'No 'ope o' catchin' it. 'E's arter rabbits in bracken. We better goo an' git ahn afore 'e scares 'em all off.'

We were about to scramble on to the path when Jippo grabbed my arm and nodded again. A man and a dog were coming towards us. Benson!

'Oh 'ell! There goes me rabbits,' sighed Jippo.

We backed out of our branches and slipped away along the edge of the wood to let the keeper get well ahead of us. Then we edged round the spinney to the lane and back home past the cemetery.

An owl hooted in the spinney. Jippo answered it. It followed us hoot for hoot right down the lane as far as the farm.

Boys who could imitate the high-pitched shrieks of a screech-owl often 'gotta bitta foon' on dark evenings frightening city folk.

One night Speedie got a bit of his own back on authority for his heavy poaching fine, with the help of a real owl.

'I were in a spinney a moile or so above Westlake wen I 'ears a bloke shahtin'. It's black as 'ell an 'e's in a panic. "Can somebody 'ear me? I'm lost," 'e shahts. I goos towards 'im an' a owl 'oots jist ahead o' me. Then I 'ears the bloke say, "I'm John Simmons. I'm a visitor at the 'All." I reckon 'e must turned roight at the fork in the path above Westlake instead o' left.

'I gits nearer an' I 'ears the owl give one o' them little "oo's" wot sometimes comes between the full 'oots. "I've told yer," the bloke says all of a dither loike, "I'm John Simmons." 'E's a-talkin' to bloody ole owl. Then it 'oots farther off an' I reckons foons uvver, so I gies a gret long shriek. "Oh my God! . . . Oh my God!" 'e yells an' 'e goes a crashin' off through bushes. Ah well! 'E were goin' roight road by then.'

CHAPTER FOURTEEN

THE FREEZING weather lasted so long that when the thaw came Crum's dad had to buy another 'top' of a tree. This was what was left of a fallen one after the trunk and the main branches had been removed. The twiggy bits made good kindlin and the branches cut up into scores of logs. A 'top' cost three shillings.

You took it home yourself bit by bit which could take weeks. You had to get a 'line' from the estate office to show to keepers that you were entitled to take it. Anyone else caught collecting sticks was made to drop them and sent packing.

Jippo, Artie, Crum and I were hiding in the edge of East Wood when we saw a keeper make old Moll and two other grey-haired women drop the sticks, which they had been gathering in their aprons, and order them off the scrubland.

'Bastard!' whispered Artie. 'Bastard!'

Now 'bastard' was the worst name you could call anybody. 'Silly boogger' was friendly. 'Bastard' was fighting talk. It was surprising to hear it from Artie. He was neither given to saying much nor to losing his temper. But now he was 'fair blazin'.

'Wen that bastard's gone, we're agoona git them sticks an' a lot more an' we're agoona leave 'em ahtside the backdoors o' them ole gels!'

So we did. We were a bit surprised that we hadn't thought of it before. Occasionally, when we thought of it, we did it again. We were careful not to be seen doing it. To be thanked for it would have been embarrassing. To give a rabbit was quite usual. Unless they were relatives, to go sticking for other folk was right out of the ordinary.

Before the spring came, Mary got influenza. I used to have to take her various concoctions which my mother or Gran had made for her.

Their cottage was in a terrace along Top Street. It had a wash-house as well as a kitchen and parlour. And upstairs it had two double bedrooms and a single one.

The kitchen was spotless. The range was polished with black-lead until it shone like a toff's boots, and the mantelpiece above had a green velvet frill a foot deep with big green tassels and under it, hanging from side to side in three loops, was a thick gleaming brass chain. The fender round the hearth had a brass rail along the top and, inside it, were two large brass kettles. On either end of the mantelpiece were two brass jugs and dangling down from beneath each of them 'joost ter rahnd things off loike' were horse-brasses on strips of black leather.

Mary's mam had a passion for brass. A brass warming-pan on a long black wooden handle hung on the wall opposite the window, with more brass kettles and jugs on a wide shelf up near the ceiling.

All this gleaming metal had to be polished every Saturday morning without fail. That was why Mary always found some job to do rather than go home before lunch on Saturdays. 'A-polishin' all that there brass allus puts mam in a bad temper. I ain't a gooin' near till she's finished.'

In 1890 her father had been apprenticed as a jockey to a trainer whose stables were near Bramley. But in the fifth year of this apprenticeship, just when he was beginning to do well, a young horse threw him. He hit his head on a stone and was unconscious for two days. Afterwards he had spells of giddiness and loss of memory. He had to give up his ambition to become a jockey and take a job as a groom.

In his middle fifties now, the spells still hit him. His wife, who was almost as small as he was, used to bully him. 'Soft ole fool!' she'd say. And 'Shuttoop ahr dad!'

But Mary told me that when her family was growing up, and he was working at Bramley as a groom, he couldn't afford to have the cost of a hot midday meal deducted from his wages. So her mam used to walk the three miles each way to take him one in a can wrapped in a towel. She made this journey every day except Sundays (when he came home) in all weathers for four years.

One day, when I went round to see Mary, her mam was doing a cleaning job down at the Hall. So, for once, I was able to have a chat with her dad. He was as bald as an egg and had a round merry face. His eyes were hazel, like Mary's, and they always seemed to be twinkling. I was surprised that he always seemed to be so happy. I didn't think he had a lot to be happy about.

He showed me the indentures, inscribed in copper-plate writing on parchment, which he had signed when he was apprenticed. These, along with a beautiful bronze statue of a horse mounted on black velvet in a glass case, were his treasures. He had won several races on the horse and, after his accident, the owner had presented the statue to him.

In the indentures, to which he had to swear before a Justice of the Peace, he undertook, among other things, faithfully to serve his Queen, his country, and his master; to go to a place of worship every Sunday; to be back at his stables by nine at night; loyally to obey all the rules of his stable; and not to frequent gaming houses nor houses of ill-fame.

'That last bit were easy,' he told me, 'we nivver 'ad none rahnd 'ere!'

'Wot's 'ouses of ill-fame?' I asked.

He blinked at that. By now I noticed that some of my questions seemed to upset grown-ups. Lucy had told me that, if a young lad was caught poaching pheasants a second time, his dad was ordered to 'git 'im aht o' village. It's the same fer a girl wot gets inter trooble.'

'Wot sort o' trooble?' I had asked.

'Oh my guy!' Lucy had said. 'Ain't yer a darvel fer arstin' things! If yer gonna keep arstin questions wot's ockurd ter answer, I ain't gonna tell yer no more. An' don't go arstin' yer mam neither . . . I were only tryin' ter show yer why it's 'andy ter 'ave relations in nearby villages.'

Now Mary's dad said, ''Ouses o' ill-fame is weer folks goes boozin an' doin' things they 'adn't ought ter. 'Ouses weer noice people don't goo.'

That seemed a satisfactory reply.

He went on quickly, 'I were to git me keep but no money the fust year. Then I were to get me keep an' foive shillin' a wick arter that one year; seven-an'-sixpence arter two years; ten shillin' arter three; an' fer the last two years o' me toime twelve shillin' plus one tenth o'any stakes I moight win in races.'

He sat looking at his parchment for a time and then looked across at the statue of what had become a famous racehorse. 'Thorough-breds was looked arter better nor a lot o' folk. Their stables was lined across ceilin' an' dahn ter floor wi' wood. Their loose-boxes 'ad fresh straw ivvery day. An' we spread sand an' sawdust ahtside theer doors ivvery day an' all in case they moight slip. An' we 'ad to plait thick ropes o' straw to put along bottom o' doors to stop draughts an' stoof a-blowin' in under 'em . . . Wen yer 'oss 'ad gone extra well fer yer in a gallop, boss'd say, "Yer can git two bottles o' stout from kitchen; one fer 'oss and one fer yersen!"'

He smiled as he refolded his piece of personal history. 'Yes, I 'ad the meckins o' a good jockey. The fust race I were in, I were that frit I could 'ardly 'old the reins. Boot I soon got uvver that. I joost lived fer racin'. Theer's nowt to beat the thunder o' hooves, the winnin'-post in soight, the crahd a-yellin', yer 'oss going a treat an' the 'eads o' the other 'osses droppin' back. An' yer knows . . . yer knows . . . yer goin' ter *win*! . . . I'll remember me wins . . . all on 'em till the day I die.'

He crouched forward in his chair, face eager, eyes gleaming, jaw set. He held the parchment flat in both hands. He began pushing it backwards and forwards and using his whole body to urge his chair on towards one winning-post which memory had brought alive for him from all the others.

Then he stopped, sat up, and put a hand to his eyes. The parchment trembled in the other one. After a bit he gave me a misty sort of smile. 'Ahr mam's roight! I am a soft ole fool!'

He stared at the fire. 'The toffs don't teck any notice o' yer till yer begins winnin' races. Then they begins ter nod ter yer. An' arter a few more wins they begins ter speak ter yer. They even knows yer name.'

His name was Harry Sanders.

After an extra hard winter there were sometimes a few corn-stacks left to be threshed when the better weather came.

At school one lunch-time word went round 'Thresher's coomin''. We ran out in time to see it coming chuffing up West Street. As it rumbled and clanked along, a housewife or two would come out and look at it and then at their thatch to make sure it wasn't puffing up sparks.

First came the engine. It had steel wheels with the back ones about three times the size of the front. A tall black funnel rimmed at the top with brass stuck up at the end of a long round boiler. Along the top of the boiler ran polished steel rods which slid in and out of black cylinders spurting steam. Behind the rods, at right angles to the boiler, was a big steel wheel with a polished rim. The driving belt went round this when the threshing began. High up at the end of the boiler sat the driver behind his steering wheel. It took strength to turn this. So to help him a handle stuck up vertically from the rim.

Hooked on behind the engine was a big, slab-sided, wooden box on wheels like a van. It had once been red but it had faded to pink. This was the 'drum': the marvellous invention which did away with the need to spread the corn on a wooden floor and then thresh at it with flails.

Hooked on behind the drum was the 'straw-jack'. Its proper name was the straw-elevator. It had a never-ending loop of steel spikes running round it to take the threshed straw up on to the new straw-stack after the corn had been removed. It could be raised or lowered and looked like a small fire-escape.

In Hibbert's yard the contractor placed the drum alongside the first stack to be threshed then turned the engine round to face it. The leather driving belt ran from the wheel beside the boiler to a wheel on the drum. From it sundry smaller belts ran to sundry other wheels on the drum and one ran on to drive the straw-jack.

The contractor told us the drum had several drums inside it which turned more than three hundred times a minute. The corn was sifted from its ears and ran down pipes into sacks at the back of the drum. The chaff was then blown out on to the ground beside them, and wooden jaws chewing backwards and forwards spat the straw on to the elevator.

All you had to do was to fork the sheaves off the corn-stack to two men on top of the drum. One man cut the twine holding the sheaf together, the other pitched it into the drum. We were fascinated.

Leftie asked Mr. Hibbert, 'Can we coom arter school an' 'elp knock off a few rats?'

Mr. Hibbert frowned. 'A few of yer can. Boot not a lot. Yer only gits in one another's way an' there's too many belts awhirrin'. Yer can bring abaht a dozen. No more.'

So after school, armed with sticks, we watched the corn-stack get lower and lower, as the straw-stack got higher and higher.

Leftie told me, 'Wen the bottom bit's reached the rats an' moice'll bust aht all uvver.'

It was the scene at the pike in the harvest field all over again. But this time we were out to kill vermin which competed for food in a hungry world. To kill a rat was a favour to the human race.

The engine chuffed, steam hissed, belts whirred, the drums rumbled, and the straw-jack squeaked and groaned.

Dust and small prickly bits of chaff flew in clouds. The men replacing full sacks with empty ones behind the drum were powdered yellow. They had their caps pulled well-down and scarves over their mouths.

Suddenly rats and mice were everywhere. They fell off the drum. They fell off the straw-jack. They weaved and leaped among our feet. One second they were on the ground. The next they were flying through the air. A rat landed on my arm, ran up to my shoulder and leapt for the straw-jack. Crum slashed it down in mid-air. It screamed as he killed it.

Sticks clattered on cobbles and walls and crunched into furry bodies. Farm-dogs snarled, snapped, and chewed. A boy did a hysterical horn-pipe, clawing at his middle. 'It's oop me britches,' he screeched, 'Gotta rat oop me britches!'

More sheaves forked. More rats. More blood. More screaming. To my shame I began to feel sick.

There used to be a cigarette advertisement which said, 'Nature in the raw is seldom mild.' Too true.

In April we began to practise songs for the May Day procession in which we went round the village and its outlying farms in decorated traps and in old Cob's wagonette. Partly, 'it were a bit o' foon an' summat to look at' and partly it was to collect money for our annual school treat.

Each year we had sung traditional songs like, *Do you ken John Peel?* and *Come into the Garden Maud* until my mother had got heartily sick of them. So she had asked Father Gregory to write us some new ones. Several were published afterwards. But the copies have all vanished. Now they exist only in the memory of those of us who were privileged to sing them. Some of them are among the most beautiful that I have ever heard. *Yonder in the heather there's a bed for sleeping*; *Give to me the life I love*; *Alan a Dale*; *There was a crooked man* and others.

On the morning before the procession we voted for the May Queen from among the senior girls. In the afternoon the parents began to bring flowers in bowls, buckets, and tubs. The school was filled with hundreds of spring flowers. Their scent was overpowering. I can smell it now.

Early in the morning of our Queen's great day we fetched and carried flowers for the parents who were decorating our vehicles. The stems were bound on with fine wire among yards of coloured paper and dozens of balloons. Before we set off we had photographs taken of the school assembled round the Queen's carriage.

Next came Rook Shoot day. Rooks like rats were vermin. They damaged precious crops. So as many of them as possible must die. Farmers, their grown-up sons, and anybody who had a gun and a licence, met the keepers at the first spinney. It was very much an occasion for the villagers and therefore beneath the notice of the toffs. Leftie's dad always took him along. One year I went with them.

The noise of dozens of double-barrelled guns blasting away together was almost deafening. Bird after bird, flying anxiously round its nest, cawing away, folded its wings and came plumetting down. In spite of the din the living stayed near their chicks. Some hens even stayed on their nests and died there as they were shot to pieces.

When finally there were no more birds to shoot at, the bodies of the slaughtered were piled in a heap at the foot of a tree, before being loaded into a cart. Rook pie was considered a delicacy. So, at the end of the day, after all the rookeries had been blasted, the guns took as many as they wanted, and the rest were shared round folk who had come to watch.

My mother, Gran, Mary, and I found the idea of eating rooks revolting. But each year parents would give my mother one or two pies. I had to smuggle them along Top Street in a bag to old Moll who was sworn to secrecy so that the givers would not be offended.

With the summer the age of mechanical adventure at last penetrated the back of beyond and reached Overton. 'My guy!' said Jebra, 'all these 'ere new fangled things. Yer dunno wot the 'ell yer gonna see next!'

First the Hall replaced its old gas plant with a motor-driven electricity generator. The church was wired up too. Until then it had been dimly lit by paraffin lamps along the walls. Now even in the evenings it was bright as day. Amazing! We altar boys, who had access to the switches kept putting a few lights on and off before the service began.

Next, I met a water-closet. My mother and I often went round to Father Gregory's billiard-room after Mass on Sundays. They discussed things about the church and the school while I rummaged about among his hundreds of books or rolled billiard balls about on the table. Then one day I had to go to the lavatory.

What a posh place. No stink at all. Even though we sprinkled a lot of carbolic powder into our roost out of a big blue tin, it couldn't really kill the stink. And this place was lined with shiny white tiles. And it had three steps leading up to a long wooden seat. A throne indeed.

There was a round hole in the seat with a white bowl half full of water under it. Beside the hole, coming up through the seat, was a thick brass rod with a spade-grip at the end of it. Father Gregory told me that to flush out the bowl you had to pull the grip up about a foot.

I had to use both hands before I could get the grip to come up. Then I only got gurgling noises. So I braced myself and gave it a big heave. There was such a hell of a clatter and such a whoosh of water that I jumped back in fright and fell down the steps. I thought that I had bust the thing and that the Hall was about to be flooded.

Then on Saturdays a bus began to run between Ashborough and Plantham calling in at out-of-the-way places like Overton. It was a ramshackle old thing with a big brass radiator, brass headlamps, wide mudguards sticking out over the wheels, and a brown canvas hood which leaked. The front of the hood was held down over the windscreen by two big leather straps anchored on the radiator. A man called Dimbleton was the enterprising owner.

That bus was Overton's entry into the big wide world. No other bus has ever been like it. This, considering the number of times which it broke down was a good thing. It won a special place in our affections and in our folklore. We even made up a song about it to the tune of *Horsey, keep your tail up*.

> Dimbo bring yer bus aht!
> Bring yer bus aht!
> Bring yer bus aht!
> Dimbo bring yer bus aht
> An' teck us fer a roide.
> If she won't go oop Brooks 'ill
> Jist gie 'er a Beecham's pill
> Dimbo bring yer bus aht
> An' teck us fer a roide!

Sometimes in fact it wouldn't go up Brooks hill or any other hill as steep. The passengers had to climb down and push. If it happened once in a way to be full, the engine boiled after a few miles. And a party of men who hired it to go to Lincoln one Sunday didn't get back until the Monday afternoon because, for once, Dimbo hadn't been able to fix it. He had learned about motors in the war.

If it was likely to rain you had to take an umbrella with you. And you had to make sure there wasn't a hole in the hood near your seat. The drips didn't matter all that much. But the canvas was slack and puddles formed in it as if in basins. When one near you began to look dangerous, the thing to do was to give it a shove either with your hands or your head and send it rolling across the roof in a tidal wave. If it found a nice hole it settled down there and spurted through it as from a hosepipe. A few of you could play a kind of volleyball with the puddles on the roof of Dimbo's bus.

However a return fare to Ashborough was only tenpence and one to Plantham one and fourpence: a penny a mile. Many Overton women, girls, and boys, were able to adventure out to the towns for the first time. It was perhaps the spirit of adventure with which we set forth in it which endeared the old thing to us.

Trips to Plantham Fair were even more adventurous. The bus was so full when it left Plantham on its last journey of the day that men were sitting on the mudguards. There had to be a stop at halfway to top up the radiator and at the hill down by the Mill all the men got out and pushed. Three-Foot, Dunkie, Tupner, and Fizzer, who had taken on too much beer, got left behind one year and had to walk the last three miles.

By now we had seen a number of motors in the village. There was a little red Renault van with a Brooke Bond advertisement on it which came round the shops, and toffs drove up the village on their way to the Park. Then the Family bought one, and Lady Sarah, under instruction, lost her head when turning it on the wide space where the lanes meet opposite the Stores. She stepped on the accelerator instead of the brake and crashed head-on into a garden wall. I was coming out of the Stores and the thunderous double bang as the front tyres burst followed by the sounds of the crash made me choke on a sweet.

Behind me Dunkie dropped his basket and shouted 'Cripes! Some boogger's shellin' us!'

But it.wasn't until Woll's dad bought a model T Ford for hire, and Mr. Stanwell was forced to do the same, that motors really hit us. For then the Agent, the parson, the Colonel, and some of the better-off farmers all bought one. Most of them were second-hand.

No longer could you pick a nice hole for marbles at the side of the street. If you wanted to race tops or hoops you had to have a look-out at the corners. There were several nice corners where folk could meet for a chat sheltered from the wind. But motors would pop round at them and scatter them.

Lucy said "'Osses 'as got more sense nor knock yer dahn wen they comes rahnd a corner. Boot these bloody motors ain't got no sense no'ow. Yer can't 'ear 'em. It were petherin' rain an' I were walkin' along Top Street in middle rut, loike I allus does. I 'ad a sack over me 'ead. Then I 'ears this foony fartin' noise. Well I knows it ain't me. Boot I can't see nobody an' can't 'ear no cloppin', so I goos on. Then I gets a tap on me'arm wot mecks me nearly joomp aht me skin. It's a feller wearin' a flyin' 'elmet an' these 'ere big specs things. 'E arsts me if I'd moind lettin' 'im past. I ain't stoppin' yer, I says. Goo on! But 'e points be'ind me. 'E's got a motor. Were that you fartin? I says. 'E laughs fit to bust an' 'e shows me the fart cooms from a trumpet thing wi' a black rubber balloon on. 'E says it's 'is 'orn. I says as 'ow 'e could git summat politer nor that. 'Tain't roight! Fartin' at folk on puppuss! 'Osses can't 'elp it!'

If you wanted to drive a motor you just went to Ashborough and paid five shillings for a licence. There were no driving tests and no proper instruction. A salesman or a friend would sit beside you and tell you how to work the controls. But once you had the hang of that you were on your own. There were no traffic signs, no white lines, and no Highway Code. Officially the speed limit on all roads was twenty miles an hour. But nobody took any notice of that, even though only motors with brakes on the front wheels as well as the back could stop quickly. Most just had brakes on the back wheels. So those with them on the front as well had to have little red triangles round their one and only rearlight to warn that they could actually pull up suddenly.

When we heard that somebody had bought a motor, we used

to hang about near their house in the hope that they would set out in their new toy. What with starting it up, moving off without jerking the passengers' heads off in a series of hiccups, and stalling the engine, new owners were usually good for a laugh. And when they got going we sometimes gave them a cheer.

Boxer had learned to drive the inn's motor. He told us that under the steering-wheel there was a lever which you had to push up to advance the engine and push down to retard it. He didn't know what the words meant. But he did know that, if you didn't push the lever up far enough, the engine wouldn't go and if you pushed it up too far you got kick-back when you turned the crank handle to start it.

With kick-back the handle flew back anti-clockwise and unless you were quick enough in snatching your hand away the thing could skin your knuckles, or split open your hand, or even break your wrist. The inn's handle had got Boxer right across the knuckles. He said he was damn sure it wasn't going to get him again. So he cleaned things called 'plugs' every week. With clean plugs, he said, motors didn't kick so much.

Now that we knew about the dreaded kick-back, it was interesting to see how new owners approached their motors. There were really two questions. First: had they been told about kick-back? Second: could they cope with it?

Some clearly hadn't been told. They casually ushered in their passengers, scowled at our posse of eager, pop-eyed, little peasants which hoped for the worst, briskly pushed up the lever, grabbed the handle, turned it, and received the father and mother of a crack across the knuckles. Some screamed oaths, much to the shame of their respectable ladies. Some just screamed. All would certainly perform a weird dance which consisted of running a few steps, then bending and placing the damaged hand between the knees, then leaping up and placing it under the opposite armpit, then blowing on it and beginning the dance again, This could go on for five minutes. The ladies would disembark and offer help or advice or both.

We were highly delighted when one farmer, known to be badly hen-pecked, was sharply told to 'Stop making such a fuss' by his battle-axe of a wife, and replied, 'Sod off, yer stupid ole 'en!'

Then there were the drivers who knew all about kick-back. Probably they had received some or seen somebody else do so. They approached their expensive new toy with more caution than they would have approached a bull. They sometimes hummed or whistled softly to themselves, pushed the lever up a fraction, patted the radiator, hoping to God nothing was going to kick them, bite them, or gore them, and gently turned the handle a couple of times. They then gave it a few real heaves before returning to the steering wheel and pushing the lever up a bit. Sometimes they decided as they gripped the handle that they had moved the lever too far and went back to split the difference rather than their hand.

Passengers would get impatient as the softly-softly ritual continued. Outside the Fox and Geese one big bluff farmer shouted to his smaller host, 'Wot the 'ell are yer mookin' abaht at, Bill?'

Bill must have explained that it was difficult to be in two places at once because, having moved the lever, he sat behind the steering wheel while his guest spat on his hand, grabbed the handle and heaved. The scream of rage and the roar of curses which went echoing round the Green as the kick-back nearly took his hand off, brought strong men rushing from the public bar.

People, especially ladies, would leave their engines ticking over while they went into shops or paid short visits. Ladies never tackled the handle anyway if they could help it. They got some male sucker to have a go. But outside the Fox and Geese men switched off their engines. So that was a good place to watch the fun.

The Colonel was a tall, thin, man with extra long legs. He had grey hair and a big grey moustache; not a floppy one, but big just the same. He would march up to his motor, set the lever, march to the front, straddle his legs, bend, grab the handle, heave, let go, and leap backwards with his legs still straddled. It was as if he was playing leap-frog the wrong way round. Sometimes the handle would kick and go whirring round backwards and he would mutter 'Missed me, you bugger!' Sometimes the engine would fire and he would slap the radiator and march in behind the wheel. Sometimes nothing happened. Then he would glare at the handle and return to the attack.

One evening when he had stalled his engine twice trying to

move off, he chased us across the Green. It was surprising just how bad-tempered motors made people.

His lady persuaded him to teach her to drive. She was splendid with horses. But she couldn't get used to motors not doing what you told them and not using their common-sense. She would come down West Street from the Stores, miss a gear, and expect the motor to carry on in a straight line while she looked down at the lever. Her zig-zags made life chancy for other folk. Soon, 'Ey oop! . . . 'Ere she cooms! . . . Roon!' was much heard in the village.

The Colonel got a beautiful new wooden garage. His lady, shouting angrily, 'Whoa, damn you! . . . Whoa!' drove in one end and out through the wall at the other.

Mr. Green bought a Humber of which he was immensely proud. He took a party of friends out shooting in it. One old chap, who had never been in a motor before, somehow got in a tangle with his gun, when trying to get out at a spinney, and blew a hole in a door. 'Ooh 'ell!' he yelled as the explosion died away. 'Ooh 'ell! I've urt me 'and!'

'Boogger yer 'and!' shouted the agonising owner, 'look at me motor. Whatcha think yer are? A bloody U-boat?'

The swings and roundabouts of the motors had folk roaring with laughter one day and raging the next. It all depended on who was suffering, the drivers, or themselves.

The thing about motors which annoyed folk most was the way they trailed a cloud of dust behind them off the limestone roads in dry weather. Soon you couldn't see the green of the hedges for their thick coating of white dust.

When they saw a motor coming trailing its cloud of dust, walkers and cyclists headed for the nearest field gate and took cover. If you couldn't get off the road and the driver didn't have the decency to slow down for you, you could hardly breathe in the choking cloud, and the grit stung your eyes. Horses as well as humans hated the stuff. It wasn't unusual to see a motorist crawling along in low gear behind a trap, honking away at his horn, while the trap held the middle of the road and its driver occasionally turned and shook a fist. Tempers were lost and blows were struck as ancient fought back against modern.

Our roads were only wide enough for two waggons to pass. So occasionally the laugh was on the motorists. When two met, one, blinded by the dust, was liable to land in a ditch. At first farmers would send a horse to haul them out free. But, as the number of rescues grew, they began to charge five shillings.

CHAPTER FIFTEEN

That year, encouraged by the spirit of adventure which had gripped our village, my mother and Father Gregory arranged a trip to London for the two top classes in the school.

Ashborough was served by the London, Midland and Scottish Railway (LMS), and Plantham by the London and North Eastern Railway (LNER). Since Ashborough was nearer to Overton and LMS offered cheaper excursion fares for school parties than LNER, we went from there.

We were astonished to see that London was packed with traffic and with people. 'Please miss,' Betty asked, 'weer 'ave all the folk come from? Is it Fair Day?'

Outside Buckingham Palace at the Changing of the Guard the sun streamed down on the scarlet uniforms and the tall black bearskins. It glittered on the swords, on the fixed bayonets, on the wheeling ranks, and on the brass instruments of the bandsmen. I was spellbound by the music and the pageantry.

In the middle of the ceremony, Cobby, completely carried away, grabbed my arm, 'Ooh look Son! There's a sparrer wi'aht no tail . . . 'tain't got a tail!'

The London trip was such a success that my mother decided the whole senior school would go in future years. To raise money to help pay the fares she organised a Christmas concert. The first half of it was taken up by a play about the French Revolution which she wrote herself.

At one time she had wanted to be an actress. In Glasgow she had been a regular theatre-goer and she had also taken part in amateur dramatics there and in Aberdeen. This play, she decided, was going to be done properly.

Now Overton had put on Children's Plays and also Nativity Plays. But never had it seen one in which the cast was properly made-up and costumed and playing in front of special scenery.

The stage was made of trestle-tables held together by wooden battens nailed on underneath. The scenery was three thicknesses of wall-paper pasted on to wooden frames and designed and painted by my mother. The lighting was supplied by new patent pressure lamps which were fitted with carrying handles, designed to be used out of doors, and guaranteed not to burst into flames. Some hung over the stage from the beams and some, backed by a strip of painted corrugated iron, were the foot-lights.

As the first night approached, the tension both in school and schoolhouse was terrific. Gran said, 'The Revolution itsel' was nothin' to this. I'll jist bide in ma room until a'body gets sane again.'

During rehearsals my mother vowed horrible vengeance on anyone who forgot their lines and even worse on anyone who went and fell through the scenery.

Because she was producer, stage-manager, dresser, and make-up artist, the dress rehearsal was on the afternoon of the opening night. That saved the costuming and make-up having to be done twice. Our sitting-room was the ladies dressing-room and make-up.

The rest of us were going through our lines in the dining-room when the door opened and a tall, beautiful lady swept in followed by another equally tall, equally proud, and equally beautiful. We all got quickly to our feet. I wondered why two members of the Family had come to watch the rehearsal. They were wearing low-cut gowns and high, white, curled wigs. Jewels glittered round their throats and on their dresses. They stood looking down their noses at us. One of them gently fanned herself. Nobody dared move. Then Millie burst out laughing and Agnes was mad at her.

They went and looked at themselves in the big mirror over the mantelpiece.

Millie said, 'Coo! That can't be me!'

But Agnes, having studied herself from various angles, said, 'That's more loike it. We are gonna shake 'em.'

The play was a success. When Agnes and Millie were led off to be guillotined and Father Gregory softly played *The Marseillaise* there was hardly a dry eye in the house.

The highlight of the second half, much to our immediate dismay, but afterwards to our astonished pride, was the performance of Artie, Leftie, Jippo, Crum and Son.

My mother had written a poem for us about a horse. We took it in turns to recite a verse and at the end of each one we all, except Artie, said together, '. . . it were a good 'orse . . .' Then Artie, on his own, shook his head and said slowly and sadly 'boot *thin!*' My mother got him to drag the last word out a bit. And she threatened to kill us if we even began to smile.

She needn't have bothered. When the curtains opened, the sight of the ranks of staring faces nearly froze us with fear. Our eyes, it seemed, stuck out like toffee apples. It was only too clear that all we wanted to do was 'roon'.

We were wearing boots, old baggy shorts, old baggy jerseys, and old floppy caps. They were several sizes too big for us. The caps were padded with paper and pushed back on our heads so that the audience could see our faces under the peaks.

My mother had cheated. We hadn't rehearsed in the caps. They kept falling forward and we had to keep pushing them back. The first time Artie shook his head his cap shot off. Thereafter he sort of shook it by stages. First he gave it a couple of wiggles, while he twisted his eyes up into his skull to see if the cap was still with him. Then he gave it a little shake and thumped himself above the ear to kill any departure before it got going. He had a big Adam's apple which bounced up and down his long thin neck. The more he worried the more it bounced.

At the end of the first verse the audience sniggered. Then, oh horrors, it began to laugh and then to howl laughing. The more it laughed the unhappier we would have looked had that been possible. By the last verse Artie's cap had settled over his eyes, and, desperate at its threatened departures, he thankfully left it there.

The verse ended like this:

CRUM: '... we 'ad ter tie a knot in 'is tail (gulp) ter stop 'im
    from (gulp) slippin' froo 'is collar

C.L.J. and S.:   '... 'E were a good 'orse ...'

ARTIE: (in a high-pitched muffled scream) ... 'boot *THIN!*'

We bowed. All our caps fell off. We snatched them up. We looked fearfully round for my mother and ran while the house came down. Gran laughed so much she hurt her ribs.

The concert ended with the whole school singing two new Christmas carols: poems by G. K. Chesterton set to music by Father Gregory. Then both audience and school sang some traditional ones.

The first verse of one of the poems was:

> There is heard a hymn when the panes are dim
> And never before or again
> When the nights are strong with a darkness long
> And the dark is alive with rain.

The dark is alive with rain. Of course. The words were exactly right. The trouble with the dark was that everything you knew in daylight seemed gone: seemed dead. You could only hear the rustling of the things you didn't know. Folks talked of the silence of the grave. And in among the black trees, out of that graveyard silence, could come the dreaded feet of the unknown creeping up behind you, or its low gliding moan. But the rain whispered to things and made them whisper back. It wakened them. It did bring them alive. Even though you couldn't see it, you knew where you were with rain. In the dark it was a friend.

The dark is alive with rain. Why couldn't I have thought of putting those words side by side?

Two things came for me from that poem. I began to be less afraid when I was walking, or more often running, at night alone, down the lanes through the black spinneys. And I began to try to make words work for me.

In the spring more change came to our village when the fifth Earl died. By tradition the coffin was taken from the church to the cemetery in a farm waggon. The gardeners lined the grave with thousands of daffodils, tulips, primroses, and violets, set among evergreens. They rose up from the bottom of the grave and foamed over its lips, covering the mouth of the moist red clay.

The new Earl, like his Countess, was friendly and approachable. Although, since his marriage, he had spent most of his time in London, the village liked him. It remembered how, as a boy, he had got off his pony to chat to folk ignoring the scowls and mutterings of the groom who rode beside him.

Now word went round that folk were no longer to curtsy or stand to attention when a member of the Family went by. And he wanted to see sports taken up by the village. So a full-sized cricket ground was laid out in the Park with a square for the pitches levelled and returfed. And a football pitch with proper goalposts was marked out in Brickles field. The school too was allowed to play cricket and football in the Park. Our bit was bumpy and you never knew what the ball would do next. Boot it were better nor nowt.

The old Countess, now the Countess Dowager, came to say goodbye to us in the school before going off to Gloucestershire to live in the Dower House.

She wrote in the log book:

'I am visiting the school to say goodbye to the children. I have seen it grow since 1881, and am pleased to know that I leave a school in Overton of which I can be proud. I hope that I will be spared to see the children of the present generation—whose fathers and mothers I have known from their birth—grow up to be a good example to all in the village.'

.'The ole Dowager' was certainly a proper Tartar and few people liked her. They weren't of course supposed to. She did what she was quite certain that she should do. And she tried to see that her tenants did what she was quite certain that they should do. For that she is remembered with respect.

Mary's mam, who worked at the Hall before she was married, and did like her, said, 'Some o' them wot says they 'ated 'er is jist sixpennorth o' nowt!'

My mother told Gran how upset the Dowager was at having to leave Overton. Gran sighed and shook her head, 'It jist shows there's nae accountin' for taste.'

More than ever now my friends and I were collectors of experience. Our talk was all about what we had seen and heard. As the seasons came and went, we watched young animals born, we watched them castrated, and we watched young horses shod for the first time.

When the huge, gleaming, shire stallions came clopping up through the village on a Saturday we followed them to the farmyards to see them 'put to' mares across a gate. If they didn't 'teck' the mares bit the stallion in the neck and reared and lashed out at the gate. If they did teck they let him nuzzle their neck and they nuzzled his before they were led through the gate and he reared and covered them.

Mares had a choice. But young heifers didn't. They were penned in a small yard with a huge bull which chased them round, cornered them, and covered them willy-nilly. They were like the hens grabbed, covered, and treaded, by the cocks.

If we had seen an animal or bird do something unusual we argued about it and came up with our own guesses as to why it did it. If we saw anything funny done by animals or humans we told the rest about it and laughed over it. And if anything unusual happened in the village, and we missed out on it, we were mad.

Sometimes, as at harvest-time or threshing, we were useful for holding horses' heads, fetching, and carrying, and killing. But sometimes we got in the road and were told that we were 'wuss nor nettles'. It was surprising how patient with us, and our endless questions, the men were. I expect this was because we were only following where generations of boys had led.

We wanted to learn how to do things. And above all we wanted to learn to do them 'proper'. 'Don't nivver do things by 'alves' was Overton's motto.

One afternoon we perched on the wall of a cattleyard to see young shire-horses 'broken-in'. The yard was knee-deep in manure and each horse was whipped, floundering, round and round it. Then it was bridled and whipped round it again on the end of a long rope. Soon its flanks were trickling with blood and it was trembling and exhausted: too broken to resist a saddle being girthed to its back.

Crum and I argued that the whole thing was too cruel. But Jippo and Leftie argued that if horses weren't properly broken they could kill people.

Artie didn't argue. He muttered, 'Some-un should whip the bloody men', slipped off the wall, and went home.

To us it was just another bit of ugliness. Overton folk hadn't much use for the gentle game of let's pretend. 'Yer 'as ter face oop ter facts,' they'd say.

Crum and I had never seen a bullock slaughtered. We didn't much want to. But the others were keen that we should fill this gap in our collection, and, one morning in the holidays, we found ourselves watching through the window of the butcher's slaughterhouse.

The place was floored with shiny red tiles and so was a passage sloping down to it from a yard at the back. A big steel ring was bolted to the middle of the floor and sundry pole-axes, meat-saws, and knives hung from the walls. It looked like a torture chamber in the Tower of London.

Two men in shiny black aprons came in and sluiced water over the floor. They did the same to the passage.

One of them came back carrying the end of a length of thick rope. He passed it through the ring in the floor and then through a block and tackle bolted to the wall near our window. He stood holding the rope and listening until bellowing started up in the yard and the rope began to twitch. He then began to take up the slack until it was taut and quivering.

The butcher and the other man came down the passage along which the rope now ran. All three men began to haul the rope a bit at a time through the block. Soon the bellowing echoed down the passage and we could hear slithering and struggling.

The bellowing changed to moans and gasps and we saw a brown bullock in the mouth of the passage. Its eyes bulged with terror. Thick, glassy, rods of slime hung from its mouth. Its legs were thrust so far forward against the pull that its hind feet were under its head where the rope was anchored.

As it was dragged out on to the floor that head was pulled lower and lower. The bullock struggled to keep its feet. Then it collapsed. Its nose was pulled tight against the ring. When it stopped shuddering the butcher swung a pole-axe into the centre of the forehead. It sounded like driving an axe into wood. The bullock stopped moaning.

I had seen plenty of sudden deaths. But this was the first I had seen which happened by stages. It is photographed in my memory.

It was a sudden death of a very different kind which brought more change to our village. The new Earl died. In less than two years Overton changed more than it had done in the past century. For when the two sets of death duties were assessed it was clear that the Family could no longer afford to live at the Hall. Its finances had been rocky for a number of years. Now it would have to go and live elsewhere.

A wealthy Baronet leased the Hall and the sporting rights on the estate. But the village of course was still run for the Family by the Agent.

The Baronet's wealth spilled back into the village in new jobs. Whereas the Family had been able to afford only one motor and had long since sold its string of hunters, the Baronet had several motors and over a score of hunters. His wife, Lady Barbara, was mad keen on hunting and a hell-for-leather rider.

Their manager took on grooms and drivers, more servants, and more gardeners. It's doubtful if our village had ever known such a rush of jobs before.

Father Gregory couldn't go on living in the Hall so the estate housed him in The Beeches. The move meant that he would have to walk close on half a mile to and from his church along the path past the Old Hall through the lawns to the terraces. But it was the only suitable house which was empty. Nobody wanted to live there.

Emma was back with us now after her illness. She said 'Father Gregory'll 'ave a job gittin' a' 'ousekeeper ter live-in oop at that 'aunted place. Strange goin's on oop there. Things don't jist fall off walls an' shelves. They gits shifted abaht. I wucked up theer once fer a bit. One mornin' I put me bag, wot I carried me shoes, apron, an' stoof in, dahn in the kitchen as usual. In evenin' it were gone. 'Ouse-keeper fahnd it in dinin'-room. I didn't put it there. So 'ow the 'ell did it git there? That were a rum do fer sure.

'Oop there a few year ago the maid wakened thinkin' summat's landed on 'er bed. She's frit and it tecks 'er a toime ter loight 'er candle. She sees a big ladle on foot o' bed. It weren't there wen she went ter sleep. So, even more frit, she 'ops aht bed an' inter passage ter goo ter 'ouse-keeper wot sleeps in next room. But summat poofs aht candle. Well! She starts 'ollerin' fit ter wake dead let alone 'ouse-keeper. She 'ammers on wall till she finds 'ousekeeper's door, falls in an' lies on floor kickin' wi' the ab–dabs an' shahtin' "It's got a ladle. It's a gonna kill me!"

'In dark the 'ousekeeper mecks sooch a grab at 'er candlestick she knocks it off table matches an' all. It lands on maid wot screeches "Ooh! Me arse! It's got me!"

''Ousekeeper's that shook oop she can't git aht bed. Maid lets aht 'ell o' a scream, gits oop, chucks 'erself on bed, an' grabs 'ousekeeper wot thinks it's the ghost. So she screams an all, "It's got me! It's got me!"'

Seeing us laughing, Emma laughed too, ''Ell of a 'owdyerdo. Boot it weren't foony for them. They both left at end of month. An' nubbody'll want, even terday, ter goo an' live oop there.'

But Agnes who had left school the year before and had no fear of things which went bump in the night, or of much else for that matter, happily went to live at The Beeches as Father Gregory's maid. This suited both her and my mother who was teaching Agnes to speak and behave properly. There was a famous school at Ashborough to which two of the school's most intelligent boys were now going after passing the scholarship exam. But there was no school nearby for which intelligent girls could win a scholarship. Agnes had her sights set on London and while working as Father Gregory's maid she could go on learning to be bilingual.

She and I became friends after I had teased her in the playground and accidentally hurt her. For one so tall and slim she was surprisingly solid and strong as I soon found out when she proceeded to give me a thumping. I never stood a chance. She could beat me, and most other boys, at everything except throwing and running. She used to tell me, 'I wish I had been a boy.' But as her curves formed I think she changed her mind about that.

She soon began to admire the tall and beautiful Lady Barbara. This was perhaps not surprising because they each had great courage and a sense of humour that was wicked even for Overton.

Lady Barbara loved dogs and horses. She went for long walks through the Grounds with a pack of dogs ranging in size from Trotsky, a black dog of some Russian breed as big as a deer-hound, to spaniels. If she was only going for a gentle canter she sometimes took several of her bigger dogs with her. But on her morning gallops, when she thundered along the rides through the spinneys, only Trotsky bounded alongside her horses. He could clear a fence or a gate as easily as they could.

For hunting she wore the proper habit and topper. But on these gallops she rode astride and bareheaded, her blonde hair and coloured scarves flying. The young men of the village thought she was magnificent. Early on Sunday mornings they used to walk up the lane near one of the spinneys just in the hope of seeing her gallop by.

It was her ladyship's other Sunday morning amusement which first alerted us to her sense of humour. We no longer had the privilege of going the short way to the church through the Nun's Door. We had to walk round the back of the Grounds past the Home Farm to the tradesmen's entrance above the kitchens. From it a path about four hundred yards long led down to the back of the Hall and the Church.

It was a funny thing but, often when the congregation was filing down this path on the way to eleven o'clock mass, Lady

Barbara just happened to be exercising her dogs not far away. They would keep rushing at groups of folk, barking their heads off and snarling at heels. The pack frightened the daylights out of the women who huddled together back to back until it rushed off to pester somebody else, while Lady Barbara watched the fun from a distance. When one day Trotsky snatched an umbrella she was clearly shaking with laughter as she turned away.

The village was not amused. It chalked one point up to her ladyship and waited, as it often did, until in time it would get the chance to even the score. No hard feelings. It just waited.

By now my love for dogs was as great as her ladyship's. One morning when I was trotting down the path to serve Father Gregory's eight o'clock mass Trotsky came barking up to me. He didn't look savage so I patted my knees and called to him. He stopped barking and frisked up to play.

He was big and rough but we were getting on fine when a voice like a whiplash snapped 'Trotsky!' He stopped mouthing my wrist and turned towards Lady Barbara who had come round the corner of a building a few paces away. Until now I had only seen her in the distance. The close-up of this lithe, golden woman, splendid in white blouse, red silk scarf, fawn breeches and shining brown riding boots fairly took my breath away. I expect I was as pop-eyed as a mesmerised rabbit.

'Don't stare at me, boy,' she snapped. 'Get on your way to God.'

She was not it seemed of a religious frame of mind. That, plus sheer boredom, may have been the reason for her fun with the congregation.

Soon, although he never complained, we heard that she was having fun letting her dogs pester Father Gregory too on his way back from his early mass to The Beeches. I had told my mother about my game with Trotsky, so she told me to go back with Father Gregory. 'See if you can deal with your big, black friend,' she said.

Sure enough, on the second morning I walked back with him, the pack came barking at us along the terrace in front of the Hall. Trotsky was leading so I called him and when he came up for a pat the rest did too. A piercing whistle soon put an end to the patting.

Her ladyship, further along the terrace, didn't like her dogs hob-nobbing with the peasants.

Father Gregory said, 'I'm not afraid of the dogs. But I can't see them properly and I don't want to fall over them.'

It seemed to me that no one so beautiful would allow her dogs to pester a man who was nearly blind. So, in spite of his protests, I took his arm and guided him down the steps from the terrace. I explained that Lady Barbara was watching and that I was doing it for her benefit.

I was right. She checked up on his sight and never let her dogs go near him again.

Shortly afterwards, it was a good thing for old Dockum that she did have a wicked sense of humour.

He was a stately sort of old chap was Dockum. He had one of the biggest bellies and certainly the biggest backside of any man in Overton, and feet to match.

One of his jobs was to pace gently along behind a lawn-mower drawn by an old cob, which wore leather boots to stop it leaving prints in the turf.

The sight of these two old characters performing their slow ritual got on Lady Barbara's nerves. She couldn't be doing with old-fashioned things. She told the manager, 'For God's sake get him a motor mower.'

Now, apart from his old mower, anything mechanical was a mystery to Dockum. He didn't even ride a bicycle. So after a smart young salesman had brought a big motor mower, covered with knobs and levers, the old chap told the public bar, 'I were fair flummoxed and frit to dead.'

''E were a sarky young sod wi' a pencil tash an' flat greasy 'air. 'E seemed ter think I were 'alf-witted becos I couldn't git the 'ang o' the splutterin', stinkin', boogger . . . "Goo on!" 'e says, "push the throttle forward an' pull back lever ter put it in gear." 'Ow the 'ell did I know abaht gears an' throttles? I coulda throttled the young darvel 'issen!

'I pulls this lever and pushes that un an' the damn thing leaps oop in air, gies 'ell o' a bang, poofs aht smoke, an' stops. I damn near shat mesel . . . 'E mecks me wind it oop wi' a little 'andle, an' wen it's roarin' again 'e says I gotta push throttle 'arder. So I gies it a good un, an' off sod shoots wi' me arter it shahtin' Whoa! 'E catches it and says shahtin' at it ain't no good . . . An' termorrer I gotta wuck boogger on me own. I'm that frit I could churn booter wi' me knees.'

Next day Millie saw him start mowing the strip of lawn on the terrace above the cedar tree and the little lake. After a few hiccups and leaps and quick grabs at the handles to stop it running away, he was doing not so badly. Then the manager arrived and Dockum got muddled. He pushed the wrong lever, missed his grab at the handles, and shouting 'Whoa! . . . Whoa!' lumbered off after the mower. Its engine roaring with glee, it swooped off down the bank of the terrace and snaked down the slope towards the lake.

Dockum shouting 'Coom 'ere ye boogger!' tried to follow its zig-zags. This was a mistake. It was a lot nippier than he was. Too late he headed for the lake to cut it off. He managed to lean out and get a despairing hand to it as it shot through the reeds. And it took him with it into the water in one of the biggest belly-flops of all time.

As Millie ran up to the hole in the mangled reeds, he sat up among the lily-pads. He looked at the handles of the sunken mower. 'Ah well!' he said, 'that's stopped the sod!'

The manager was raging and he sacked Dockum on the spot. But Lady Barbara had appeared on the terrace. Millie said she 'were laughin' fit ter bust'. Dockum was taken on again and went on providing her ladyship with fun until, in the end, he got the hang of the job.

A week or so after his ducking I found him laying new paving slabs near the entrance to the church. The manager was with him. I heard him tell Dockum, 'Make sure you get them accurate.' Then he saw me, sneered at me, and went off.

Dockum 'fair flummoxed' gaped after him. 'Ey, Son,' he said, 'wot 'ave I gotta 'ack 'em oop fer? I'm jist puttin' booggers dahn!'

'Nar!' I said, ''e means yer gotta git the edge straight.'

'Well!' said Dockum, glaring after the manager, 'as if I wouldn't. That bloody manager is wuss nor wireworms!'

These days Mary had gone all quiet and sad. I knew it was because her favourite brother Pip was ill. He had been in bed for several weeks and I used to go with Mary to see him. In spite of his illness he told me funny stories about our village. But I didn't know how ill he was until I heard my mother telling Gran that he had tuberculosis—consumption we called it—for which there was no cure.

One morning a boy came to tell us that Pip was worse and that Mary would be staying at home with him. At lunch-time my mother sent me to find out how he was.

Their back door was open and as I reached it I saw Mary's mam coming downstairs. She put her apron up to her face as she went into the kitchen. I could hear Mary sobbing upstairs so I tiptoed up to see if I could help.

Mary was kneeling beside Pip's bed with her head on it, buried in her arms. He was lying on his back with his head lolling towards me. His eyes were frozen, staring through me. A trickle of black vomit oozed from his mouth and ran down on to his pyjamas. His hair was rumpled, his face putty-coloured, and his hands clawed into the sheet.

There was nothing I could do. So I ran home and told the awful news to my mother. She said it would be better if I didn't just remember Pip the way I had seen him. So I went back with her that evening to tell Mr. and Mrs. Sanders and Mary how sorry we were.

Lucy had laid out Pip in white. His face was white now too: waxy, like a candle. His hair was brushed, his eyes and mouth closed and his hands were folded across his chest. He looked calm and peaceful. I knew that he had been received back where he came from; that this was not the end of Pip. But I knew too that this was not the face of death.

While we were talking to the family, friends and neighbours came knocking at the door. They were bringing small gifts as tokens of their sympathy. When it came to deep feelings, Overton folk didn't much go in for words. 'Sorry to 'ear abaht Pip' was about all they could manage. They didn't think it was enough, even though some of the women had tears streaming down their faces. So they pressed little packages into Mrs. Sanders' hands before hurrying away. In them might be sugar, or butter, or tea. It had to be something which they had bought. No matter how poor they were home-made things or things from their garden or allotment wouldn't do.

Again, I got a lot to think about. I knew my Overton folk. They joked about anything and everything. They looked hardship, and hunger, and pain, and loss, slap in the face and sneered at them. They wore poverty like a suit of armour.

But these were new people: soft people. Lucy came. And Emma. Emma was crying. As more folk came to the door I began to feel muddled and a bit angry. My Overton folk could stand up to anything. They didn't cry.

I had known them. Now, I didn't. This new problem would take a bit of sorting out.

CHAPTER SIXTEEN

AFTER PIP died Mary told my mother that she would like to get away from Overton. She had relatives in Leicester and wanted to go and live with them while she trained to be a nurse. Our doctor thought that she would make a good nurse and he arranged for her to have an interview at the Leicester hospital. She was accepted for training and moved out of our lives.

Freddie, who hadn't been able to find a job when he left school, joined us as odd-job man. My mother hated to see any of her former pupils out of work. I couldn't use his nickname, Duckie, in front of her. She said it was a daft name for a boy.

For my tenth birthday she gave me a bicycle and Freddie taught me to ride it. It was a bit big for me and for some silly reason I claimed that I couldn't swing my leg back over the saddle to dismount. So when I practised riding round the village, Freddie had to wait beside our gate to hold the saddle while I got off.

He soon got fed up with having to do this and solved my

dismounting problem in the good old Overton way. One day as I set off he could see from up in the playground what I couldn't see for the corner: a herd of cows coming up the street and filling it with gleaming horns.

As I pedalled round the corner he shouted down to me, 'Now, Son, yer'll 'ave ter git off!'

So I did.

Soon afterwards my mother gave me another present: a four-month-old black puppy called Prince. I had been pestering her for months to buy me one without success. Perhaps it was my dealings with Trotsky that made her change her mind.

Prince was a cross between a labrador and a spaniel. In shape he was like a labrador but he only grew to be half-way between the two breeds in size.

I thought he was magnificent. But Smuttie thought he was a menace. She just would not accept him. She kept shooting out, clawing at his big brown eyes, from under furniture, and he kept scuttling away yelling for the nearest human.

We thought that after a week or so she would get used to him. But she didn't. My poor pup was soon a bundle of nerves. He made a note of her favourite ambush places and scooted past them, eyes popping, and tail between legs. And if he thought she was about to make a dash at him out on the open floor he would leap up on to the nearest knees for safety. This led to difficulties with books, newspapers, knitting, and cups of tea. It wasn't so bad when you saw Smuttie come into the room. You knew then that somebody was about to collect a pup in the lap. It was when he imagined that he smelt, saw, or heard her that anything might happen.

Visitors were quite surprised to find that if Prince twitched or sat up suddenly, we, with shouts of 'Look out!' would bend forward as if smitten with the stomach cramps to protect whatever was on our knees; or we might leap up to protect their knees.

The colonel's lady came to tea. In the middle of the proceedings, Prince, who was lying on the hearth-rug, suddenly raised his head. Gran who was nearest yelled, 'Look out!' And we all got the cramps. Prince went back to his doze.

The lady was fascinated. 'Why do you do that?' she asked.

'It's the cat,' my mother said.

The lady looked round. 'But there isn't any cat.'

'No,' said my mother. 'But there might have been. You never know, you see.'

'No. I don't see.'

Just with that a draught clicked open the sitting-room door and its hinges creaked. Prince, fearing the worst, picked Gran who was distracted by the talk, otherwise she would have handed him off. He collided with her cup and saucer, deluging her with hot tea.

'Ach!' she screeched, shaking him off and dancing while the china flew. 'Ye wee demented black gomeril! Will ye stop seein' imaginary cats!'

Prince bounced off the carpet and shot quivering into my stomach while I held my cup above my head.

The colonel's lady hooted with laughter. 'Now I see!' she said.

Clearly this cat-and-pup game could not go on. One of them would have to leave. I was annoyed with Smuttie. She was being entirely unreasonable. And I did so want to have a dog. But I couldn't just give my cat away.

Father Gregory solved my problem. It is a little over a mile from the schoolhouse to The Beeches. So instead of him coming to have tea with us we went to have tea with him twice a week. Earlier Smuttie had become a great friend of his. She would curl up in his lap, purring away, in spite of the pipe-smoke clouding ceiling-wards above her.

'There are mice in the house here,' he said, 'and Agnes has seen a rat in one of the out-houses. Why not see if Smuttie would be happy here with me?'

So we took her up to The Beeches and she soon settled in to polishing off the mice and starting a war with the rats.

When I took Prince for walks I was careful to keep him on a lead because folk kept warning me that if he strayed into the spinneys beside the roads he was liable to get shot or to pick up poison.

I was even more scared after my friends and I made an expedition to check on a discovery of Artie's. He claimed that he had found a flight of steps in a fenced off bit of waste ground up the avenue;

that they led to a tunnel which in turn led to a big underground sort of cellar.

Leftie and I believed him. But Crum and Jippo said he was having us on. So, one Saturday in early summer, we took torches, sandwiches, sweets, and a bottle of water each, and set out to see this place. Since the tunnel sounded a long one, Leftie also brought a ball of twine. He had just read a book in which the hero fastened twine at the entrance to some deep caves and unrolled it behind him so that he could follow it to get out again.

Artie took us to the waste ground towards the far end of the avenue and there, sure enough, hidden by bushes, was the flight of steps. It was a good thing for Artie that they were there. It was hot and we had walked over two miles, eaten all our sandwiches and sweets, and drunk nearly all our water.

With Artie leading we clambered down into the perilous adventure of exploring the long dark tunnel. But Artie had groped his way along it in the dark and struck matches when he got to the cellar. Now that we had torches we were disappointed to find that the tunnel was quite short. Moreover the cellar was full of rubble at one end and full all over of a terrible stink and nothing else. Artie's popularity took a sharp dip. We found out later that it was an old brick-kiln.

We were about, grumbling somewhat, to go off in search of a real adventure when I shone my torch on the pile of rubble. I saw something sticking out of it. When I went closer I found that it was the paw and part of the hind-leg of a dog. I found too that this was where the stink was coming from.

'Ey oop!' I croaked. 'I reckon I've fahnd a dead dog.'

The others crowded round. The day had not been wasted after all.

'Cor! Wot a stink!' Leftie said. 'Boot that's a dog's leg all roight!'

We didn't have hankies to cover our mouths and noses. But in the country there's no need to get stuck over little things if you know what's what. We went back up the tunnel and got ourselves some of the big rhubarb-like leaves of the burdocks, smoothed their backs, and tied them round our mouths with twine.

Leftie doubled up the rest of the twine for extra strength and tied one end of it to the dog's leg. While Jippo and Artie took turns at scraping away the rubble with a length of rusty iron, we pulled gently on the twine and eventually the body came out. Leftie recognised it as that of a young golden retriever which belonged to a retired schoolmaster who lived on the avenue. 'Some blasted keeper's shot it twoice,' he said. 'Once in the body and once through the 'ead from close in to finish it.'

We stood round the filthy remains of the golden dog with the shattered head and we thought bitter thoughts.

'Let's drag it oop tunnel,' said Leftie, 'an' leave it weer ivverybody passin' can see it. Wichever o' the bastards shot an buried it will be mad as 'ell.'

So we left the body on top of a pile of stones by the roadside. Then we went with Leftie to tell the old schoolmaster that we had found his dog. It had been missing for over a week.

He reported the shooting to our policeman. But all the keepers denied that they had done it. 'I can't nivver prove owt abaht these shootin's,' he said. 'Even if anybody saw one of 'em do it, I don't suppose they'd be willin' ter stand oop in court an' say so.'

So I was even more careful to look after Prince. My great worry was that someone would leave our gate open and that he would go off exploring on his own.

That was the summer in which Freddie introduced me to the patient craft of fishing. He suggested to my mother that if she would buy me a rod and tackle he would borrow his brother's bike now and again and take me fishing in the lake at Saxford. You needed a permit from the Agent to fish the Overton lakes and, since he reserved these for his favoured few, my mother was convinced that he would take great pleasure in refusing me one. But you didn't need permits to fish the lonely lake at Saxford.

My mother bought me a good ten-foot rod with a cork grip. It cost five shillings, the reel and the line one shilling each. The rod licence cost two shillings.

I hadn't been to the lake since I got too heavy for my mother's pillion. Now it seemed smaller than I remembered it and more overgrown. But the old clock still chuntered out the hours on its cracked bell.

We were armed with worms and bread paste for our hooks, and with a mixture of pig-meal, bran, and chopped worms for ground-bait. Freddie taught me how to cast out my float. 'Wen it bobs pick oop yer rod. Boot don't strike until float gooes under else roons one way or t'other.'

But our floats moved not. They stuck upright, maddeningly toffee-nosed and aloof, not to say prim. I got fed up with them and went for a walk.

Below the iron sluice-gates I found a pool which the over-flow had dug out in wet weather. It was about twenty yards in diameter and lined with reeds. On its surface small fish skittered. Tiddlers they were. But at least they were there. The lake seemed empty of everything except water-fowl and rats.

I told Freddie about the tiddlers. 'All roight, Son,' he said, 'they ain't mooch. But they'll do fer yer ter learn on.'

We baited our hooks with paste and cast in. Mine instantly boobed and twirled. ''Old 'ard, Son,' said Freddie, 'wait wile it gooes under.'

Then his own did a little dance. We crouched, rods quivering. The floats went prim again. We waited. I got fed up and reeled mine in. No paste. Freddie checked his. No paste.

We rebaited and cast in. The floats bobbed, went prim. We waited. I reeled in. No paste.

'Foony!' said Freddie. We rebaited. The floats twirled. We reeled in. No paste.

Soon Freddie got mad as fire and I got fed up. 'Are yer sure we're doin' it roight?' I asked. 'Seems soft ter me!'

That did it. He glared at me, swallowed what was probably a cuss word, cast in again and crouched with a life-or-death look on his face. I found out afterwards that his mam had told him he'd lose his job if he used cuss-words while working for Teacher. He was doing his best but an explosion was nigh.

His float danced. He struck like lightning. A fish glittered up. 'Ah! Got un!' yelled Freddie full of glee. The fish kept going. It hit Freddie between the eyes and fell back into the pool. His eyes bulged. He bashed his free hand on his rod butt. He shouted 'Aah! Boogger the blasted little sods!'

I laughed so much I nearly fell in.

I cast out my own float. It twitched. I knew I wasn't going to catch anything so I twitched my rod-hand in reply. The float shot off across the pool. I gently raised the rod. Behold a fish. Freddie glared. Neither of us spoke.

I cast in again. The float twitched. I twitched. Another fish. And another.

After I had bagged my fifth, Freddie, driven to it, asked, 'Wot the 'ell are yer doin'?'

'I'll teach yer,' I said grandly.

He was peevish all the way home.

Years later, in Scotland, I annoyed another friend in the same way. He was nice but pompous. He would, he announced, teach me to fish dry-fly for trout. He made a big thing of it. Any fool could fish wet-fly. As a great favour he was about to help me to join that select band of purists who fished the dry. I had fished the wet? Then he supposed that I could cast. We would soon see.

He didn't think much of my casting but for the time-being it would have to do. He watched me raise a trout and miss it. Then he gave me an involved account of what I was doing wrong. I couldn't really make out what he meant and missed another rise.

'Never mind,' he said kindly. 'It is difficult. Watch me. You'll get the hang of it perhaps before the day's out.'

Soon he hooked a trout and landed it. He explained just how he had done it. I was as wise as ever. But something in his wrist action reminded me of a reedy pool and a cracked bell.

The next time I saw a swirl near my fly I did a Saxford twitch and the reel screamed.

'What a bit of luck,' he said, 'see if you can do it again.' He obviously wasn't hopeful.

But I did it again. And again.

He looked at me in amazement, 'Why did you pretend?' he said. 'I don't think it funny. You have obviously fished dry-fly before.'

He was so hurt that I had to explain about the tiddlers. Even then I don't think he believed me. To him coarse fishing was the sport of clowns. But later he saw that I had only wet-flies in my box.

Back at Saxford Freddie and I competed to see who could catch the most tiddlers in one day. Once we caught seventy between us. I think he won.

When the dark evenings came in the autumn, Leftie got an acetylene lamp for his bike. It worked by mixing a little water with carbide powder to make gas which, when lit at the burner, was brighter than the electric battery lamps.

The carbide powder came in long, thin tins and he invented a new Overton joke. He would sneak into roosts in the dark, just before folk went to pay their bed-time visits, and sprinkle carbide into the pans. It sizzled and bubbled when water got to it. And folk came out worried about what terrible new ailment they had picked up.

The joke might have gone on for weeks if it hadn't been for one old grand-dad. He went into the family roost and was just about to sit down when he found his pipe had gone out. So he lit it again and, as he turned to sit, tossed the match still burning, into the pan. Leftie's gas exploded with a whoosh. The old chap shot out of the door with his trousers at half-mast, turned, saw blue flames flickering through the seat, and shouted, 'Oh yer boogger! Oo's pissed paraffin?'

'Better stop,' said Leftie. 'If 'e'd sat dahn, could've knackered 'im.'

Sunday newspapers were no longer banned and more people were buying the daily ones. There was a lot in them these days about the wireless and about the British Broadcasting Company which ran it. And there were advertisements from magazines like *The Wireless Constructor* about plans and kits you could buy from them to make your own crystal set. Woll's elder brother Boy was a dab hand with anything mechanical so he sent off for one of the kits.

He managed to get his dad to pay for the aerial by explaining that they would be able to get the latest news, racing, and football results.

The aerial was about thirty yards of twisted copper wire slung from a pole in your garden to the chimney of your house. The wire ran down into one side of a black box on your window sill, an earth wire ran into another side and a wire from your set went into another. There was a switch on the box which disconnected the aerial from the set and sent it direct to earth. It was argued that if your aerial was struck by lightning when it was switched to your set, it could set fire to your house.

The set itself was about a foot square, usually a wooden box with a plate of insulating material called vulcanite screwed flat on top of it. On this plate was a small glass cylinder with a piece of crystal in it the size of a pea. Sticking out of one end of the cylinder was a thin metal rod which had a spring-shaped piece of metal at the end of it. This spring was the cat's-whisker. Fixed to the side of the box so that they pivoted at their bottom ends like a pair of wings were two coils which looked like large rolls of sellotape. You turned a little knob to open them or close them.

To tune your set to a station you stuck your cat's-whisker into the crystal and moved your coils further open or further shut. Once you found a station you might get a stronger signal by fiddling the cat's-whisker about on the face of the crystal. It was very much a hit-or-miss business and finicky too.

Boy was going to have his set finished on a Saturday evening when Jack Payne and his Orchestra were playing in one of the programmes. We had read about him in the papers. But when the time came Boy, wearing earphones, was still fiddling with his set. Woll, Leftie, and I, plus his dad in an armchair puffing at his pipe and scowling, looked on.

Boy fiddled away. Woll said, 'Ave yer got owt?' Boy couldn't hear him. Dad muttered, 'Waste o' good money!'

The tension was tremendous. Were we or were we not about to hear a band actually playing at that moment in London? How could the sound possibly travel through the air? It seemed un-believable.

Eventually dad got up, muttered, 'Piece o' nonsense!' and stalked towards the door. But he stopped short and nearly dropped his pipe when Boy suddenly took off in a leap, waved his arms about and shouted, 'I got it! . . . I got it! . . . They're singing "Wen day is done an' shadows fall."'' The earphones fell off and he had to grab them before they hit the floor. He then passed them round so that we could all have a listen.

The impossible had happened. Overton was in direct touch with London through the air. It was 1926.

But a wireless licence cost ten shillings, messing with coils and cat's-whiskers was too chancy for most people, and two-valve sets with separate tinny trumpet-shaped loudspeakers cost over five pounds. On top of all this, most women in the village were quite sure that a wireless could burn your house down.

Later, although Mr. Stanwell never admitted it of course, it was well-known that his wireless went and killed Jebra's pig what was in a sty on the other side of the allotment fence from Mr. Stanwell's aerial pole. Pig was all right one day and dead the next. 'Wot else,' demanded Jebra, 'coulda killed it bar this 'ere bloody wireless? It jist ain't natturral! It's soomat devilish!'

So only a few enthusiasts bothered with the wireless that year. Besides, there were only a few programmes in the evenings and none during the day. And these were mostly talk and a thing called 'Chamber Music'. This name puzzled Overton for 'chamber' was the posh name for the pot under the bed.

But one great influence over the life of our community was removed almost at once by the wireless. Bill, the postman, got a set. Now when folk asked him, 'Wot's Ashborough toime, Bill?' he would reply, 'That ain't no good. T'aint allus ackerat. The *woireless* toime is . . .' Soon few people remembered that 'Ashborough toime' had ever controlled our lives.

1926 was the year of the slump and the General Strike. The strike didn't affect us in the back of beyond of course, but in the hard winter which followed many men were laid off and others had to accept a cut in wages to twenty-eight shillings a week.

Father Gregory's sight was so bad that I used to cycle up to The Beeches to do odd jobs for him. One of them was to count the pennies and halfpennies which made up most of his church collection and to store them away in the big tins in which his incense grains had come. He said he was keeping the coins 'against emergencies'.

'What's he mean by emergencies?' I asked Agnes.

She laughed. 'What he calls loans to folk with children when they're out of work. Lately the loans—which he never expects to get back of course—have mostly been to pay fines for poaching rabbits. Only rabbits. He won't pay for poaching pheasants, because they're not wild but specially bred.'

Times were so bad that men who hadn't gone poaching since they were boys were driven back to it as they struggled to make ends meet on the P.L.I. or the Lloyd George. Desperate for food they sometimes took silly risks which experts like Speedie would never take. And they got caught.

'Oh dear, Mr. Taylor,' Father Gregory would say, 'not again. It will be fifteen shillings this time won't it? You really should be more careful.'

Then either I or Agnes would have to count out the necessary one hundred and eighty pennies. These the man would take to the court in a soft leather bag of Father Gregory's which looked rather like a long purse on strings.

After I had put the pennies in the bag I always had to go and wash the sickly smell of the incense off my hands. It hung about in the tins and seemed to penetrate the pennies.

Soon, folk began to notice that, in court, when an Overton man was called, the official who had to count the money for the fines always looked to see if the accused was carrying the dreaded bag. If he was, then the official usually put his head in his hands. The poor chap had been brought up to look on incense as an instrument of the devil.

What happened one afternoon just before Christmas was probably not unconnected with that dreaded bag. Agnes was down in the village shopping when Father Gregory heard a shot in the spinney which was about two hundred yards behind The Beeches, running beween it and Ashborough road.

When Agnes got back she found him wandering round the garden, very upset and calling Smuttie. He told Agnes about the shot and said he was sure that a keeper had shot our pet.

He was right. Smuttie never came back. But we didn't find the remains of her body until three years later.

Agnes was quite sure that the keeper at the Single Lodge had shot Smuttie. 'Ooh, I wish I were a man,' she said, 'I'd beat that keeper into a pulp. Fancy shooting a blind priest's cat.'

News of the shooting of course went quickly round the village. It followed hard on news which folk thought too good to be true.

The Baronet was to give a Servants Ball and all the keepers, it seemed, had been invited to it.

'Can't be true,' said Speedie. ''E couldn't be that soft.'

More in hope than anything else the village began to make more little nets on poles for hooking pheasants, dazzled by torch beams, out of trees.

When, on the evening of the Ball, word came from the Hall that all the keepers had in fact arrived, half the men in the village set off quick for the Park and its woods. It was a black night. But that didn't matter. The roosting places were well known. Soon the dark was alive not with rain but with poachers.

When the raid was over came the master-stroke. A breathless boy arrived at the kitchen door of the Hall where the festivities were at their height. 'The Park woods is full o' poachers,' he gasped, and scooted.

Suitably concealed behind hedges and bushes, the poachers watched the four keepers, in their Sunday suits, pedalling like mad up the lane. It rounded off the night a treat. One point had been crossed off the keepers' score. And the village was quits now with her ladyship for the dogs terrifying the congregation. Quite apart from this, of course, whereas Christmas hadn't been too good a feast in some homes, New Year would be a lot better.

'I don't reckon them keepers'll ivver be invoited again,' said Speedie.

He was right. The following year the keepers got so fed up with being asked, ever so sweetly, 'Are yer gooin' ter the Ball this year?' that, in the end, all they did in reply was snarl.

CHAPTER SEVENTEEN

IT WAS a pretty miserable Christmas for me. But now that Smuttie was dead, I could take Prince with me on the evenings I went up to The Beeches. I had to walk instead of cycle because bikes and dogs on leads just don't go together.

It was dark on the way up to The Beeches. But I usually met people. On the way back however, after I had done my jobs for Father Gregory and perhaps played cards or ludo with Agnes, I rarely met anybody.

I always ran past the spider tree even if the night was so black that I couldn't see the ghastly thing crouching on its bent legs ready to shoot two of them out and grab me like a fly. Prince was no help. He was a bigger coward in the dark than I was. He would leap back into me at fears of his own. The lead would get tangled in our legs so that I nearly fell. And then I would have to stop to untangle it; sometimes right in front of the dreadful tree. I used to tell him that if he didn't stop tripping me up I would leave him behind. But it never made any difference.

He was no better in the spinney. The first time an owl hooted right above our heads he yelped and shot round behind me. If he heard a rustling in the undergrowth, instead of going to see what beastie was making it, he would buck and shy away from it as far as the lead would allow. Then he would slink along looking left and right expecting something terrible to land on his back at any moment.

I only used to run through the spinney on the blackest nights. But I stopped doing even that, partly because the tangles we got into slowed us down anyway, and partly because his stupid fears made me laugh and stop being stupid myself. If I stood still in the middle of the spinney he used to sit on my foot and tremble against my leg. It was a year before he got over his fear of the dark.

Another reason why I stopped being afraid in the spinney, even if it wasn't raining, was what I read in a book about what foxes, stoats, weasels, rabbits, squirrels, owls, woodmice, dormice and so on, got up to after dark. I knew that if only I could see them I would be fascinated. So why be afraid of the noises which they made?

Soon more ripples of the sea of technology, which was to batter at our old way of life, reached our village.

Dimbo got competition from a daily bus service which ran from Ashborough to Plantham four times a day. It called in at all the villages near the main road.

The first bus to Plantham got to us about eight in the morning. Women and girls, therefore, could get jobs in shops, hotels, and cafes, and come home on the bus which left Plantham at six in the evening. Not many did yet because it was such a revolutionary idea. Fancy working in Plantham and living in Overton eight miles away! But the pioneers who launched themselves out into the unknown that year opened the way for others later.

The men were not so well placed. The big engineering works at Plantham opened before the first bus arrived. But Boy, Sparks, Winkle, and a few other mechanically-minded lads bought ancient motorbikes on the 'never-never' monthly payments. They got jobs at the works, unskilled to start with, but skilled later.

Winkle's was the oldest motorbike. It was a Zenith. I remember it because he gave me a ride round the village on it. I had to sit on my folded jacket on the back because he didn't have a pillion. It wasn't low and compact like modern bikes but high and spread out with a long thin petrol-tank. Instead of a foot-change, or a gear lever which went up and down in a line beside the tank the Zenith had one like a small crank-handle with a black knob on it. You turned it clockwise to change up and back again to change down. Sometimes it jammed in between gears and Winkle had to lift the back wheel and push it round with his foot to free it.

Our young adventurers roared through the village in leather flying-helmets and goggles looking like Great War fighter pilots. Winkle said, 'I gotta git a pillion fer the gels. Offer 'em a pillion roide an' yer've clicked!'

Even men on horseback were not as glamorous as those old stinking bikes. Girls who had regular pillion rides took to wearing leather helmets with the chin-strap undone when walking round the village, much to the envy of most of the other girls. But this fashion came to a sudden end when cheap helmets for kids reached the town shops and many of us got one. Mine kept my big ears nice and warm in frosty weather.

Then the same young pioneers began to make two-valve wireless sets.

Next came the 'picters'. From time to time there had been film shows in halls in Plantham and Ashborough. Now a proper cinema called 'The Picturedrome' opened in Plantham. Although for the first two years the films were silent, they quickly caught on with the village. The best seats were one shilling and the cheapest sixpence.

My mother took Gran and me to see Charlie Chaplin in *The Gold Rush*.

One way or another Overton was getting to be 'in the picter' about national affairs. But Jebra and his cronies were disgusted. 'These 'ere things is spoilin' village,' the old man said. 'Yer can't git a good chat in the pub no more. All gassin' on abaht this 'ere film or that there programme. Lot o' roobish!'

In the early summer my mother bought a brand-new 1927 Morris Cowley Occasional Four. It cost her one hundred and seventy five pounds on the 'never-never'. It was the fore-runner of the hatch-back because the two back seats folded up to leave a space for luggage if required, and all the seats were covered by the canvas hood. Earlier models were either four-seaters, or two-seaters with two more dickey-seats outside the hood at the back.

Our car (we had discovered from the wireless that although people who went in 'motorcars' were 'motorists', the short for motorcar was 'car' not 'motor') had the red triangle round the rear-light to show it had front and back brakes, and it had two new features: a windscreen wiper worked by suction from the carburettor and a switch to put out the off-side headlamp when meeting other traffic. The salesman explained that headlamps were so bright nowadays that it was as well to get into the habit of using the switch to avoid dazzling oncoming drivers. We had a self-starter too.

While I sat fascinated in the back one evening he gave my mother a three-hour lesson. The next evening he brought the car back and gave her another. At the end of this he said, 'Yer got the 'ang o' it nah. Jist droive me back inter Ashborough an' then yer can droive yerself 'ome.'

On the way home my mother kept stopping and practising starting off smoothly with none of the hiccuping leaps which Lady Sarah and the colonel's lady did. Thanks to them, lady-drivers had a bad name in our village and she wanted to show, right from the start, that she was different.

Mr. Stanwell had sold Kitty and he rented her old stable to us as our garage. I washed our car up there every Saturday morning and polished the body-work with *Mansion* and the big bull-nosed chromium-plated radiator with *Brasso*.

In the afternoons my mother drove Gran and me into Plantham for shopping. We didn't realise at the time of course, but now the days of our three grocers' shops, and our baker's, our cobbler's shop, and our butcher's shop, were numbered.

Now that there were more cars and buses, the clouds of dust which they whooshed up on side-roads were making journeys dangerous as well as uncomfortable. The County Council had begun a programme of spraying all roads and streets with tar, spreading them with gravel, and then packing it down with huge steam-rollers. Eventually the programme reached Overton. New drains were dug in our streets, the old ruts and pot-holes were levelled, the new surface rolled in, and even some of the foot-paths tarred and gravelled. Our village looked quite posh. The mud and the puddles had disappeared. But not of course the horse-muck and the cow-pats.

After she had been driving for a few weeks my mother said she was going to take us down the Great North Road to St. Neots, sixty miles away, for lunch. We would have supper in Plantham on the way back. We would set out on the following Saturday.

'Sixty miles!' said Gran. 'You're nae ready for it. You're nae ready for a' the traffic you'll meet. It would jist be temptin' Providence.'

So, of course, that settled it. We would definitely go.

'I'm nae comin',' said Gran.

This suited my mother and me because Gran was a terrible back-seat driver and got on our nerves. She sensed perils on the road quicker even than Prince did in the spinneys. However, when it was all fixed that Father Gregory would come with us, she changed her mind and came in the back with me and Prince.

I too had been worried about that first long journey. No yachtsman about to set out to sail round the world was more excited and apprehensive than I.

It was a beautiful morning and when eventually we reached the Great North Road I was surprised at how wide and smooth and shiny black it was.

'You're goin' too fast Neldie!' Gran said. Neldie went faster.

'You're never goin' to overtake yon lorry.' Neldie overtook it.

Then Neldie found a way of silencing her parent. 'I better watch now,' she would say, 'there's a lorry coming up this hill . . .' or: 'Now watch, there's a car coming out of that side-road.' She saw dangers just that bit quicker than Gran and talked her-self out of them. Gran, beaten to the punch, went into a huffed silence.

Next, my mother decided that we would go up the Great North Road to Scotch Corner through Newark and Doncaster. Gran was horrified. But she came. She also came to Oxford and to the seaside at Hunstanton and Skegness.

I began to realise for the first time that my mother often got bored with Overton life and that she was revelling in these adventures into the unknown.

Motoring was full of hazards. Bad roads and old-fashioned tyres led to punctures. And engines often conked out.

I got expert at jacking-up our car and changing a wheel and I learned to repair two kinds of break-down.

On the way to Scotch Corner the engine began to cough and spit. Then it stopped and we couldn't start it again. My mother sat on the off-side mudguard, looking suitably forlorn and helpless, and in no time at all a nice man stopped to help us.

'Did it stop all of a sudden with perhaps a back-fire, or did it sort of fizzle out bit by bit coughing and spitting?' he asked.

'It coughed and spat,' said my mother.

'Ah! Then I bet you've got grit in your jets.'

'Really?' said my mother.

'It often happens,' the man said. 'Come here young man and I'll teach you how to remove the float chamber and use the jet-spanner.'

Breakdowns were so frequent that most cars were equipped with a box of tools fixed to the running-board.

From then on I could cope with fizzling stops. But on the way to Skegness the engine back-fired then conked.

'That,' said my mother, 'will be the other kind. I'll have to go all forlorn again.'

Eventually a man stopped who said, 'You've lost your spark.'

'Really?' said my mother.

I watched him slide a metal clip off a brown bakelite cover on the side of what he said was the magneto, clean two contacts underneath it, and re-set them.

Now I could cope with both bangers and fizzlers. For once I could do what my mother couldn't do. She had to rely on me. We became a team.

Luckily Gran wasn't with us when we skidded on wet leaves into a ditch, nor, in the winter, when we skidded on ice through a hedge. Once we conked out in a flooded hollow and once all the lights went out and we had to drive home by moonlight because I had never heard of fuses.

My mother seemed to enjoy these adventures too. One day she

said, 'Let's see if we can get the needle up to seventy,' and roared down a straight bit of road. The car bucked and rattled on its primitive springs and the wind howled gale-force round the windscreen while she clutched the wheel eyes wide with excitement. Then she laughed in triumph, 'We've done it! We've done it.'

What had happened to my respected and prudent mother whose word was law and who was forever urging me to be careful and not to take stupid risks? All of a sudden I realised that my mother was not a provider and a law-giver and a being from a superior world but a human being like me and my friends. From now on she and I also became friends. It was one of the great discoveries of my life. By now she was thirty-five.

When a new 'talkie' cinema opened in Plantham she drove Artie, Jippo, Crum, and me to see a film. In the film a blonde heroine suffered from a series of dastardly deeds.

My friends, who had never been in a cinema before, weren't sure that we were safe. We had read a week or two earlier that there had been a fire in a cinema and that several people had been trampled to death.

When the lights dimmed Jippo jumped up. 'Ey oop!' he said, 'Let's git aht! Soomats oop!' Then, reassured, but forgetting that his seat had tipped-up, he sat down where it wasn't and disappeared with a thump and an 'Ooh . . . boogger!' which luckily my mother didn't hear.

The people in the row behind us were most amused. When the main feature started however we no longer amused them.

In the darkened cinema the big glowing screen seemed to mesmerise Artie and he began to live the scenes with the actors. He wriggled in his seat, crouched and ducked in the fights and threw short jabs. 'Goo on . . . 'it 'im again,' he muttered, and, 'Coo! I bet that 'urt!' He got shushed front and rear.

Then, when the heroine was in trouble again he muttered, 'Leave 'er alone yer rotten sod!' and threw a jab which brushed the hair of the man sitting in front of him. This drew a glare and a 'Keep quiet!' from the man.

Artie subsided and only twitched for a bit. But, sitting next to him, I could tell that he was 'fair fizzin'' inside.

The villain grabbed the sobbing heroine and Artie exploded out of his seat. 'Leave 'er alone! . . . Leave 'er alone!' he shouted and he grabbed the man in front by the shoulders and shook him.

The man got up, turned, and, but for a whiplash 'Sit down' from my mother, would have smitten Artie. Shushes now frothed round us like the ripples on the beach at Skegness. My mother, seeing that a section of seats across the aisle was empty, moved us quietly into them, so that Artie could join in the action as much as he liked. He was pretty tired by the end.

I would soon be twelve and my mother decided that I could no longer go on roughing it as a village boy. I needed to go to a boarding school to get a secondary education and a little polish.

So in September 1928, with a trunk full of new clothes and a large lump in my throat, I said goodbye to Gran, Father Gregory, Prince, and my friends, and my mother drove me off to start a new chapter in my life. I was only going away for three months. But, to me, it seemed to be for ever.

Prince too, was miserable for a week or so after my disappearance. He wandered round the house whining and refused to eat. On the second morning my mother heard terrible wolf-howls coming from my room. She found Prince sitting in the middle of my mattress, from which he had stripped all the bed-clothes and pillows in looking for me. He had his nose pointed to the ceiling and in front of him was the present of a muddy bone which he had decided he would give me if only I would come back.

When my mother came to collect me for the Christmas holidays I picked up again with my friends exactly where I had left off. They had to hear all about my new school.

'Cor!' said Jippo. 'Yer gits this 'ere rugger else runnin' ivvery arternoon?'

'Ar,' I said, 'but don't fergit we 'as ter wuck in the evenin' an' all. We don't knock off at four o'clock.'

Speaking Overton was a bit strange after speaking posh for three months.

Father Gregory, my mother, Gran, Agnes, and I walked down to Midnight Mass through the Grounds. Snow had fallen the week before and now we had a heavy frost. Half a moon lay on its side in a blue velvet sky. To its light millions of stars added their twinkles. They lit up the snow-covered lawns and trees. We sang carols all the way to the church and all the way back again.

I remembered how enormous the white lawns had seemed at my first Christmas Treat. Already it seemed an age ago.

At the end of the month, the day before I was to go back to school, my mother began packing my trunk, as usual, on my bedroom floor. Prince, who hated the thing, slunk off in a fit of the miseries.

That evening we couldn't find him anywhere. Agnes and I went through the spinney whistling and calling him. But there was no Prince. I was sure that he had been shot.

We had a very sad dinner. I couldn't eat. Afterwards my mother and I went upstairs to finish my packing.

There curled up in my trunk was my friend. He refused to come out. 'Kill me if you like,' he said, 'otherwise, this time, I'm coming with you.'

CHAPTER EIGHTEEN

I WAS ONLY spending four months out of every year now in the thatched village. By 1931 I was playing in the school's second fifteen and in the second eleven and I had won the cup for the best athlete in the under-twelve and under-fourteen groups, breaking the records for the sprint, high-jump, and long-jump. For me lessons came a long way second to sport and my new interests had swamped my old ones.

All my friends had left school at fourteen, so I only saw them now and again at week-ends. Their worlds and mine were so different that, if it hadn't been for the interest which we shared in the ups and downs of our village, we would have had little in common. They were changing and so was I.

And so was our village. Nearly every home had a wireless now, mostly two-valve sets with a separate speaker. But mass-produced sets with built-in speakers had arrived in the shops. They didn't sound tinny at all.

We had a set which folded like a small suitcase. The speaker was in the top half and the valves and tuner in the bottom half. You could carry it from room to room. But you had to have separate leads from the aerial to each room and you had to carry the battery on its own in case you spilled the acid.

Farm wages had gone up to thirty shillings again and, at the ironstone quarries, to thirty-two shillings. But the young adventurers who had gone on motorbikes to the engineering works at Plantham were now earning more than their dads.

A bus started out on the circuit now from Plantham at the same time as the one which started from Ashborough. So you could get to work in either town before nine in the morning. Men, as well as women and girls, now went to work by bus. The girls could earn fifteen shillings a week and the women a pound.

Working clothes hadn't changed much in our village. The women still wore thick skirts with aprons over them, knitted jumpers, and good, strong lace-up boots. The men wore old jackets, thick corduroy trousers tied with twine below the knees, collarless flannel shirts and hobnailed boots.

On my way up to The Beeches one afternoon I met Artie. It was pelting rain. I was snug in a water-proof mackintosh, but he was just wearing his old tweed jacket.

'Yer'll git soaked,' I said.

'Nar, Son,' he said, 'this 'ere jacket's a grand rain-tunner. Yer can't beat tweed fer tunnin' rain. Runs offen it loike offen a sheep.'

But on Sundays now and on special occasions Overton folk were transformed.

Except for the oldies, men no longer wore black suits with stiff white celluloid collars and black ties and boots. Instead they wore worsted suits of various colours or sports jackets and grey flannel trousers.

But the change in the dress of the men was nothing to the change in dress of the women and girls. 'Gooin' ter picters on bus' was no longer an adventure but a regular treat. The fashions in the films were two or three years out of date. But the news-reels showed Overton what the smart set was wearing.

We didn't come up to Park Lane of course, but the old home-made style of clothing was out. Smart suits—we called them

costumes—in winter and linen or cotton dresses for summer were
in. Now that the streets were no longer deep in mud and you no
longer had to wear boots and carry your shoes in a bag, many girls
wore high-heels and with them silk stockings instead of woollen.
Some even wore lipstick and powder, and worked to get their
hair to curl like the film stars' by clamping it into tongs heated in
the fire.

Young courting couples, all togged out in their Sunday best,
had begun to use the special late night bus on Saturdays, to go to
dances in Ashborough. They no longer walked a yard apart on the
Sunday promenade up Ashborough road, but went arm-in-arm
or even with their arms round one another's waists.

'God knows wot they'll be oop ter next,' said Emma. 'D'yer
know as 'ow lads is givin' their gels boxes o' chocklets on their
birthdays! My Guy! I were born thirty year too soon!'

Her daughter Lizzie had a job now in a shop in Ashborough.
The thin waif in the darned skirt and jersey had turned into a tall
girl with curly brown hair, high-heeled shoes, a smart blue linen
dress, powder, lipstick, and a figure. I met her one day and didn't
recognise her until she said, 'Allo, Son.'

'Coo!' I said, 'Yer a smasher. Wot they call yer nah? Miss
Walton?'

'No,' she said, very posh and looking down her nose at me like
Lady Sarah used to do, 'I'm Elizabeth I am.' Then we had a good
laugh.

But although our folk looked different on posh occasions, they
hadn't changed all that much in themselves.

I came home one Easter to find the village more excited than I
had ever known it. We were in the final of the County League
Football Cup. We only had to beat Ashborough the following
Saturday and we'd won it.

'Fancy Overton winnin' coop!' said Crum.

'We ain't won it yit,' said Jippo.

'We will,' said Crum. 'Yer mark my words.'

It had been arranged that everybody would gather on the Green
on the Saturday afternoon and that Sparks would come back on
his motorbike, immediately the game ended, to tell us whether or
not we had won. If we had, there would be a surprise party for the

team at the inn. The farmers and the colonel would buy a barrel of beer and some of the housewives had already made piles of sandwiches, pies and cakes.

The truth was that, win or lose, Overton was going to have a party. Our village didn't get all that many.

As we waited opposite the inn the suspense was thirst-making for some. But the bar wasn't open.

About five o'clock we heard a motorbike roaring down Ashborough road. The excitement was unbearable. 'Sharp enoof ter sour milk,' Jippo reckoned.

Sparks came flying up from the Oss Pond, waved both arms at once, and nearly killed himself plus two dogs. As he missed a tree by a whisker a great cheer went up. Boys jumped up and down. Men slapped each other on the back. The wives or girl-friends of the players threw their arms round one another. Cries of 'We've won!' mingled with 'We've beat the booggers!'

The team would be arriving on the eight o'clock bus from Ashborough. Meanwhile everybody old enough shoved their way into the Fox and Geese 'ter git party ready'. The bar shouldn't have been open. But it soon was.

Everybody gathered on the Green again to meet the bus. When it arrived a tide of beery cheers surged round it. They hiccuped into silence. 'Oo yer! Weers team?' Only two old folk got off and they didn't even know that a cup-final had been played.

Sparks set off to find out what had happened. Everybody old enough went back into the inn 'ter see nubbody starts on eatables yit'.

Sparks came back with sad news. Our team had been having a nice quiet celebration in the Lion Hotel when some Ashborough supporters had provoked them into a fight. The police were sent for. Even then there wouldn't have been trouble if the police hadn't sided with the Ashborough lot. As it was, three of our men had been locked up for punching police officers and the rest of the team had disappeared. Sparks had searched the town; no team.

'Ah well! Pity ter waste good stoof. They'll git 'ere sometoime,' said Romeo-Jack.

Just before the eats ran out, the survivors of the team trudged wearily into the inn after walking from Ashborough. Sparks hadn't seen them because they had taken a few short-cuts across fields.

Nobody welcomed them, until, hot and with hangovers, they arrived in the middle of the party in the big dining-room. By then some folk had forgotten what the celebration was in aid of. Now they remembered and gave a few cheers muffled by food and drink; mostly drink.

'Ooh! We ain't 'arf thirsty,' said Speedie, 'We've sweated aht last lot. Weers drinks?'

''Ang on! 'ang on!' said Mr. Green. 'Proper thing is ter fill coop an' pass it rahnd.'

'Ar!' said Speedie. 'That's roight.'

There was a pause.

'Well coom on! Oo's got it?' said Mr. Green.

''Ave yer got it Watto?' asked Speedie.

'Nar!' said Watto. 'I 'ad it wile arf-way.'

Mr. Green raised his voice, ''Old 'ard! . . . 'Old 'ard ivverybody! Oo's got coop?'

Silence.

'Ah well,' said Speedie, 'we did 'ave it wen we started.'

Next day most of the survivors managed to drag themselves out of bed and then back across fields and through leafy lanes to Ashborough. No cup. On the way back they found it in a bed of nettles beside a hole in a hedge through which someone had tossed it. He had then forgotten to pick it up after he had crawled through the hole himself.

It cost twenty-five shillings to take the dents and scratches out of Overton's first trophy.

At the end of September my mother drove me back to school. My trunk and other gear filled the back of the car and, now that I had grown bigger, there was no room for Prince to come too. So he was left behind with Father Gregory at The Beeches. Alas, a gate was left open. A shot was heard and no Prince came when he was called.

Agnes went into the spinney and whistled and called. Then she went to the keeper's house at the Single Lodge. His wife said he was still out on his beat.

When my mother got back, she remembered how the body of the golden retriever had been hidden and she organised a search-party on the Saturday to go through the spinney looking for a place where a dog might have been buried or hidden.

They found an old, dried-up, well in the middle of some thorn-bushes. When Jippo went down it with a torch on a ladder, he found Prince, newly shot, the remains of another dog, and of three cats. One of the cats had once had long black fur and four white paws. Smuttie.

My mother reported the shooting to our policeman. But, as always, he could prove nothing. She went to see the Agent and pointed out that it was against the law for keepers to shoot a dog in an unfenced spinney beside the public highway. But he said there was no evidence to show that one of his keepers had shot the dog. And anyway it was customary to shoot dogs which were disturbing game.

But now the village took a hand. No one would speak to the keeper in the pub. In the shops he was served politely but with ice. Pebbles thrown by small boys out of the darkness clanged into the spokes of his bike.

It may have been this treatment which caused him to overreach himself. No poisoned baits had been laid in recent years in the spinney on Ashborough road or in those along the Avenue because Lady Barbara sometimes took her dogs with her through them. She was away in London, however, and wasn't expected back until October. So poison intended for the village dogs was put down again.

But Lady Barbara came back unexpectedly. She took her dogs with her on an early morning ride up the Avenue. One of them picked up poison and died, as was usual, in convulsions.

In a rage, she questioned her servants about the poisoning of dogs and had the spinneys searched. Another poisoned bait was found. Her ladyship gave the Agent forty-eight hours to get the keeper on whose beat the poison was found off the estate.

When the Family received her complaint it too was horrified. From then on its keepers were forbidden to put down poison for dogs, or to shoot them, in the spinneys.

Soon afterwards the Agent left the village. But the events were probably not connected. And anyway Smuttie and Prince were dead.

During the Christmas holidays after Prince had been shot, I was lonely and depressed. I blamed myself for leaving him behind. Leftie and Artie were working in Plantham and I rarely saw Crum and Jippo. Agnes had gone off to London. The village which once had been all my world was now becoming just a place where I spent holidays. Folk had begun to treat me like a toff; not like a proper toff, of course, but as a bit of a stranger. They didn't call me 'Son' now or if they did they looked at me quickly to see if I minded. They knew they were 'lower class' and imagined that I thought I was 'middle class' or even 'upper class'. Which class you were in, or thought you were in, mattered a lot. Only a few people realised that to me, with my upbringing, it didn't matter a damn. I felt that my old world was rejecting me. And I didn't want to be rejected. I consoled myself by learning to drive my mother's car.

Then in the summer Mr. Stanwell brought me back into the life of the village again by inviting me to play for our cricket team.

There was no messing about in our cricket. When you batted the idea was to thump the ball away as hard as you could; and when you bowled to thump the ball down as fast as you could. Whether you got the batsman out or laid him out didn't much matter just so long as he went.

Mr. Stanwell, who learned his cricket in Australia, was the only member of our team who used guile. He was our one and only spin bowler. Soapie, Clackie, and Watto were our fast bowlers. Boover—so-called because his speciality was hitting sixes over the wooden changing-booth—and Jiffla were mighty hitters. The new Agent, who didn't suffer from feudal ideas, was our wicket-keeper.

I was a medium-fast bowler and the first time I played for the team I hit an opponent slap between the eyes with a ball which reared up off a length. That did it. Son was accepted as a useful addition to the team by one and all. I was also an opening batsman for the school. But I didn't score runs quickly enough for Overton and propped up the middle order along with the Agent.

If we thought our bowlers were faster than our next opponents' were, we prepared a pitch with one of our secret weapons on a length. But if they were as fast or faster than ours we tried to find a pitch which didn't have one—which wasn't easy to do because our ground was near the East Wood.

These secret weapons were the little scrapes which a rabbit makes when prospecting for a home or when making up to a fierce doe who knows how to look after herself. They were only about three inches long but if a fast ball hit them it fairly flew.

One week we made a mistake. We didn't know that our opponents had a new fast bowler. He was a huge farmer's son who roared up to the wicket snorting like a runaway steam-roller.

This steam catapult found one of our scrapes just right. By the time I got in he had clean bowled two of our batsmen and laid out two others with balls which whipped into their groins.

In my first over, a ball whipped into my groin off the handle of my bat. The slips and wicket-keeper trotted forward happily again to pick up the fallen.

I shrugged, pushed down my shield—unheard of in village cricket—and went and gave the scrape a jab with the bottom of my bat.

The bowler looked not merely disappointed but outraged. That I should be upstanding instead of rolling on the pitch in agony was unjust. It was unfair to bowlers. It was depriving him of his rights. He glared at the umpire 'Ow is 'e?'

''E looks o.k.,' the official said. 'But God knows 'ow. 'E ain't aht, "balls before wicket", that's fer sure!'

As I settled down to face the next ball, the wicket-keeper solved the problem. In a stage-whisper he told the slips ''E ain't got none!'

To raise funds for our team the Baronet sportingly agreed to field a team from among his friends to play us in a Gala Match. It was held on a beautiful afternoon. The sun beat down on the lines of deck-chairs where the dresses of Lady Barbara and the wives of the Hall guests made a splendid splash of colour.

They batted first. Soapie was thumping the ball down. Clackie was fielding close in at short-leg. I was fielding on the boundary right in front of the gorgeous ladies.

Soapie dropped a ball short. The batsman hooked it viciously straight at Clackie who brought off a brilliant catch.

'Oh well held, sir!' came from the deck-chairs, followed by a burst of clapping.

'That'll show you we're not just a bunch of peasants,' I thought.

As the clapping died away, Clackie made an Overton joke of it to hide his embarrassment at all the posh applause. ''Ad ter catch it,' he shouted to Soapie, 'else I'da bin knackered!'

For a moment there was silence from behind me. Then her ladyship's golden chuckle triggered off peals of laughter. I was more embarrassed than Clackie had been.

We only got three of their side out before they declared. They won easily. But Jiffla smote sixty for us while I kept my end up.

During the match a formation of Hawker Fury fighters flew over the Park. A few weeks later one of our new airships, looking like a huge silver cigar, flew over the village.

On the wireless we were hearing more and more about a German called Adolf Hitler and his Nazi Party; and about Winston Churchill who kept going on about the danger of war. Soft sort of chap. We'd just fought the war to end all wars.

The papers had funny cartoons about a German scientist who had said that rockets would one day take man to the moon. The one we laughed at most showed him clinging astride a huge Guy Fawkes rocket standing on a stick in a German beer jug. How soft could yer get!

In the autumn electricity at last reached the village. There were still no street-lamps. But people who could afford to pay the cost of having their houses wired-up could get rid of their candles and lamps.

I came home for Christmas to find that both The Beeches and the schoolhouse had been transformed. There were bowl-shaped fittings hanging from the ceilings in the main rooms and saucer-shaped white enamel ones in the kitchen and the passages. The old ranges and the paraffin stove had been replaced by shiny electric cookers.

'Cor, Son!' Emma said, 'yer don't 'alf grow. 'Ow d'yer loike the electric then? Boot o' course yer used ter it at school. Ain't it grand? I don't 'ave to loight foires 'ere fust thing o' a morning no more. I jist switches 'em on. An' wot wi' them there electric kettles an the geyser wot yer mam's 'ad put in beside kitchen sink I don't 'ave ter be everlastin' puttin' kettles an' pans on ter boil. An' wi' that there big geyser she's 'ad put in wash-'ouse I don't 'ave ter loight a fire under the copper nor 'ump buckets o' water no more ter do the washin'. Wot a difference it mecks! Saves hours!'

She laughed. It was the good old wheezing-sheep affair. But these days she wore a close-fitting net thing called a snood over her hair instead of a man's cap. So she had no peak to peck with.

''Ow's Lizzie?' I asked. ' . . . I mean Elizabeth.'

'Lizzie's good enough.' Her face lit up. 'She's engaged to an Ashborough feller oo's dad owns 'is own shop. Quite the young lady she is.' Then she frowned. 'I don't mean as 'ow she looks dahn on 'er old 'ome.'

'Why the 'ell should she?' I said.

Emma nodded. 'Yer looky! Yer loike yer mam. All this schoolin' don't meck no difference ter yer.'

'Wotcha mean looky?'

'Looky in yer mam.'

'I know that.'

She glared at me. 'An' don't yer nivver fergit it neither.'

The Village Hall had been wired-up too. It even had two lamp-standards outside it. They made a pool of light in the village dark. My mother had arranged a concert and dance in the Hall on the Saturday before Christmas.

It was the last time I saw my friends together. Mary was on holiday and came with her brother Johnnie and her mam and dad. Freddie was there and Emma and Lucy. And of course Leftie, Artie, Jippo, Crum, Speedie, Perce, Pickles, Cobby, Boy and Woll. Agnes alone was missing.

Time in the thatched village and at school was running out for me. Soon I would have to make the leap on to the upright of the great question-mark of life from the dot underneath. Sometimes I looked forward to the leap. Sometimes it scared me. I had no one to pull strings for me and not the faintest idea how I would make my living. But, like Shakespeare, I fully believed that:

> 'There's a divinity which shapes our ends
> Rough-hew them how we will.'

Isn't it odd how, when the end of a chapter in our lives approaches, the clock gallops forward to meet it? In no time at all my days at school, and of living in the thatched village, ran out. Away I went. I was not like a fox-cub chased away from the earth by its parents and trotting off into the great unknown carrying its favourite toy, perhaps the wing of a bird, or an old tin-can. Nor was I like a young girl, straight from school, forced by poverty out of our village into a frightening world and a life of city drudgery. But I was a bit taken aback just the same.

The year was 1935. The year that saw the dawning of one of the world's great changes. The year in which Mussolini sent his Fascist armies marching into Abyssinia.

The armies would go on marching for another eleven years. By the end of those years the old way of life in many countries in the world would have disappeared. It would have disappeared too in a small village at the back of beyond on the road to nowhere, of which only a privileged few had ever heard, and fewer, even more privileged, had ever seen.

POSTSCRIPT

'A YER BIN oop an' 'ad a look at ole school, Son?' asked Speedie.
''Ad a look round garden, but 'ouse were locked o' course.'
I didn't even notice at the time that I had dropped straight back
into broad Overton.

'There's a bar in Centre nah,' said Crum. 'Let's goo oop an' see
oo's there. Dan roons it. 'E'll be pleased ter see yer.'

The street-lamps had already come on. But it was still shadowy
under the sycamores as we crossed the Green.

'Do yer remember me ole cat?'

'Not likely ter fergit it,' said Crum. 'My guy, I were frit. So
were Jippo. Yer've jist missed 'im. 'E died a couple o' months
back . . . Artie, o' course, were killed in Normandy. Boot Leftie's
still goin' strong. 'E lives in Melton. Yer jist missed Agnes an' all.
She were 'ere a fortnoight back, lookin' smart as ivver. She still
lives in Lunnon.'

The street-lamps gave the honey thatch and the stone walls the out-of-this-world look which floodlights give to old castles. Before we went off up West Street I looked back at the Green and its surrounding cottages. 'Ole Jebra used to say this bit, an' the centre bit o' village, 'adn't changed since 'e were a boy. An' 'e were over seventy. An' it ain't changed since we were boys. An' that's anoother sixty years.'

As we got near the school Crum pointed to the Pump with its Chinese hat. 'The ole well oonder there dates back ter Middle Ages they reckon. It's the oldest thing in village.'

'Overton's a bit of an ancient monument,' I said.

'Ain't we all!' said Speedie.

We went up the steps, across the playground, and in through the top door of the school. A false ceiling now covers the old beams in the gabled roof and it made the place look half as big as I remembered it. Small tables with lamps on them with red shades made it look quite sophisticated.

There was nobody in the school. But we heard voices coming through the open door into what used to be our sitting-room.

Crum led the way. 'Bar's in 'ere,' he said.

The place was full and all the chairs along the wall beside the window were taken. Only one chair was empty. As I came in through the school door it was against the wall facing me. It stopped me in my tracks. As I stared at it, the young people in the room turned and looked at me. Everybody stopped talking.

The bar ran along the wall on my right. Dan came out from behind it. ''Allo, Son!' he said, 'yer see we found yer mam's chair.'

There was a sort of gasp. A girl said, 'Oh!' As Dan introduced them, they all came up and shook hands with me. I might have been flattered. But I ''ad more sense'. I knew that I was only a small part of a village legend, which, for them, had suddenly come to life.

A grey-haired man leaning on the far end of the bar grinned at me. He was as long-legged and lean as ever. ''Allo Bacca!' I said.

'Surprised yer knew me,' he said. 'Ain't seen yer fer thirty year.'

''Ow would I fergit yer seein' as yer the only feller as beat me in a sprint.'

'Ar! Boot I were a bit older nor you.'

The young ones had been speaking posh. Now we all spoke Overton.

We got to talking about the importance in the old days of the pig, the poultry, and the allotment. 'Course nobody bothers with pigs an' poultry nah,' said Crum.

'That's it!' I said. 'I knew summat were wrong soon as I got aht me car. Couldn't make out wot it were.'

They stared at me.

'Too quiet!' I said. 'Overton's too quiet! No pigs a-gruntin', no 'ens a-cacklin', no cocks a-crowin'. Yer could allus 'ear 'em. That's what's wrong! Scores o' pigs an' 'undreds o' poultry. All gone! Well I nivver!'

'Nah yer mention it,' said Speedie, 'yer roight. Folks got rid o' 'em gradual loike. That's why we nivver noticed. Fancy yer noticin'!'

'Well 'e would notice, wouldn't 'e,' said Dan, 'arter all the years 'e 'eard 'em in full cry.'

''Ow abaht the gamekeepers?' I asked. 'One of 'em shot me cat an' then me dog. I don't suppose they'd git away wi' that nah.'

'They're all roight these days,' Speedie sighed. 'Nobody bothers ter poach nor goo stickin' no more yer see. So they ain't Enemy Number One. They turns strangers back wot wants ter goo drivin' all uvver. Boot they don't bother us.'

'Big T wouldn't stand fer no dog shootin' nor poisonin' loike in the ole days,' said Crum. 'There's nowt wrong wi' Big T.'

'Oo the 'ell's Big T?'

Everybody chuckled.

''Is lordship the Earl,' said Crum.

'Cor!' I said, ''e must be the first Earl ivver ter git a nickname.'

'Ar!' Speedie nodded. 'That's becos, like yerself, 'e belongs Overton. 'E lives 'ere. An' 'e wucks 'ere. 'E don't spend most of 'is toime somewheers else. 'E's sold some o' 'is cottages off ter commuters. Boot not a lot. Overton folk can still git cottages at a good rent. Be a tragedy if 'e ivver sells aht ter some company wot only cares abaht profits an' don't care owt abaht people . . .'

'O' course 'e were jist a boy wen 'is dad died,' I said.

Crum said, ''E's growed oop wi' village. 'E's knowed us all fer uvver fifty year. I 'ope 'e sees me aht.'

'Talkin' o' nicknames,' I said, 'do the little ole boys still git 'em?'

'Oo ar!' said Speedie, 'Overton's nivver lost that tradition. One of the few villages 'ereabouts wot's kep it oop. We gotta new doctor. T'other wick 'e says ter me, "It's no good. I'll 'ave to learn all the nicknames, then perhaps folks'll be able to tell me weer other people live. Do you know weer John Taylor lives?" I 'ad to think. I tells 'im it's either Bummie else Scrabby. "Oh my God!" 'e says, I 'ad ter laugh.'

'Why ain't yer "Pickles" no more?' I asked Dan.

'Ar well! I were away from village for over twenty year an' it got fergot. Weren't really my nickname any road. It were me dad's. I got it wen 'e died . . . D'yer want ter see round the 'ouse?'

The door from the sitting-room into the front lobby has been bricked up. So I had to go behind the bar and through into what used to be Emma's wash-house. The old pan lavatory is a store now, the pantry a posh new toilet, and the kitchen has been tiled and modernised, while the boxroom upstairs is now a bathroom. But the rest of the house looked just the same. My rocking-horse stable in the big walk-in cupboard under the stairs is still full of junk. I bet if you were to rummage with a torch right at the back of it you would find stuff from my mother's day.

When the school was closed the priest lived in the house. But for years now the parish has been served from Ashborough. So the old place is just let to visitors from time to time.

Memories of my bright-haired, quick, young mother, of Gran, of Father Gregory, of Mary, of Duckie, of Emma, and of Lucy, crowded in on me. My mind couldn't absorb them all and it went numb in self-defence. I followed Dan through the place like a zombie. As for the old man in Masefield's poem the clock ticked to my heart. But no withered wire moved a thin ghost of music at that time. I knew that I would have to go back alone and sit in each room before the old house would come alive again. I did. And it did.

West Street gleamed smooth under the lights as I walked back down to the Green with Crum and Speedie. 'Yer could fairly wack 'oops an' tops down 'ere!' I said.

'Too many cars in daytoime,' said Speedie. 'Any'ow we got a playin' field down Plantham End wi' tennis courts an' a bowlin' green an all sorts. Kids don't bother wi' 'oops an tops no more. An' in winter o' course they watches the telly.'

'Commuters is allus in a 'urry,' said Crum. 'Big T's sold a few cottages down Pudden Bag. Folks lives there wot wucks as far away as Leicester.'

'Do they join in the life of the village?'

'Nar! I don't even know their names.'

'Nor me,' said Speedie.

'Yer livin in another world from the one we knew as kids.'

'We are and we ain't,' said Crum. 'Yer mam used to call Overton "the back o' beyond on the road to noweer". Well in a way it still is, becos we still ain't on the road to anyweer bar us. We don't get many visitors. Jist the odd few in the summer 'olidays. So cars and the telly and all that 'as changed us. But Big T's kep' the village the same an' so long as it ain't tecken over by commuters we can keep oop some o' the old traditions. It's oop to 'im an' us reely.'

'In the old days the place must have run at a loss.'

'Reckon it moight do still,' said Speedie. 'Boot the Family nivver expected it to do owt else. They 'ad a dooty to their tenants an' their tenants 'ad a dooty to them . . . Money didn't enter inter it.'

'We know now,' said Crum, 'that wen we were kids they didn't 'ave mooch. An' o' course two lots o' death duties, coomin' so quick, damn near bankrupted 'em.'

When, next day, I walked round the village I found that my friends were right. Outwardly the old part of it was hardly changed from my boyhood world. The new development has been at Plantham End where the Council has built blocks of houses and bungalows.

The only cottages I saw which had not been renovated were Old Moll's and Choc-eye's, next door, on Top Street. The door of his old shop was overgrown with ramblers. When I pushed them aside, I found the old metal strip above it with the faded words 'T. Bottomley licensed to sell tobacco'.

Down Brooks, where my mother and I used to race sticks and where we boys made our pool, is the new sewage plant for the village. Of course all the houses have water laid-on and proper bathrooms and electricity now. Emma was wrong, she did 'live ter see that day'.

One evening I walked up to the cemetery where she and Father Gregory and Gran and so many old friends are buried. On the way back down the lane I met a group of teenage youngsters on bicycles: all smart in T-shirts and jeans. By now of course they knew who I was. So while I sat on a fence and they on their bikes we had a chat about our village. They go by bus to school in Ashborough where they mix with the children from all the surrounding places. So the folk of Blackwell and Goodham, of Springwell and Ashborough, are no longer 'furriners!'

'Do you often go to London?'

'Not a lot,' one boy said. 'It's less than two hours down the motorway. But the traffic's terrible. Leicester's all right though. We went to Paris on a school trip. But that's as crowded as London.'

'Did you fly?'

'No. We went by train. But we flew when my dad took us to Majorca on holiday.'

'So you know what's at the back of Overton.'

'Eh?' they said.

I laughed. 'Never mind.'

I stayed for a week in our village. In a world where the pace of the rat-race gets faster and faster, the pace of life in Overton has slowed down. It runs along as quietly and as unruffled as Smuttie after her morning wash and polish. Electricity, and modern kitchens, have cut out so many of the old chores, and cars and buses and the new roads have cut out the hours spent in getting to nearby places. Folk have more time for leisure; more time for the playing-field, the Community Centre, the telly, and the pub. They no longer have to get up at 5 am.

In a world beset by worry Overton is less worried. Folk no

longer worry about what the children are going to eat if a hard winter follows a wet summer. There is no pig 'ter go an' git bad' just as it is getting nice and fat. And, if you need a bit o' veg, well Castlie has always got frozen stuff. He is Miss Bennett's nephew and he married Florrie, one of Mr. Stanwell's daughters. Between them they run the only shop left in the village.

At the end of the week I went round and said goodbye to my friends and, the next afternoon, started off on the first leg of my journey back to Scotland.

I was feeling sad because I knew that it was most unlikely that I would ever live in Overton again; that when I got back to Aberdeen the wheel which, for me, had begun to turn in 1919 would have reached full circle.

It was only fitting that my return journey should begin from the schoolhouse. So, after I had said goodbye to Mr. and Mrs. Findon, I drove up to it.

The house, of course, was locked, but I had another walk round the garden. Some of the trees and bushes which my mother planted were still there. The white paint which I had plastered fifty years ago on the back of one of the shed doors was still there too. And old Prince's claw marks still showed clearly on the back door from under layers of paint.

In the crumbling playground I sat on the step outside the top door of the deserted school; sat on that big block of stone scraped over the years by the tackety boots of hundreds of children, including Son's. From in front of it my mother used to bowl to us.

Her wheel-chair was a world away from that worn step.

When she collapsed, the doctor said that the cancer would kill her inside a fortnight. If 'ed a knowed Teacher 'e'd a 'ad more sense. She fought it for another twelve weeks. During those days and nights we kept her heavily sedated against the pain. Soon, most of the time, she knew neither who nor where she was. But occasionally the blue-grey eyes would light up and for a few minutes she would be herself again.

The doctor suggested that she might go into a home. But this my wife and I could not accept. Son was beside Teacher at the end. And that was proper.

Like me Overton was dreaming again in the sunshine. For once no motor broke the magic spell. But I could hear the clatter of a long-gone bucket under a long-gone tap, the clop of dead hooves, the grind of steel-rimmed wheels in smoothed-out ruts, and the sound of vanished children singing:

> 'There is heard a hymn when the panes are dim,
> And never before or again,
> When the nights are strong with a darkness long,
> And the dark is alive with rain.
> Never we know but in sleet or in snow,
> The place where the great fires are,
> That the midst of the earth is a raging mirth,
> And the heart of the earth a star.
> And at night we win to the ancient inn,
> Where the child in the frost is furled,
> We follow the feet where all souls meet,
> At the inn at the end of the world.'

Not everyone is lucky enough to have roots which go so deep that they can never be torn up; lucky enough to be able to go back to their childhood world and find that it looks so much the same. To my friends in Overton it has never mattered whether I grew rich or poor. To them I have always been neither more nor less than 'Son'. When, occasionally, they heard me broadcast from Scotland on the BBC's *Radio Newsreel*, or in later years, saw my name on the television screen, they used to say 'That's Son. 'E's from Overton.'

This is how it has been for sixty years and this is how it will be for what time remains to us to complete our journey. I 'belong' to them and they to me; and all of us, wherever we are, to the thatched village.